Contemporary Chinese Civil and Commercial Law

Peicheng Wu

Trade Secrets and Market Dominance

Legal and Economic Perspectives in China

Springer

Peicheng Wu
Guanghua Law School
Zhejiang University
Hangzhou, Zhejiang, China

ISSN 2524-6194 ISSN 2524-6208 (electronic)
Contemporary Chinese Civil and Commercial Law
ISBN 978-981-95-1151-8 ISBN 978-981-95-1152-5 (eBook)
https://doi.org/10.1007/978-981-95-1152-5

This Springer imprint is published by the registered company Springer Nature Singapore Pte Ltd.
The registered company address is: 152 Beach Road, #21-01/04 Gateway East, Singapore 189721, Singapore

Preface

In the modern commercial society, more and more undertakings rely on intellectual property to compete in the market, particularly in new-emerging and high-tech markets. That is, intellectual property has been more than a type of intangible asset, but has become a competitive tool of companies to survive in the market, which makes it closely related to competition law.

Existing antitrust research mainly focuses on the interplay between competition law and intellectual property (as a whole). However, there are many categories of intellectual property, such as patents, copyright, trademarks and trade secrets. Some may ask the question: whether antitrust law should treat them equally in specific cases?

From my perspective, different kinds of intellectual property share some similarities, while they have differences at the same time. It is arguable that these differences are bound to have implications on antitrust analysis. As a result, I try to research on the impact and choose the trade secret as the underlying intellectual property.

A trade secret is different from other typical intellectual property (e.g. patents). Some may even question if antitrust rules should apply to trade secrets as long as they are kept secret. Indeed, the secrecy of a trade secret makes it very special in the family of intellectual property. However, a trade secret holder can actively take advantage of its secret information by means of licensing. Therefore, there is no doubt that antitrust laws should apply if there are anti-competitive practices in the exercise of trade secrets.

During the recent years, China has made great efforts to improve the protection of trade secrets for both domestic and foreign companies. Meanwhile, noteworthy is that a trade secret holder may abuse its secrets in commercial practices, which might give rise to competition concerns. In that regard, I believe that the protection of trade secrets and the prohibition of the abuse of trade secrets are just like 'two sides of the same coin'.

All in all, I hope this book may contribute to the antitrust intervention of intellectual property by recognizing the differences of various types of intellectual property on anti-monopoly analysis. This book may not be comprehensive, but can be a very beginning in this area.

Hangzhou, China
March 2025

Dr. Peicheng Wu

Acknowledgements

This book is based on my doctoral research. In 2018, Shanghai Jiao Tong University (SJTU) and the University of New South Wales (UNSW) cooperated to start the double joint Ph.D. program. It is my honour to participate in this program. I would like to thank these two institutions for providing me with the valuable opportunity to conduct my Ph.D. research in China and Australia.

I would like to express my great gratitude to my supervisor at SJTU KoGuan Law School, Prof. Xianlin Wang, for his continuing support during my academic journey. Professor Wang is the leading antitrust scholar in China, particularly in the area of anti-monopoly intervention of intellectual property. I benefit greatly from his supervision and professional guidance. In particular, his guidance about the differences of different kinds of intellectual property on antitrust analysis has contributed substantially to my ideas of this research.

I want to thank Prof. Deborah Healey, my primary supervisor at UNSW Law. Her patience and support are of great help to this book. I also learnt a lot from her long-time competition law expertise. I am also grateful to my joint and secondary supervisors, Associate Professor Charlie Xiao-chuan Weng and Associate Professor Alexandra George. They have assisted me in providing specific comments of my Ph.D. research on Chinese law and intellectual property law.

My sincerely gratitude to my parents for your parenting and unchanging love. My milestone of this book is dedicated to both of you.

Finally, I acknowledge that some parts of this book have been published:

Chapter 3 contains some materials from Peicheng Wu, 'How does China Prohibit the Abuse of Market Dominance? A Comparative Analysis with the US and EU Approaches', published by the Polish Research Centre for Law and Economy of China (Warsaw University, Poland) in (2021) 1 Journal of Law and Economy of China. Chapter 5 contains some materials from Peicheng Wu, 'The Refusal to License Intellectual Property as an Antitrust Violation in China: How should the Current Approach be Improved?' (2024) 14 (1) Queen Mary Journal of Intellectual Property; Peicheng Wu, 'Bad Faith Litigation of Intellectual Property as a Violation of China's Anti-monopoly Law' (2024) 32 (1) Asia Pacific Law Review.

Contents

Abbreviations

AML	Anti-Monopoly Law
AUCL	Anti-Unfair Competition Law
CFI	Court of First Instance
DOJ	Department of Justice
DTSA	Defend Trade Secrets Act
ECJ	European Court of Justice
EEC	European Economic Community
EU	European Union
FTC	Federal Trade Commission
GC	General Court
HMT	Hypothetical Monopolist Test
IP	Intellectual property
MOFCOM	Ministry of Commerce of the People's Republic of China
NDRC	National Development and Reform Commission
NPC	National People's Congress
PRC	People's Republic of China
SAIC	State Administration for Industry and Commerce
SAMR	State Administration for Market Regulation
SEPs	Standard Essential Patents
SPC	Supreme People's Court
SSNIP	Small but Significant and Non-transitory Increase in Price
TFEU	Treaty on the Functioning of the European Union
TRIPS	Agreement on the Trade-Related Aspects of Intellectual Property Rights
US	United States
WIPO	World Intellectual Property Organization
WTO	World Trade Organization

Chapter 1
Introduction to the Book

In 2012, the European Commission required Microsoft to disclose trade secret information to its competitors:

> The requirement that Microsoft disclose [secret] information to its competitors so as to allow interoperability between the dominant Windows architecture and rival workgroup servers brought significant benefits to users. A range of innovative products that would otherwise not have seen the light of day were introduced on the market.[1]
>
> — Joaquín Almunia[2]

Companies are entitled to protect their valuable information as a trade secret. Trade secret law prevents competitors from misappropriation of secret information held by an undertaking. Under the protection of trade secret law, a secret holder is usually not obligated to disclose trade secrets to its rivals. In other words, only if the secret holder agrees to a license contract with others can the underlying secret information be disclosed. Despite these facts, why did Mr. Joaquín Almunia require Microsoft to disclose its secret information to competitors without Microsoft's permission?

The short answer is: because the competition law will limit the exploitation of a trade secret if the exercise of a trade secret leads to concerns about anti-competitive impact. Although Microsoft can freely decide whether to disclose its information in principle, the competition law may require the secret holder to disclose secret information if the refusal to disclose harms competition.

Why can the competition law require the holder to disclose the trade secret? One may bring up the question how can competition law apply in the complex overlap domain of trade secrets and antitrust? This book will answer these questions derived from the above *Microsoft* case circumstance.

---

[1] European Commission. 2012. Statement by Vice President Joaquín Almunia following General Court Judgement in Case T-167/08 Microsoft versus Commission. https://ec.europa.eu/commission/presscorner/detail/en/MEMO_12_498. Accessed 25 March 2025.

[2] Joaquín Almunia was the vice president of the European Commission and the European Commissioner for Competition (2009–2014).

P. Wu, *Trade Secrets and Market Dominance*, Contemporary Chinese Civil and Commercial Law, https://doi.org/10.1007/978-981-95-1152-5_1

1.1 Introduction

This book is designed to analyse the abuse of market dominance related to trade secrets from a competition law perspective. It is important to have an overview of the study before conducting substantive research on this competition law issue. This chapter provides an introduction to the whole book.

This chapter is organized as follows. Firstly, this chapter articulates the background of the book in Sect. 1.2. It then provides the research objective and question of this study (see Sect. 1.3). Section 1.4 outlines the structure of this book in compatible with the organization of each chapter. The next section (see Sect. 1.5) defines the significance and scope of this book. Section 1.6 introduces some anti-monopoly rules in China for a better understanding of the analysis in the subsequent chapters for international readers. This chapter explains the doctrinal method as the main methodology applied in this book (see Sect. 1.7). The last section (see Sect. 1.8) concludes the introductory chapter.

1.2 Background of the Book

1.2.1 Trade Secrets as a Category of Valuable Assets of Companies

Trade secrets are defined as commercial information that is not readily accessible by the public and has commercial value, and for which the holder has adopted reasonable protection measures.[3] Many jurisdictions, such as China and the US, consider a trade secret as a type of intellectual property.[4]

A trade secret is a crucial asset of firms in modern society, described as the 'crown jewels' of an undertaking's intellectual capital.[5] Recent research shows that nearly 70% of undertakings' valuable intellectual assets are trade secrets.[6] Companies also

[3] Chapter 2 of the book introduces the definition and characteristics of a trade secret in detail.

[4] Some common law jurisdictions, including the UK and Australia, use common law (breach of confidence doctrine) to protect confidential information. Nevertheless, this book uses comparative experience from the US and the EU to solve antitrust problems in China. Chapter 2 of the book will further explain that competition agencies in these three jurisdictions consider a trade secret as a type of intellectual property.

[5] Jorda, Karl. 2007. Trade secrets and trade-secret licensing. In *Intellectual property management in health and agricultural innovation: A handbook of best practice,* eds. A. Krattiger, RT Mahoney, and L Nelsen, 1043, 1046. Oxford: MIHR.

[6] Brant, Jennifer. 2016. Trade secrets: Tools for innovation and collaboration. ICC. https://iccwbo.org/publication/trade-secrets-innovation-process/. Accessed 25 March 2025.

believe that proprietary technology encompassing trade secrets is a critical source of their competitive advantages.[7]

Commentators from both sides of the Atlantic have noted the importance of trade secrets of companies in the market. It is suggested that US companies become more reliant on confidential information to compete in the market.[8] According to recent estimates, trade secret misappropriation may cost US firms between 1 and 3% of US GDP annually.[9]

The EU unified the trade secret protection by enacting the *Directive on the Protection of Undisclosed Know-how and Business Information (Trade Secrets) against their Unlawful Acquisition, Use and Disclosure* (Trade Secret Directive) in 2016. The EU lawmakers recognized the great value of trade secret as much as other forms of intellectual property.[10] European companies use trade secrets as a competitiveness and research innovation management tool, the categories of which may vary from technological knowledge to commercial data.[11]

Chinese companies witness a similar situation where trade secrets are significantly valued.[12] For example, when the US and China decided to pause their 'trade war' from 2018, in early 2020, these two super economies signed a trade agreement[13] (China–US Agreement). Under the China–US Agreement, China sees itself experiencing 'transforms from a major intellectual property consumer to a major intellectual property producer'.[14] Trade secrets are a key element of 'optimizing the business environment'[15] in China.[16]

In conclusion, trade secrets have become an important and competitive asset of firms across nations. Companies doing business in China are dependent on trade secrets as valuable intellectual property to compete with rivals.

---

[7] Intellectual Property Owners Association. 2004. MITSloan, Survey on Strategic Management of Intellectual Property. https://sloanreview.mit.edu/article/strategic-management-of-intellectual-property/. Accessed 25 March 2025.

[8] Almeling, David. 2012. Seven reasons why trade secrets are increasingly important. *Berkeley Technology Law Journal* 27:1098–1117, 1091, 1112.

[9] Varanini, Emilio. 2017. United States of America. In *Abuse of dominant position and globalization & protection and disclosure of trade secrets and know-how*, eds. Pranvera Këllezi, Bruce Kilpatrick, and Pierre Kobel, 622. Berlin: Springer.

[10] See para. (2) of the Trade Secret Directive.

[11] Ibid.

[12] Bai, J. Benjamin, and Guoping Da. 2010. Strategies for trade secrets protection in China. *Northwestern Journal of Technology and Intellectual Property* 9: 351–376, 351.

[13] It is known as the 'phase one' deal because the two countries are still discussing other subject matters. For the official version of the agreement, see http://www.mofcom.gov.cn/article/ae/ai/202001/20200102930845.shtml. Accessed 25 March 2025.

[14] See Section A of Chapter 1 of the China–US Agreement.

[15] See Section B of Chapter 1 of the China–US Agreement.

[16] The Chinese government states in China's 14th Five Year Plan that China will bolster intellectual property protection operation systems and provide undertakings with high-level intellectual property protection. See State Council of China. 2021. Outline of the 14th Five-Year Plan (2021–2025) for National Economic and Social Development and Long-Range Objectives for 2035. http://www.gov.cn/xinwen/2021-03/13/content_5592681.htm. Accessed 25 March 2025.

1.2.2 Concerns About Competition Arising from the Exploitation of Trade Secrets

Companies may choose to protect their crucial information as a trade secret. The ownership of a trade secret is legal. However, it may raise concerns about competition if a company abuses its secret information, particularly when the firm has substantial market power, or market dominance.

There have been some antitrust cases relating to trade secrets in the EU and the US.[17] One leading case was the EU *Microsoft*[18] case. There Microsoft protected the interface information of its Windows system as a trade secret. By refusing to disclose the interface information to competitors, Microsoft prevented rivals from entering the relevant market and harmed competition. The European Commission considered that Microsoft's refusal to disclose the trade secret had constituted an abuse of market dominance under the EU competition law. Antitrust scholars from the EU, the US and China have critically examined the *Microsoft* case from their own perspectives.[19]

Owing to economic globalization, many transnational corporations, such as Microsoft, Qualcomm and Sony operate business in China. It is possible for dominant undertakings, such as these companies, to use their trade secrets to hamper competition in China. For instance, the Chinese anti-monopoly agency is investigating Microsoft's refusal to disclose trade secrets as a possible abuse of market dominance,[20] which is similar to the EU *Microsoft* case. Similarly, it is also possible for Chinese companies to use trade secrets to hamper competition in China and overseas.

In conclusion, despite the fact that companies may possess trade secret as valuable intellectual property, the exploitation of trade secrets may result in concerns about the impact on competition and therefore should be under antitrust scrutiny.

---

[17] See generally First, Harry. 2011. Trade secrets and antitrust law. In *The law and theory of trade secrecy:A handbook of contemporary research,* ed. Dreyfuss Rochelle, 358–365. Northampton: Edward Elgar.

[18] *Microsoft v European Commission* (T-201/04) [2007] ECR II-3601. Chapters 4 and 5 will further discuss this case.

[19] See e.g. Drexl, Josef. 2011. Refusal to Grant access to Trade Secrets as an Abuse of Market Dominance. In *Intellectual Property and Competition Law-New Frontiers,* 165. Oxford: Oxford University Press; First, Harry. 2011. Trade secrets and antitrust law. In *The law and theory of trade secrecy: A handbook of contemporary research,* ed. Dreyfuss Rochelle, 358. Cheltenham: Edward Elgar; Hou Liyang. 2012. The Essential Facilities Doctrine—What Was Wrong in Microsoft? *IIC International Review of Intellectual Property and Competition Law* 43(4): 251–271, 451.

[20] The investigation began in 2014 and is still pending. See *State Council of PRC*. 2014. 工商总局对微软的反垄断调查正深入进行 [The SAIC is Investigating further into Microsoft's monopolistic Behaviours]. http://www.gov.cn/xinwen/2014-08/26/content_2739925.htm. Accessed 25 March 2025.

1.2.3 *The Anti-monopoly Intervention in Intellectual Property in China*

China enacted the Anti-monopoly Law (AML) in 2007, effective from 1 August 2008. In 2022, China amended the AML for the first time. Compared to competition rules in other jurisdictions, such as the US Sherman Act in 1890, China's AML is a 'young boy'. Chinese competition agencies and courts therefore have limited experience in dealing with anti-monopoly cases, including those relevant to intellectual property.[21]

Article 68 of the AML provides a general provision regarding intellectual property,[22] stating that abusive practices related to intellectual property should be under anti-monopoly scrutiny.[23] Additionally, the Anti-monopoly Commission of the State Council of China enacted *Anti-monopoly Guidelines in the field of Intellectual Property* (IP Guidelines) in 2019. These IP Guidelines guide Chinese competition agencies and courts dealing with antitrust cases concerning intellectual property.

One feature of the above Chinese legislation is that Chinese intellectual property laws look at intellectual property as a whole. However, the intellectual property at issue in an antitrust case is specific. It should be either a patent, or copyright or a trade secret in one case because the issues in relation to each are different. Despite the IP Guidelines intending to solve anti-monopoly problems in the field of intellectual property, the provisions in these Guidelines are general and fail to consider the characteristics of specific intellectual property. Arguably, although a trade secret shares many similarities with other categories of intellectual property (e.g. patents), it has some unique characteristics that may have implications for the antitrust assessments.

This feature of Chinese legislation influences the application of China's anti-monopoly law. Chapter 5 will discuss *Hytera v Motorola*,[24] the only case where the exercise of trade secrets was alleged to have constituted the abuse of market dominance in China. In line with Chinese legislation, the court in this case considered the secret information in question as intellectual property, and did not examine the possible impact arising from the characteristics of a trade secret in an anti-monopoly case.

---

[21] See 王先林 [Wang Xianlin]. 2020. *知识产权与反垄断法* [*Intellectual Property and Anti-monopoly Law*]. 北京: 法律出版社 [Beijing: Law Press China], 423.

[22] Article 68 of the AML says that '[T]his Law shall not apply to the exercise of intellectual property by undertakings pursuant to the relevant laws and administrative regulations on intellectual property; however, this Law shall apply to the abuse of intellectual property by undertakings to exclude or restrict competition.'

[23] It is suggested that article 68 of the AML (article 55 of the 2007 version) is too general to provide guidance on the application of competition law in the field of intellectual property. See e.g. Healey, Deborah. 2008. An anti-monopoly law for China: weapon or mirage? *Competition & Consumer Law Journal* 16: 220–245, 231.

[24] 海能达与摩托罗拉滥用市场支配地位纠纷案 [Hytera v Motorola— Disputes of the Abuse of Market Dominance], 北京知识产权法院 [Beijing Intellectual Property Court, People's Republic of China], 北京知识产权法院 (2017) 京73民初1671号 [Economic Appeal No. 1671], 31 December 2019.

1.2.4 Some Legal Theories Applied in the Book

This book deals with the issue of how competition law (the abuse of dominance law) can be applied to the use of intellectual property (trade secrets). This book primarily relies on two theories to explain legal issues in this book: the theory of complementarity and the family resemblance doctrine.

1.2.4.1 Theory of Complementarity Between Competition and Intellectual Property

General Assessment

This book applies competition law to the exploitation of trade secrets. Recognizing a trade secret as a category of intellectual property, this book is a project based on the interplay between competition policy and intellectual property in a broader sense. This book chooses the theory of complementarity as the legal theory to explain the relationship between competition law (in particular, the law of the abuse of market dominance) and intellectual property (trade secrets).

At first glance, the function of intellectual property law seems to contradict competition policy.[25] Intellectual property rights are usually regarded as a type of 'monopoly rights' because intellectual property law artificially establishes monopoly over intangible objects, such as inventions (patents), ideas (copyright), symbols (trademarks) and information (trade secrets).[26] By contrast, competition law aims at maintaining effective competition law in the market, and is referred to as anti-monopoly law in some jurisdictions (China).

However, this first impression is not the case in modern competition law. Current competition policy introduces a theory of complementarity to explain its interactions with intellectual property matters.[27] For example, as competition policy has potential implications on trade between nations, its interplay with international trade has been discussed under the framework of the WTO. The WTO working group issued a report

---

[25] For example, the origin of the modern patent law was called 'Statute of Monopolies (1623)' in England.

[26] See George, Alexandra. 2012. *Constructing intellectual property.* Cambridge: Cambridge University Press, 6.

[27] See e.g. Drexl, Josef. 2007. Abuse of dominance in licensing and refusal to license-a 'more economic approach' to competition by imitation and to competition by substitution. In *The interaction between competition law and IP law,* eds. Claus Dieter Ehlermann, Isabela Atansiu, 647–648. Oxford: Hart publishing; Drexl, Josef. 2011. Intellectual property in competition: How to promote dynamic competition as a goal. In *More common ground for international competition law?(ASCOLA competition law series),* eds. Josef Drexl, Warren S. Grimes, Clifford A. Jones, Rudolph J.R. Peritz and Edward T. Swaine, 210. Cheltenham: Edward Elgar Publishing.

to reveal its views,[28] and the relationship between intellectual property rights and competition policy was addressed.

The WTO report argued that there is 'a basic complementarity between intellectual property law and competition law'.[29] Intellectual property law guarantees that the intellectual property holder can be rewarded (e.g. by charging royalties for the license), encouraging further inventive or creative activities.[30] The encouragement of innovation as the goal of intellectual property law will finally 'provide better conditions for price, quality and diversity of products',[31] which is compatible with the objective of competition policy. In other words, competition rules ensure a fair and efficient market for the use of intellectual property.[32]

Apart from the WTO report, it has been suggested that the two primary jurisdictions of competition law (namely the US and the EU) accepted the theory of complementarity described in their domestic antitrust guidelines.[33] For instance, the US IP Guidelines (1995) say that '[T]he intellectual property laws and the antitrust laws share the common purpose of promoting innovation and enhancing consumer welfare.'[34]

The EU Technology Transfer Guidelines (2004) set out the theory of complementarity more explicitly by providing that:

> The fact that intellectual property laws grant exclusive rights of exploitation does not imply that intellectual property rights are immune from competition law intervention...both bodies of law share the same basic objective of promoting consumer welfare and efficient allocation of resources...Intellectual property rights promote dynamic competition by encouraging undertakings to invest in developing new or improved products and processes. So does competition by putting pressure on undertakings to innovate. Therefore, both intellectual property rights and competition are necessary to promote innovation and ensure a competitive exploitation thereof.[35]

Such ideas have also come into IP Guidelines of younger antitrust jurisdictions, such as China, as the targeted jurisdiction of this book. For example, article 1 of China's IP

---

[28] See Report of the Working Group on the Interaction between Trade and Competition Policy to the General Council (WT/WGTCP/2, 8 December 1998).

[29] See ibid para. 113.

[30] See ibid.

[31] See Oliveira, Gesner and Thomas Fujiwara. 2007. Intellectual property and competition as complementary policies: A test using an ordered probit model (WIPO). https://www.wipo.int/export/sites/www/competition-policy/en/docs/study_ip_competition_oliveira.pdf. Accessed 25 March 2025. This paper also conducted empirical research based on more than 4000 firms in 36 countries to demonstrate that intellectual property and competition are not contradictory policies.

[32] See Report of the Working Group on the Interaction between Trade and Competition Policy to the General Council (WT/WGTCP/2, 8 December 1998) para. 113.

[33] Report by the Max Planck Institute for Intellectual Property and Competition Law (authored by Professor Josef Drexl), 'Copyright, Competition and Development' (December 2013) 37–38.

[34] See Antitrust Guidelines for the Licensing of Intellectual Property (April 6, 1995) issued by the US Department of Justice and the Federal Trade Commission. The statement was still valid in its 2017 version.

[35] See Commission Notice-Guidelines on the Application of Article 81 of the EC Treaty to Technology Transfer Agreements (2004/C 101/02) para. 7.

Guidelines (2019) provide that '[A]nti-monopoly and intellectual property protection have common purposes, i.e. to protect competition and stimulate innovation, improve economic efficiency, and safeguard the interests of consumers and the public'.

Overall, the theory of complementarity considers that competition law shares the same objectives as intellectual property law, both aiming to provide better products (or service) for consumers in the market. The above spells out complementarity in a general sense. Arguably, the two dimensions that should be noted arise from the ideas of complementarity between competition and intellectual property.

The Dichotomy of the Existence and Exercise of Intellectual Property

Although competition and intellectual property law share complementary goals, they play different roles in specific cases. As to the relationship between competition and intellectual property, competition law should only apply when the holder exploits its intellectual property. The ECJ, for the first time, clarified the existence/exercise dichotomy in the *Établissements Consten S.à.R.L. and Grundig-Verkaufs-GmbH*.[36] It was a competition case related to trademarks, yet its rule applied to all kinds of intellectual property. The ECJ claimed that although the plaintiffs were entitled to have a trademark issued under the French national law, this did not imply that the EU competition law could not apply since the exercise of trademark obstructed the free trade between member states. The case indicated that national laws govern the existence or ownership of intellectual property, but their exercise should follow competition rules.[37]

The existence/exercise dichotomy is of great significance to this book by providing a legal foundation for competition agencies or courts to deal with competition cases involving intellectual property. According to the dichotomy, it is the task of intellectual property law (instead of competition law) to determine whether the underlying intellectual property exists (or whether an object should be protected by intellectual property law).

Competition law only intervenes when the owner begins to exercise its intellectual property. In other words, if the owner merely creates the underlying intellectual property but does not use it, there is no room for competition law to apply. It is competition law which stipulates the circumstances under which the exercise of an IPR should be prohibited absolutely.[38]

This book is thus organized pursuant to the existence/exercise dichotomy. As a competition-oriented book, it does not examine why information can be protected as a trade secret or why a trade secret should be protected. These questions are more

---

36 *Établissements Consten S.à.R.L. and Grundig-Verkaufs-GmbH v Commission of the European Economic Community* (Joined cases 56 and 58–64) [1966].

37 See Korah, Valentine. 2000. *An introductory guide to EC competition law and practice,* 258. Oxford: Hart Publishing. The ECJ further explained the very significance of existence/exercise dichotomy in the *Centrafarm BV et Adriaan de Peijper v Sterling Drug Inc* (Case 15–74).

38 Schmidt, Hedvig and Steven Anderman. 2011. *EU competition law and intellectual property rights, the regulation of innovation.* Oxford: Oxford University Press, 38.

appropriate for trade secret law to answer. Instead, this book focuses on whether the exercise of trade secrets may constitute the abuse of market dominance under competition law. Consequently, this book provides critical analysis mainly relevant to the establishment of abusive practices regarding trade secrets conducted by a dominant company (see Chapters 4 and 5).

Competition by Imitation V Competition by Substitution

Arguably, the theory of complementarity does not deny some potential conflicts between intellectual property protection and competition. In this regard, it is necessary to distinguish competition by imitation from competition by substitution.

As discussed, intellectual property protection aims to promote further innovation, benefiting consumers. It has been suggested that intellectual property protection should not be used to prevent the holder from competition in the market, but should encourage intellectual property owners to engage in competition for the sake of long-term investment.[39] The question then becomes: what kind of 'competition' does this refers to?

As noted by the US IP Guidelines, '[R]apid imitation would reduce the commercial value of innovation and erode incentives to invest, ultimately to the detriment of consumers.'[40] Indeed, intellectual property law proscribes rivals from imitating the owner's intellectual property, which reflects the characteristic of the exclusivity of the intellectual property. By preventing competitors from imitating, intellectual property law protects the incentives to innovate. As a result, it is legal for intellectual property holders to prevent 'competition by imitation'.[41]

Modern economics has identified dynamic competition as the great driving force of economic growth. The Austrian economist Joseph Schumpeter described dynamic competition in his famous monograph:

> …competition from the new commodity, the new technology, the new source of supply, the new organization…competition which commands a decisive cost or quality advantage and which strikes not at the margins of the profits and the outputs of the existing firms but at their foundations and their very lives.[42]

This is also known as the Schumpeterian idea of 'creative destruction'. Competition by providing better products (or services) is the driving force of economic growth.

---

[39] Barnett, Thomas (Assistant Attorney General of the US Department of Justice). 2006. Interoperability between antitrust and intellectual property. US Department of Justice. https://www.justice.gov/atr/speech/interoperability-between-antitrust-and-intellectual-property#N_3_. Accessed 25 March 2025.

[40] Antitrust Guidelines for the Licensing of Intellectual Property (January 12, 2017) issued by the US Department of Justice and the Federal Trade Commission.

[41] Report by the Max Planck Institute for Intellectual Property and Competition Law (authored by Professor Josef Drexl). Copyright, Competition and Development (December 2013) 38.

[42] Schumpeter, Joseph. 1976. *Capitalism, socialism and democracy.* New York: Harper Perennial, 84.

In this regard, despite being entitled to restrict competition by imitation, intellectual property owners will only continue to invest in innovative or creative activities if they undertake competitive pressure.[43] Under the Schumpeterian idea, even though the owner can have substantial power derived from the exclusivity of the underlying intellectual property, its competitors with superior technology can 'destroy' the existing market position on any occasion.[44]

Accordingly, when it comes to the intervention of the exercise of intellectual property, competition law should protect 'competition by substitution'.[45] Rivals are entitled (and are encouraged) to compete with the intellectual property holder by supplying better substitutes of the intellectual property products to consumers. If the exploitation of intellectual property by the holder hampers the competition by substitution, competition law should apply for dynamic competition in the market.

Theory of Complementarity in This Book

This book focuses on a sub-section of the area between competition and intellectual property. It analyses when the exercise of a trade secret (as a type of intellectual property) may constitute the abuse of market dominance from a competition law perspective. According to the complementarity theory, this book argues that trade secret protection and the abuse of dominance law do not contradict each other. This book applies the theory of complementarity from the following aspects:

Firstly, this book accepts the existence/exercise dichotomy to address the interplay between trade secret law and the law of the abuse of market dominance. This competition-oriented book concentrates on when the exercise of trade secrets may constitute the abuse of dominance. This book thus does not provide critical analysis on trade secret protection only because it is an issue best handled by intellectual property law.

Secondly, this book considers the (limited) exclusivity as a noticeable characteristic of a trade secret.[46] Therefore, the secret holder is entitled to prevent competitors from misappropriating the secret information, i.e. to proscribe the competition by imitation. The law of abuse of dominance should apply when exploiting trade secrets may harm competition by substitution. For example, this book critically examines the relationship between the exclusivity of a trade secret and the market power it

---

[43] Report by the Max Planck Institute for Intellectual Property and Competition Law (authored by Professor Josef Drexl), 'Copyright, Competition and Development' (December 2013) 38.

[44] Drexl, Josef. 2011. Intellectual property in competition: How to promote dynamic competition as a goal. In *More common ground for international competition law?(ASCOLA competition law series),* eds. Josef Drexl, Warren S. Grimes, Clifford A. Jones, Rudolph J.R. Peritz and Edward T. Swaine. Cheltenham: Edward Elgar Publishing, 210.

[45] Ibid.

[46] See Chapter 2 of this book.

may bring about,[47] and whether the 'new product' standard in the refusal to disclose trade secrets cases is reasonable pursuant to the complementarity theory.[48]

Last but not least, as the WTO report cited, the compatibility of the two policies (competition and intellectual property) heavily relies on the competition law being properly applied to the exploitation of intellectual property.[49] Competition agencies and courts need to facilitate the predictability and transparency of competition assessments.[50] To this end, this book provides clear-up tests based on thorough competition analysis to identify different types of abusive practices regarding trade secrets.[51]

1.2.4.2 Doctrine of 'Family Resemblance'

As discussed earlier, the topic of this book is a sub-group of the antitrust intervention in the exercise of intellectual property. It is thus necessary to briefly analyse the concept of 'intellectual property' and its implications for this book.

It is difficult to give a precise definition of intellectual property from a legal point of view.[52] It is suggested that the term 'intellectual property' is like Hans Christian Andersen's story about the emperor's new clothes because different people may have various opinions on this term.[53] Despite this, some scholars argue that the 'family resemblance' doctrine may well explain some common features of intellectual property,[54] which is sufficient for the assessments in this book.

Austrian-British philosopher Ludwig Wittgenstein argues that it may be impossible to provide a concept (or definition) for everything. Compared with a definition, the looser kind of structure, named 'family resemblance', can be used to described things that necessary and sufficient conditions cannot define.[55] Philosophers often consider objects such as games or languages as examples of a 'family resemblance'.[56]

According to Wittgenstein's doctrine, things that are in a class have a 'family resemblance':

---

[47] See Chapter 4 of this book.

[48] See Chapter 5.2 of this book.

[49] See Report of the Working Group on the Interaction between Trade and Competition Policy to the General Council (WT/WGTCP/2, 8 December 1998) para. 117.

[50] Ibid para. 116.

[51] See Chapter 5 of this book.

[52] There are some abstract descriptions of intellectual property but arguably none of these provides a satisfactory definition in itself. Dr Alexandra George summarizes some approaches to defining the intellectual property, such as enumerated approaches, property approaches, rights approaches, a stipulated approach and an intuitive approach. See George, Alexandra. 2015. The metaphysics of intellectual property. *The WIPO Journal* 7: 16–28, 17–18.

[53] George, Alexandra. 2012. *Constructing intellectual property.* Cambridge: Cambridge University Press, 38.

[54] See e.g. ibid Chapter 5 ('Family Resemblance' and Intellectual Property).

[55] See McGinn, Colin. 2011. Definition and family resemblance. In *Truth by analysis: Games, names and philosophy,* ed. Colin Mcginn, 15. Oxford: Oxford University Press.

[56] See ibid 16.

> I can think of no better expression to characterize these similarities than "family resemblance"; for the various resemblances between members of a family: build, features, colors of eyes, gait, temperament, etc., etc. overlap and criss-cross in the same way.[57]

As noted above, it is difficult for lawyers to agree on the definition of 'intellectual property'. Instead, the doctrine of 'family resemblance' can be helpful in describing the notion of 'intellectual property'. From the perspective of 'family resemblance', different forms of intellectual property have some similarities, placing them in the class of 'intellectual property'. For example, Dr George says that:

> The department of intellectual property is like a family whose members (doctrines) have various resemblances: abstract objects of regulation defined in terms of creatorship and originality, documented forms, associated rights, and so on…[58]
>
> and
>
> Intellectual property law can 'encourage creators to invest in designing or making creative new documented forms that might be of cultural or economic value.[59]

The above resemblance is described from the perspective of intellectual property law. This book analyses trade secrets issues from a competition law perspective. It may be difficult to define intellectual property, yet the 'family resemblance' doctrine may help realize the features of a trade secret as opposed to other forms of intellectual property in view of competition law.

As the existence/exercise dichotomy shows, competition law concentrates on the exploitation of intellectual property. Therefore, from a competition law perspective, trade secrets have many similarities with other typical intellectual property (such as patents), placing a trade secret in the same class. For example, trade secrets, as other forms of intellectual property, are intangible property. All types of intellectual property, including trade secrets, can be licensed. If any intellectual property rights are infringed upon, the intellectual property owner, including a trade secret holder, is entitled to sue the infringer for civil remedies. Accordingly, a trade secret is a member of the intellectual property family.

The similarities a trade secret shares with other categories of intellectual property are important to the antitrust analysis in the subsequent chapters. For example, Chapter 5 analyses some abusive practices derived from the exercise of a trade secret. One of them is the refusal to disclose trade secrets. Because all forms of intellectual property can be licensed, this book can borrow experience from the extensive literature on refusal to license intellectual property (e.g. patents and copyright) to assess the less discussed field of refusal to disclose trade secrets. In short, this book may apply experience from the abuse of dominance regarding other categories of intellectual property to the abuse of dominance cases regarding trade secrets due to the similarities that a trade secret has with its family members.

---

[57] Wittgenstein, Ludwig. 2003. *Philosophical investigations*, Trans. G.E.M. Anscombe. 27ᵉ–28ᵉ §67. Oxford: Blackwell.

[58] George, Alexandra. 2012. *Constructing intellectual property*. Cambridge: Cambridge University Press, 257.

[59] George, Alexandra. 2015. The metaphysics of intellectual property. *The WIPO Journal* 7: 16–28, 26.

As established, the trade secret is similar to other forms of intellectual property since they are in the same 'family'. These similarities enable this book to apply some antitrust experiences concerning other types of intellectual property to trade secret cases. Nevertheless, this book argues that a trade secret is different from other intellectual property in some ways. To some extent, the originality of this book comes from these differences a trade secret has with its family members and their implications on antitrust assessments. Chapter 2 of this book, which briefly introduces the framework of trade secrets, takes a patent as an example to reveal the differences between a trade secret and a patent. Chapters 4 and 5 of this book, which provides critical antitrust assessments, also articulate the implications of these differences on the antitrust analysis regarding trade secrets.

1.2.5 Conclusion

Transnational or domestic undertakings are becoming reliant on trade secrets as valuable assets to compete in modern commercial practices. The ownership of a trade secret is legal, yet the exploitation of a trade secret by a dominant firm may bring about competition problems. China does not have abundant experience in dealing with anti-monopoly cases relevant to intellectual property, including trade secrets. In a specific anti-monopoly case, Chinese legislators or competition authorities may not pay attention to the characteristics of a trade secret which may have implications on the antitrust assessments of the case. This book uses the complementarity theory and family resemblance doctrine to explain legal issues in the following chapters.

1.3 Research Aim and Research Questions

The exploitation of trade secrets by dominant companies may result in competition problems in China. Simultaneously, the Chinese competition agencies or courts have little experience in dealing with such cases. As a consequence, this book intends to fill the gap as to how the AML could be applied in situations where dominant firms use their trade secrets illegally. In other words, the aim of this book is to determine in what situations the use of trade secrets by a firm may constitute the abuse of market dominance in China.

The following discussion reveals the main research question of this book in line with the research aim. It also outlines some sub-questions derived from the main research question.

The main research question of this book is the following:

In which circumstances does the use of trade secrets constitute an abuse of market dominance pursuant to China's Anti-monopoly Law (AML) and how can the approach to determining this be improved?

The main research question is supported by the following inquiries:

(a) What is the current legal framework of trade secrets in China?
(b) What is the framework of the abuse of market dominance under competition law?
(c) How should the relevant market and market dominance be defined in trade secrets cases under China's AML?
(d) What constitutes prohibited unilateral conduct in relation to trade secrets under China's AML?
(e) How could Chinese competition law and enforcement in relation to the abuse of dominance concerning trade secrets be improved?

This book intends to answer the research questions from the following perspectives: firstly, it will define trade secrets, particularly under Chinese law and describe the characteristics of a trade secret; secondly, it will provide an overview of the abuse of market dominance from the perspectives of the US, the EU and China; thirdly, it will define the relevant market and assess market dominance in relation to trade secrets; fourthly, it will examine relevant prohibited unilateral practices that may arise from the abuse of trade secrets; lastly, the research will provide suggestions for Chinese law and competition enforcement relevant to the abuse of market dominance regarding trade secrets. By answering these research questions, this research helps China develop its competition rules and enforcement in relation to the abuse of dominance in trade secrets, helping maintain healthy market competition in China.

1.4 Structure of the Book

In order to address the main research question—in which circumstances does the use of trade secrets constitute an abuse of market dominance pursuant to the AML and how can the approach be improved?—This book has been structured as follows:

Chapter 1—Chapter 1 serves as an introductory chapter of the book.

Chapters 2 and 3—Chapters 2 and 3 provide the basic analysis of a trade secret and the abuse of market dominance. It is necessary to illustrate the concepts and characteristics of these two subject-matters because this book considers the extent to which competition law (law against the abuse of dominance) can apply to trade secrets.

Specifically, Chapter 2 outlines the legal definition and characteristics of a trade secret. The WTO TRIPS Agreement[60] provides an international common standard for trade secret protection across jurisdictions. In China, the EU and the US, trade secrets refer to commercial information which is not known to the public and has commercial value and for which the holder has adopted reasonable confidentiality measures. The Chinese civil Code treats a trade secret as a type of intellectual property. There are some characteristics of trade secrets. For instance, the categories of trade secrets may vary from technical information to business information or data. The secret owner

[60] Agreement on Trade-Related Aspects of Intellectual Property Rights.

can protect its secret information indefinitely. The exclusivity of a trade secret may be limited. Chapter 2 also articulates some differences between a trade secret and a patent.

Chapter 2 examines a crucial concept of this book: trade secrets. Chapters 4 and 5, which analyse the market definition and the abusive practices regarding trade secrets, will consider the definition and characteristics of a trade secret when assessing specific antitrust cases.

Chapter 3 helps to organize Chapters 4 and 5 by examining the legal history and application of the abuse of market dominance provision. Even though this book mainly focuses on China's AML, the development of the abuse of market dominance in the EU and the US is also discussed because the concept and assessment methods arise from these two jurisdictions, and because the book will look at the way those laws consider abuse of dominance in relation to trade secrets.

Generally, Chapter 3 sets out the doctrine of prohibiting the abuse of dominance—A company with substantial market power may affect market outcomes by limiting output and raising prices or otherwise adversely modifying terms of trade. Therefore, a dominant firm should not abuse its market power, impairing competition and harming consumers' interests. More importantly, through an examination of the abuse of dominance provisions, Chapter 3 uses a two-step method for analyzing cases involving the abuse of market dominance. The first step is to examine whether the undertaking has market dominance in the relevant market. If the undertaking is dominant, it becomes vital to investigate whether the dominant firm engages in illegal abusive conduct. Accordingly, Chapters 4 and 5 which resolve around the market dominance in trade secrets and the abusive practices are organized pursuant to the two-step methods concluded in Chapter 3. Chapter 3 uses doctrinal methodology to study the relevant Chinese, EU and US legislation, case law and literature and compare the similarities and differences as well as the social contexts when necessary.

Chapter 4—Chapter 4 is divided into two parts-defining the relevant market in trade secrets and assessing market power related to trade secrets.

The threshold for identifying market dominance is to define the market which the undertaking competes in. Competition agencies or courts usually consider two dimensions of relevant market—product and geographic markets. When it comes to trade secrets as a type of intellectual property, a secret holder can license the secret information to competitors. Therefore, this book also discusses the definition of a technology market. Chapter 4 mainly uses both quantitative and qualitative approaches to define the relevant markets.

After market definition, it is necessary to assess factors that influence market power in relation to trade secrets. This Chapter 4 briefly examines the relationship between market power and market dominance from a competition law perspective. It also critically discusses the potential relationship between the exclusivity of a trade secrets and the market power the exclusivity may lead to. This chapter also analyse some indicators of market dominance relevant to trade secrets, namely market share and barriers to entry. In this chapter, guidance is taken from previous decisions of competition agencies and judgment of courts in China, as well as in the EU and the US to help improve China's decision-making process.

Chapter 5—According to the two-step method provided in Chapter 3, if a company is a dominant firm in the relevant market, it is necessary to assess whether the underlying conduct of an undertaking constitutes the abusive practices that may harm competition. Therefore, Chapter 5 critically examines some abusive practices relevant to trade secrets.

As stated, the possession of a trade secret, even by a dominant firm, is legal. It is the exploitation of trade secrets that may raise competition concerns. This chapter analyses three typical abusive practices as to trade secrets from a competition law perspective.

To be more specific, this chapter considers the refusal to disclose trade secrets, as a sub-set of the refusal to deal, and this may constitute the abuse of market dominance. If a dominant undertaking files trade secret misappropriation litigation against competitors in bad faith, this litigation may constitute an anti-competitive abuse. Additionally, a dominant firm is likely to license trade secrets to competitors. If the dominant company forces its licensee not to challenge the existence of the secret information in question, the imposition of non-challenge clauses in relation to a trade secret might constitute the abuse of dominance.

Chapter 6—China does not have significant experience in dealing with cases of the abuse of market dominance in trade secrets. This book helps China facilitate its anti-monopoly rules and enforcement concerning this topic. In line with analysis in previous chapters,Chapter 6 provides several suggestions for revising relevant Chinese competition rules and improving for anti-monopoly enforcement in China.

Chapter 7—Chapter 7 concludes the whole book.

A flow chart illustrates the structure of this book (Fig. 1.1):

1.5 Significance and Scope of the Research

1.5.1 Significance of the Research

Section 1.2 of this chapter has described the background of this book. In short, a trade secret has become a vital asset of many companies nowadays. Firms conducting business inside or outside of China are taking advantage of trade secrets to compete in markets. Comparative experience in some western jurisdictions, such as in the EU or the US, has demonstrated that the exploitation of trade secret may constitute the abuse of market dominance in specific circumstances.

China's AML has only been in effect for a mere decade. It is arguable that China does not have sufficient experience in addressing the abuse of dominance cases regarding intellectual property, including trade secrets. According to the author's

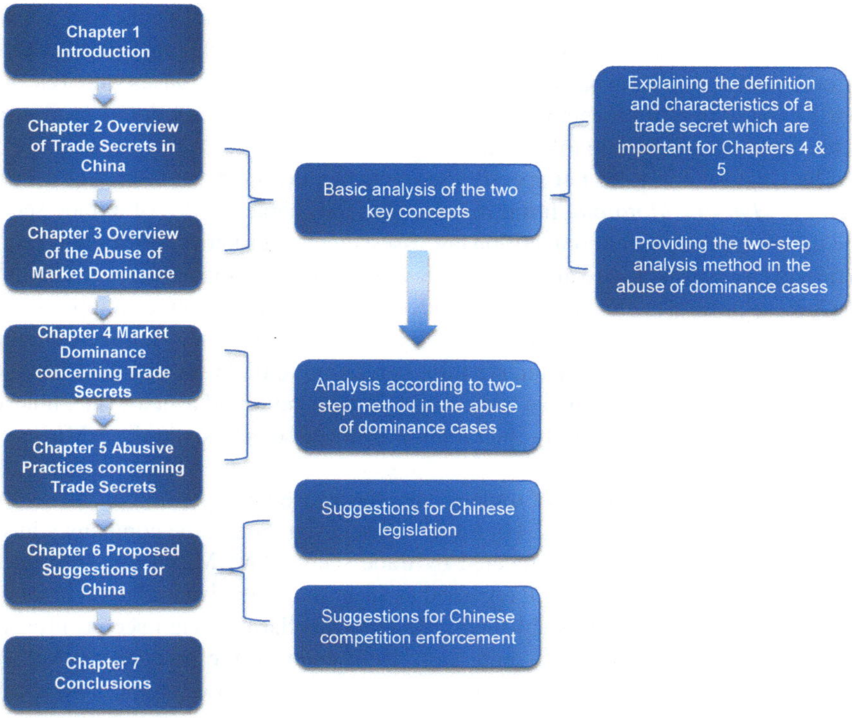

Fig. 1.1 Chart illustrates the structure of this book

research,[61] there have been only three abuse of dominance cases as to intellectual property reported in China. They are:

(1) *Huawei v InterDigital* (2013)[62]
(2) *NDRC v Qualcomm* (2015)[63]
(3) *Hytera v Motorola* (2019)[64]

---

[61] The following lists three cases that have been concluded by the Chinese courts or competition agency. As stated earlier, the China Microsoft case, although concerning intellectual property, is still pending.

[62] 华为公司与交互数字公司滥用市场支配地位案 [Huawei v InterDigital—Abuse of Market Dominance case], 广东省高级人民法院 [Guangdong High People's Court], (2013) 粤高法民三终字第306号 [Economic Appeal No. 306], 21 October 2013.

[63] 高通公司滥用市场支配地位案 [NDRC v Qualcomm— Abuse of Market Dominance case], 国家发展和改革委员会 [National Development and Reform Commission of the PRC], (2015)发改办价监处罚 [2015]1号 [Decision of the NDRC [2015] No. 1], 9 February 2015.

[64] 海能达与摩托罗拉滥用市场支配地位纠纷案 [Hytera v Motorola— Disputes of the Abuse of Market Dominance], 北京知识产权法院 [Beijing Intellectual Property Court, People's Republic of China], 北京知识产权法院 (2017) 京73民初1671号 [Economic Appeal No. 1671], 31 December 2019.

Chapter 5 of this book, which analyses relevant abusive practices concerning trade secrets, will consider these three cases in depth to describe the existing anti-monopoly enforcement and its drawbacks in China. Generally, the first two cases were relevant to the exploitation of patents while the third one was an abuse of dominance cases as to secret inter-operation information.

The Chinese court did not specify the intellectual property at issue was a trade secret in *Hytera v Motorola.* It did not consider the characteristics of a trade secret and their implications for competition law assessments. Furthermore, the court failed to provide a clear-cut test to analyse the abuse of market dominance cases in China.[65]

Chinese antitrust scholars often consider how competition law can apply in the field of intellectual property as a whole.[66] By contrast, there is very limited literature discussing the anti-monopoly intervention in relation to trade secrets. According to the author's research, there have been only four peer-reviewed articles (in Chinese) that address the anti-monopoly intervention in trade secrets since the AML came into force in 2008.[67]

In reality, the exploitation of trade secrets has caused competition problems. As stated earlier, in the famous EU *Microsoft*[68] case, even though the company's inter-operability information was protected by trade secrets law, Microsoft's refusal to disclose the information was still regarded as an anti-competitive unilateral practice. This is because Microsoft established a de facto standard through secret information in order to prevent other competitors from entering the relevant market. As a consequence, Microsoft was compulsorily forced to disclose the interoperability information to its rivals.[69]

China's AML may apply to the use of trade secrets. Economic glocalization has made China deeply involved in world markets. For example, as discussed, Microsoft's refusal to disclose secret information also raised anti-competition concerns in China. Aside from Microsoft, many transnational or domestic undertakings are using trade

---

65 For detailed analysis of *Hytera v Motorola*, see Sect. 5.2.2.2 in Chapter 5 of this book.

66 Professor Xianlin Wang's monograph titled 'Intellectual Property and Anti-monopoly Law: Study on Anti-monopoly Issues of Abuse of Intellectual Property Rights' is the first monograph in China which examines the anti-monopoly intervention in the domain of intellectual property. It was first published in 2001 and republished in 2008 and 2020. See 王先林 [Wang Xianlin]. 2020. *知识产权与反垄断法* [*Intellectual property and anti-monopoly law*]. 北京: 法律出版社[Beijing: Law Press China].

67 See 曾雄 [Zeng Xiong]. 2018. 商业秘密滥用行为的反垄断适用规则之完善研究 [Research on improvements on the application of anti-monopoly law in the abuse of trade secrets]. *研究生法学 [Graduate Law Review]* 33(5): 77–85; 胡良荣 [Hu Liangrong]. 2016. 利益平衡: 论商业秘密的竞争法保护与规制 [Balance of interests: Research on the protection and regulation of trade secrets from a competition law perspective]. *知识产权 [Intellectual Property]* 12: 52–57; 郭德忠[Guo Dezhong]. 2015. 商业秘密滥用的反垄断规制 [The anti-monopoly regulation of the abuse of trade secrets]. *情报理论与实践 [Information Studies: Theory & Application]* 38(11): 36–39; 刘磊 [Liu Lei]. 2009. 浅析滥用商业秘密权的反垄断法规制 [Research on the anti-monopoly regulation of trade secrets]. *科学之友 [Friend of Science Amateurs]* 1:145–146.

68 *Microsoft v European Commission* (T-201/04) [2007] ECR II-3601.

69 For more details on the EU Microsoft case, see Chapters 4 and 5 of this book.

secrets as an efficient competitive tool against rivals, and more antitrust disputes concerning trade secrets are anticipated in China in the future.

In this regard, if Chinese anti-monopoly rules are too general to guide Chinese competition authorities when addressing cases of trade secrets, the failure to fight against abusive practices may eventually harm competition and consumers' interests in China. This book fills the current gap in how Chinese anti-monopoly agencies and courts should handle abuse of dominance cases regarding trade secrets.

Specifically, the significance of this research can be divided into the following four parts.

(1) This book is significant because it is designed to contribute to scholarship about how the law against the abuse of dominance applies to a new area—trade secrets. Despite the fact that western jurisdictions have more mature experience (than China) in handling abuse of dominance cases as to trade secrets (e.g. EU *Microsoft*), antitrust literature from both sides of the Atlantic on this topic is limited.[70]

    As stated earlier, Chinese competition lawyers often consider all categories of intellectual property together in anti-monopoly literature. This is also the case in the west. For example, there have been many discussions on the application of competition law in the field of intellectual property by international organizations, such as the Organization for Economic Cooperation and Development (OECD)[71] and the World Intellectual Property Organization (WIPO).[72]

    Leading antitrust scholars in the US and the EU have continuously examined the relationship between intellectual property and competition. However,

[70] The author has found a few antitrust literature on the abuse of dominance regarding trade secrets. For example, Dr Gintare Surblyte critically examines the refusal to disclose trade secrets in her monograph. See Surblyte, Gintare. 2011. *The refusal to disclose trade secrets as an abuse of market dominance-microsoft and beyond*. Bern: Stämpfli. Some antitrust lawyers analyse the antitrust intervention of trade secrets in journal articles or book chapters. See e.g. Drexl, Josef. 2011. Refusal to grant access to trade secrets as an abuse of market dominance. In *Intellectual property and competition law-new frontiers*. Oxford: Oxford University Press, 165; First, Harry. 2011. Trade secrets and antitrust law. In *The law and theory of trade secrecy:A handbook of contemporary research*, ed. C Dreyfuss Rochelle. 358. Northampton: Edward Elgar; Czapracka, Katarzyna. 2008. Antitrust and trade secrets: The US and the EU approach. *Santa Clara High Technology Law Journal* 24(2): 207–273; Oliver, Michael. 1989. Comments: Antitrust liability for bad faith assertion of trade secrets. *University of Baltimore Law Review* 18: 544–569; Jr. Yoerg, Norman. 1977. Should a trade secret misappropriation claim lie in the procrustean antitrust bed. *Antitrust Bull* 22(1):1–65.

[71] See e.g. OECD. 1998. Competition Policy and Intellectual Property Rights (Research Paper, OECD); OECD. 2019. Licensing of IP rights and competition law. OECD. https://www.oecd.org/en/publications/licensing-of-ip-rights-and-competition-law_6a74221e-en.html. Accessed 25 March 2025.

[72] See e.g. Oliveira, Gesner, and Thomas Fujiwara. Intellectual property and competition as complementary policies. (Research Paper, WIPO project on Intellectual Property and Competition Law); WIPO. IP and competition policy. *WIPO*. https://www.wipo.int/ip-competition/en/. Accessed 25 March 2025.

they generally refer to patents or take patents as examples when analyzing competition cases related to intellectual property.[73]

This book argues that although trade secrets share similarities with other forms of intellectual property (such as patents), they have some distinct characteristics.[74] These characteristics may have implications for the antitrust assessments of the abuse of dominance cases regarding trade secrets.[75] Hence, it is vital to consider the characteristics of a trade secret in antitrust cases when necessary.

The book will borrow antitrust experience in relation to other intellectual property (mostly patents) to critically analyse the abuse of market dominance concerning trade secrets. This research will contribute not only to Chinese competition literature but also western literature regarding antitrust intervention in the exercise of trade secrets.

(2) This book will assist Chinese competition agencies and courts when handling cases of the abuse of dominance in trade secrets. There have been two abuse of dominance cases involving trade secrets in China as discussed—the China *Microsoft* case (pending) and *Hytera v Motorola.* It is expected that there will be more anti-monopoly cases concerning trade secrets in the future in China.

Doctrinal methodology is used as the main research methodology of this book.[76] This methodology is also the primary method used by Chinese competition agencies and courts to handle competition cases. This book will assist Chinese anti-monopoly agencies and courts to interpret the general competition rules and establish clear tests in specific antitrust cases.

(3) This book is also significant because it explores comparative experience of other jurisdictions (mainly the EU and the US),[77] helping shape China's AML

[73] See e.g. Drexl, Josef. 2011. Intellectual property in competition: How to promote dynamic competition as a goal. In *More common ground for international competition law?* eds. Josef Drexl, Warren S. Grimes, Clifford A. Jones, Rudolph J.R. Peritz and Edward T. Swaine, 210–229. ASCOLA Competition Law series. ('...patents— as IP rights that are expected to create incentives for innovation— are hence pro-competitive. Indeed, they exclude only a specific form of competition namely competition by imitation...'); Jones, Alison and Nazzini, Renato. 2019. The effect of competition law on patent remedies. In *Patent remedies and complex products: Towards a global consensus,* eds. B. Biddle et al. Cambridge: Cambridge University Press. ('It is often said that patent law (and intellectual property (IP) law more broadly) and competition law "constitute complementary components of a modern industrial policy' which aim to improve innovation and consumer welfare.'); Hovenkamp, Herbert. Intellectual property and competition (Research Paper, University of Pennsylvania Law School, December 2016). Professor Hovenkamp mostly uses patent cases as examples to explain the relationship between intellectual property and competition is this paper.

[74] Chapter 2 of this book introduces characteristics of a trade secret and compares a trade secret with a patent.

[75] Chapters 4 and 5 considers characteristics of a trade secret when analyzing the abuse of dominance cases regarding trade secrets.

[76] See Sect. 1.6 of this chapter.

[77] Section 1.6 of this chapter will further explain the reasons that the EU and the US are selected comparative jurisdictions in this book.

to promote and protect effective competition in China. By reviewing comparative experiences, this book highlights the advantages and disadvantages of the approaches taken by different jurisdictions. Meaningful lessons can be drawn to help China regulate abusive practices involving trade secrets to promote competition and protect consumer interests.

(4) This book is original because it gives specific recommendations within the Chinese legal context. China is the targeted jurisdiction of this book. After critically analyzing the abuse of market dominance with regard to trade secrets from a competition law perspective, this book provides specific suggestions for Chinese anti-monopoly rules and enforcement.

1.5.2 Scope of the Research

Firstly, the legal framework of this book concentrates on the abuse of market dominance (prohibited unilateral conduct) under China's AML. Competition law, including China's AML, prohibits three types of economic monopolistic conduct: anti-competitive agreements between undertakings, mergers that may have effects of restricting competition and the abuse of market dominance.[78] The book will not include analysis of all kinds of monopolistic conduct but will focus on the law against abuse of market dominance.

Secondly, the book explores the abuse of dominance regarding trade secrets rather than in relation to other intellectual property. As indicated, IP-related competition issues have been much-discussed. Nonetheless, most discussions on the IP-related fields in competition law are relevant to patents, while there are few on trade secrets in China or western countries. This book will borrow antitrust experience concerning other forms of intellectual property to research on competition issues about trade secrets.

Lastly, the book will study relevant comparative experience from the EU competition law and the US antitrust law. Competition law practices in these two jurisdictions matter to China's AML because, firstly, the EU competition law was a foundational model for China's AML[79] and secondly, as the ancestor of modern competition

---

[78] Antitrust scholars noticed that in addition to these three economic monopolistic practices, China's AML provides a special chapter that prevents administrative monopoly. See e.g. Fox, Eleanor. 2008. An anti-monopoly law for china— scaling the walls of government restraints. *Antitrust Law Journal* 75(1): 173–194; Wu Changqi and Liu Zhicheng. 2012. A tiger without teeth? Regulation of administrative monopoly under China's anti-monopoly law. *Review of Industrial Organization* 41: 133–155, 133–136.

[79] The then vice minister of the Ministry of Commerce of the PRC (MOFCOM) used to claim in 2005 that the enacting China's AML would learn from the EU competition law from many aspects. See China News, people.cn (18 November 2019) https://www.big-bit.com/wap/news/13041.html.

law, the US antitrust enforcement greatly impacts China's competition law enforcement.[80] The following section will further explain the implications that the EU and US competition laws have on Chinese anti-monopoly practices.

1.6 Introduction to Anti-monopoly Rules in China

This book focuses on competition law practices in China, and uses some Chinese legal documents in the following chapters to reveal the landscape of Chinese anti-monopoly enforcement. This part introduces several anti-monopoly rules in China so that international readers may have a better understanding of the antitrust analysis in this book.

One fundamental characteristic of the civil law system is that "the courts' main task is to apply and interpret the law contained in a code, or a statute to case facts."[81] In a jurisdiction with civil law traditions, Chinese competition authorities and courts attaches importance to codified rules. The following briefly explains the existing framework of codified anti-monopoly rules in China.

The current framework for these anti-monopoly rules has been shaped since the enactment of China's Anti-monopoly Law (AML) in 2007. The Standing Committee of the National People's Congress (NPC) passed the AML on 30 August 2007, effective from 1 August 2008. According to the Constitution of the PRC, the NPC as well as its Standing Committee is the highest organ of state power,[82] and one of its duties is to enact and amend laws.[83] The AML is the fundamental anti-monopoly (competition law) rule in China. The AML was amended once in 2022.

Prior to 2018, there were three competition agencies in China. They were responsible for different antitrust tasks. These agencies were the National Development and Reform Commission (NDRC), the State Administration of Industry and Commerce (SAIC), and the Ministry of Commerce (MOFCOM).[84] Chinese antitrust lawyers

---

[80] The US antitrust economics and legal theory affect the application of China's AML in many ways, such as the application of SSNIP and influences from Harvard and Chicago school of economics. See 李剑 [Jian Li]. 2014. 中国反垄断法实施中的体系冲突和化解 [System conflict and resolution in the implementation of China's anti-monopoly law]. *中国法学 [China Legal Science]* 6: 138–153, 139.

[81] See Pejovic, Caslav. 2001. Civil law and common law: Two different paths leading to the same goal. *VUWLR* 32: 817–842, 819.

[82] Article 57 of the Chinese Constitution provides that '[T]he National People's Congress of the People's Republic of China is the highest organ of state power. Its permanent body is the Standing Committee of the National People's Congress.'

[83] See articles 62 and 67 of the Chinese Constitution. According to the Chinese Constitution, only those regulations enacted by the NPC and its Standing Committee can be called 'laws' in China. Other regulations enacted by administrative or judicial organs must not contravene laws.

[84] In short, the NDRC was responsible for cases of price-related monopoly agreements and the abuse of market dominance. The SAIC was responsible for other types of cases of monopoly agreements and the abuse of dominance. The MOFCOM was responsible for cases of merger control.

called for a unified competition agency after the establishment of the AML.[85] In 2018, China established an integrated anti-monopoly authority, the State Administration for Market Regulation (SAMR).[86]

Chinese competition agencies (including the previous three agencies and the current SAMR) are not independent authorities. They are ministerial administrative agencies under China's central administrative government (namely the 'State Council' of the PRC). According to the Legislation Law of China, ministries of the State Council can enact administrative regulations (in Chinese '行政规章'), which must not contravene laws promulgated by the NPC and its Standing Committee. These administrative regulations are binding for the agency by which they are enacted and the local branches of this agency in China.[87]

When it comes to antitrust rules, the SAMR can enact antitrust administrative regulations as a ministry of the State Council. For instance, the SAMR issued *Provisions on Prohibitions of Abuse of Intellectual Property Rights to Exclude and Restrict Competition* in 2020.[88] The SAMR, as well as its local branches, must follow this administrative regulation when it conducts antitrust investigations with respect to the abuse of intellectual property rights.

Another type of antitrust rule in China is the anti-monopoly guidelines. Article 12 of the AML authorizes the State Council to establish an Anti-monopoly Commission,[89] one of whose duties is to formulate and issue anti-monopoly guidelines.[90]

---

[85] See e.g. Wang Xiaoye. 2008. Highlights of China's new anti-monopoly law. *Antitrust Law Journal* 75(1): 133–150, 145 ('[C]ompetition law enforcement agencies would not only be inefficient, but it may also create conflict and friction among the three agencies.').

[86] Jingyuan Ma introduces the structures and functions of NDRC, SAIC, MOFCOM and SAMR in detail. See Ma Jingyuan. 2020. *Competition law in China:A law and economics perspective.* Berlin: Springer, 168–172.

[87] For example, if the SAMR issues an administrative regulation, this regulation is binding for SAMR and the local branches of SAMR in all provinces in China.

[88] The SAIC enacted this antitrust regulation in 2015. The SAMR amended this regulation and reissued it after the SAMR became the exclusive competition agency in China.

[89] Different from the SAMR, the Anti-monopoly Commission does not take any specific antitrust investigations. This Commission is mainly responsible for policy formulation and co-ordination.' See Ma Jingyuan. 2020. *Competition law in China:A law and economics perspective.* Berlin: Springer, 19.

[90] Article 12 of the AML provides that '[T]he State Council shall establish an anti-monopoly commission to be responsible for organizing, coordinating and providing guidance for anti-monopoly tasks and perform the following duties:

(1) study and draft the relevant competition policies;
(2) organize investigation, evaluation overall market competition, and issue evaluation reports;
(3) formulate and issue anti-monopoly guidelines;
(4) coordinate anti-monopoly administrative enforcement tasks; and
(5) perform any other duties stipulated by the State Council.

The composition and working rules for the anti-monopoly commission of the State Council shall be formulated by the State Council.'

The Legislation Law of China does not stipulate anti-monopoly guidelines as a category of 'law'.[91] Anti-monopoly guidelines, as its name 'guidelines' shows, are not a type of enforceable rules in China. Despite these facts, Chinese scholars believe that anti-monopoly guidelines play an essential role in China's antitrust enforcement, as the guidelines often provide specific instructions on antitrust issues.[92] The SAMR and the SPC have used the anti-monopoly guidelines when dealing with competition cases.[93] One example of the anti-monopoly guidelines is the *Anti-monopoly Guidelines in the field of Intellectual Property (2019)* ('IP Guidelines').

The SPC, China's top court, also plays a part in enacting antitrust rules in China. The Legislation Law authorizes the SPC to enact judicial interpretations which are legally binding for all Chinese courts.[94] Again, these judicial interpretations must not be in contravention of laws formulated by the NPC (and its Standing Committee). In terms of anti-monopoly rules, the SPC has published one judicial interpretation regarding the AML, namely *Interpretation on Several Issues Concerning the Application of Law in the Hearing of Civil Cases Involving Disputes over Monopolistic Acts.* This judicial interpretation is applicable in civil antitrust cases, which are brought by an undertaking as a plaintiff. This judicial interpretation is not binding on administrative agencies like the SAMR. The judicial interpretation mainly concerns the civil procedure of an antitrust lawsuit and the burden of proof between parties.

1.7 Research Methodology

The main research method applied in this book is doctrinal methodology. This section is divided into two parts. The first part explains the doctrinal method to be used in this book in a general sense. The second part particularly articulates why this

[91] In China, it is the task of the Legislation Law to determine which types of regulations are enforceable. Some Chinese scholar regards anti-monopoly guidelines as a type of 'soft law' as it guides (rather than 'enforces') the competition agencies and courts. See 郑鹏程, 刘长云 [Zheng Pengcheng and Liu Changyun]. 2016. 我国反垄断相关市场执法实践检讨与反思 [Rethinking on the practice of relevant market definition in Chinese anti-monopoly]. *中南大学学报(社会科学版) [Journal of Central South University (Social Science)]* 22(5): 46–51, 49.

[92] See 王先林 [Wang Xianlin]. 2020. *知识产权与反垄断法* [*Intellectual property and anti-monopoly law*]. 北京: 法律出版社 [Beijing: Law Press China], 432.

[93] For instance, the Chinese competition authority and courts referred to the Guidelines on the Definition of a Relevant Market in specific cases. See e.g. 阿里巴巴滥用市场支配地位案》[Alibaba-The Abuse of Market Dominance Case], 国家市场监管总局 [SAMR], 国市监处[2021]28号 [Administrative Decision of the SAMR No. 28], 10 April 2008; 北京奇虎科技有限公司诉腾讯科技 (深圳) 有限公司、深圳市腾讯计算机系统有限公司滥用市场支配地位纠纷案 [Beijing Qihoo Technology v Shenzhen Tencent Technology—Abuse of Market Dominance Case], 最高人民法院 [Supreme People's Court], 2013民三终字第4号 [Economic Judgement No. 3], 8 October 2014.

[94] Article 104 of the Legislation Law says that '[T]he interpretations made by the Supreme People's Court and the Supreme People's Procuratorate on the application of laws in the judicial or procuratorial work shall be mainly targeted at specific legal articles, and shall conform to the purpose, principle and original intention of legislation.'

book chooses the EU and the US as two selected jurisdictions to analyse their well-established experience for China.

1.7.1 *Doctrinal Methodology as the Primary Methodology in This Book*

It is suggested that lawyers, judges and jurists have been using doctrinal methodology for legal reasoning since the nineteenth century, establishing this method as the 'traditional genre of research in legal field'.[95] For a long period, doctrinal research has been the predominant legal methodology both in common law countries[96] and in the civil law system.[97] This book will be guided by doctrinal legal methodology. This methodology involves systemic analysis of law provisions and the relationship between them, anticipating the trends as well.[98]

It is difficult to provide a precise definition of doctrinal methodology.[99] Yet researchers across the Atlantic identify some common characteristics of doctrinal methodology.[100] For example:

(1) The authoritative sources, including laws, cases and academic literatures, may provide primary arguments in doctrinal work[101];
(2) Doctrinal method intends to make the legal system more predictable as it concentrates on established rules and publications[102];
(3) Doctrinal method often helps courts (or other authorities) about the application of legal doctrine to specific cases[103];
(4) Doctrinal method examines rules governing a specific legal category and assesses the relationship between rules, explains difficulties and maybe predicts developments.[104]

---

[95] Kharel, Amrit. Doctrinal legal research. SSRN. https://www.researchgate.net/publication/323762486_Doctrinal_Legal_Research. Accessed 25 March 2025.

[96] Hutchinson, Terry. 2015. The doctrinal method: Incorporating interdisciplinary methods in reforming the law. *Erasmus Law Review* 8: 130–138, 131.

[97] For instance, the Methodenlehre der Rechtswissenschaft [Methodology of law] written by German jurist Karl Larenz has a great influence on civil law jurisdictions like Germany, France and China.

[98] Hutchinson, Terry and Duncan, Nigel. 2012. Defining and describing what we do: Doctrinal legal research. *Deakin Law Review* 17(1): 83–119, 101.

[99] Rob van Gestel, and Hans-W. Micklitz. Revitalizing doctrinal legal research in Europe: What about Methodology?(Working Paper, European University Institute, May 2011) 26.

[100] Ibid.

[101] Ibid.

[102] Kharel, Amrit. Doctrinal legal research. SSRN. https://www.researchgate.net/publication/323762486_Doctrinal_Legal_Research. Accessed 25 March 2025.

[103] Ibid.

[104] Hutchinson, Terry and Duncan, Nigel. 2012. Defining and describing what we do: Doctrinal legal research. *Deakin Law Review* 17(1): 83–119, 101.

This book uses doctrinal methodology because the research topic and aims are compatible with its features. Firstly, this book examines the research topic from the perspective of competition law, which is a particular legal category. Secondly, this book studies relevant laws, cases and scholarly publications and to put forward arguments derived from these materials. Thirdly, this book aims to help Chinese competition authorities and courts interpret anti-monopoly rules in the abuse of dominance cases regarding trade secrets. Lastly, this book provides some clear-cut tests for the assessment of abusive practices, which may make the competition enforcement in China more predictable.

Doctrinal methodology often requires a researcher: first to select the proper legal materials, and then to conduct deep analysis of these materials. The subsequent list contains some (but not all) of the crucial legal documents and competition cases used in this book:

China:

- The Anti-monopoly Law (AML)
- Anti-monopoly Guidelines in the field of Intellectual Property (2019)
- Provisions on Prohibitions of Abuse of Intellectual Property Rights to Exclude and Restrict Competition
- Interim Provisions on Prohibition of the Abuse of Market Dominance
- *Qihoo v Tencent* (2014)[105]
- *Huawei v InterDigital* (2013)
- *NDRC v Qualcomm* (2015)
- *Hytera v Motorola* (2019)

Eu:

- Treaty on the Functioning of the European Union (TFEU)
- *Microsoft v European Commission*[106]
- *Oscar Bronner*[107]
- *Magill*[108]
- *IMS Health*[109]
- *ITT Promedia*[110]

---

[105] 北京奇虎科技有限公司诉腾讯科技（深圳）有限公司、深圳市腾讯计算机系统有限公司滥用市场支配地位纠纷案[Beijing Qihoo Technology v Shenzhen Tencent Technology—Abuse of Market Dominance Case], 最高人民法院 [Supreme People's Court], 2013民三终字第4号 [Economic Judgement No. 3], 8 October 2014.

[106] *Microsoft v European Commission* (T-201/04) [2007] ECR II-3601.

[107] Case C-7/97, Oscar Bronner GmbH & Co. KG v Mediaprint EU:C:1998:569.

[108] Joined cases C-241/91 P and C-242/91 P, Radio Telefis Eireann (RTE) and Independent Television Publications Ltd (ITP) v Commission EU:C:1995:98.

[109] Case C-418/01, IMS Health GmbH & Co. OHG v NDC Health GmbH & Co. KG EU:C:2004:257.

[110] Case T-111/96, ITT Promedia NV v Commission of the European Communities EU:T:1998:183.

- *Windsurfing*[111]

Us:

- The Sherman Act
- Antitrust Guidelines for the Licensing of Intellectual Property (2017)
- *Colgate*[112]
- *Aspen Skiing*[113]
- *Trinko*[114]
- *CVD v Raytheon*[115]
- *Lear v Adkins*[116]

Additionally, two issues that arose from the doctrinal methodology applied in this book must be addressed.

Firstly, as discussed earlier, there is very limited literature or cases that discusses antitrust issues of trade secrets. In that regard, this book analyses relevant competition cases or literature relevant to intellectual property as a whole or regarding other forms of intellectual property (such as patents). This book will apply the above experience to the abuse of dominance cases related to trade secret and consider the features of a trade secret simultaneously.

Secondly, the mainland China is a jurisdiction with civil law tradition. Judges apply codified rules to decide cases. Cases usually cannot constitute precedents and judges are not bound by previous cases.

This book also conducts some cases studies of Chinese anti-monopoly cases. This does not mean that these cases are precedents and binding for competition agencies or courts. There are only a few anti-monopoly cases related to intellectual property in China. For example, when analyzing the refusal to license intellectual property (or the refusal to disclose trade secrets),[117] there has been merely one case (*Hytera v Motorola*) in China. Consequently, this book conducts doctrinal research on Chinese anti-monopoly cases in order to reveal the landscape of anti-monopoly enforcement in China and viewpoints of Chinese agencies and courts on the application of competition law.

---

[111] Windsurfing International Inc. v Commission of the European Communities, Case 193/83, EU:C:1986:75.

[112] United States v Colgate & Co., 250 U.S. 300 (1919).

[113] Aspen Skiing Co. v. Aspen Highlands Skiing Corp., 472 U.S. 585 (1985).

[114] Verizon Communications v. Law Offices of Curtis V. Trinko, LLP, often shortened to Verizon v. Trinko, 540 U.S. 398 (2004).

[115] CVD, Inc. v. Raytheon. Co., 769 F.2d 842, 850 (1st Cir. 1985).

[116] Lear, Inc. v. Adkins, 395 U.S. 653 (1969).

[117] The refusal to disclose trade secret is discussed in Chapter 5 as an abusive practice.

1.7.2 Selected Jurisdictions to Learn from: The EU and the US

This book conducts doctrinal analysis on Chinese materials. More importantly, this book takes examples from the EU and the US to shape anti-monopoly enforcement in China. The following details the reasons of a focus on the EU and US competition law in this book.

The EU competition law has a considerable influence on China's AML. China's modern legal framework shares the civil law traditions of EU countries such as Germany. This is also the case when it comes to China's AML.

China has no history of anti-monopoly rules. The enactment of the AML was an achievement drawing on comparative experience in jurisdictions with well-established competition laws, particularly the EU competition law.[118] A small group of Chinese scholars and officials began to study foreign competition law in the late 1990s and established anti-monopoly rules in China.[119] Some of them studied in Germany and brought the European model to China.[120]

Article 22 of China's AML, which proscribes the abuse of dominance, is similar to Article 102 of TFEU in form and substance.[121] Ordoliberalism is the legal philosophy of Article 102,[122] which favors a social market economy, and is more suitable for China's socialist market economy than laissez-faire economics.[123] Accordingly, this book chooses to conduct doctrinal research on the EU competition law materials to improve Chinese legal practices.

---

[118] See Healey, Deborah. 2008. An anti-monopoly law for China: Weapon or mirage? *Competition & Consumer Law Journal* 16: 220–245.

[119] Gerber, David. 2019. Comparative competition law. In *The Oxford Handbook of Comparative Law*, eds. Mathias Reimann, and Reinhard Zimmermann, 1184–1185. Oxford: Oxford University Press, 1169.

[120] The most famous and leading competition scholar who contributed to the enactment of the AML is Professor Xiaoye Wang. Some scholars comment that the AML 'would not even been enacted without her relentless efforts to push the competition law agenda in China'. See Emch, Adrian and Wendy Ng. 2019. *Wang Xiaoye liber amicorum: The pioneer of competition law in China.* New York: Institute of Competition Law. Professor Xiaoye Wang achieved her PhD in competition law from the University of Hamburg, Germany in 1993. Additionally, Professor Xiaomin Fang, who contributed a lot to the enactment of the AML, obtained her PhD in competition law from the University of Goettingen, Germany in 2003.

[121] In fact, most civil law regions choose EU competition law as their legislation blueprint to enact competition rules. Kovacic, E.William. 2008. Competition policy in the European Union and the United States: convergence or divergence in the future treatment of dominant firms. *Competition Law International* 4: 8–17, 8–9.

[122] Chapter 3 of this book will further analyse the ordoliberal thinking which influences the EU competition law.

[123] For example, in 2004 ten European nations joined the EU, most of which were former communist states and had the similar reforming problems to China. Li Guangjie. 2018. *Revisiting China's competition law and its interaction with intellectual property rights.* Baden: Nomos Verlagsgesellschaft mbH & Co. KG., 38.

In addition to the EU competition law, US antitrust laws also have noticeable implications for Chinese competition enforcement. For example, experts from the US Department of Justice and the US Federal Trade Commission, the two main antitrust agencies in the US, actively participated in discussions around the enactment of the AML before 2007.[124]

As the world's largest and second largest economies, the US and China have closer economic ties than ever,[125] and this is what makes Chinese authorities and scholars pay more attention to US legal practices in economic-related law. It has been observed that more young Chinese scholars who are trained in the US have moved to a US-style approach to analyzing competition law issues following the enactment of the AML.[126]

Chinese legal scholars believe that even though the AML was inspired by the TFEU, the US antitrust analysis methods such as the SSNIP test in market definition are introduced to Chinese legal practices.[127] This book takes both the EU and US models into account when dealing with the abuse of dominance cases associated with trade secrets in China.

This book does not prefer either the EU or the US model. Indeed, these two models share many similarities when dealing with the abuse of market dominance cases. However, they also have substantial differences. This book critically analyses viewpoints from both sides of the Atlantic by using doctrinal methodology and selects the approach that may be appropriate to Chinese anti-monopoly practices on a case-by-case basis.

1.8 Conclusion

Chapter 1 serves as the introductory chapter of this book. This chapter explains the background of this book, outlining the importance of a trade secret in modern society and the possible anti-competitive effects derived from the exercise of trade secrets. This chapter uses the theory of complementarity between competition and intellectual property and the so-called 'family resemblance' doctrine to explain legal

[124] See Wang Xiaoye. 2008. Highlights of China's new anti-monopoy law. *Antitrust Law Journal* 75(1): 133–150, 134.

[125] For instance, the US-China trade relationship supports around 2.6 million jobs in America. The US-China Business Council, Understanding the US-China Trade Relationship, January 2017.

[126] Gerber, David. 2019. Comparative competition law. In *The Oxford handbook of comparative law*, eds. Mathias Reimann, and Reinhard Zimmermann, 1184–1185. Oxford: Oxford University Press, 1169. One example is Judge Li Zhu, who is the most well-known judge majoring in anti-monopoly law in China's Supreme People's Court. He studied the US antitrust law at Antonin Scalia Law School of George Mason University. He used to handle the very leading competition case in China—*Qihoo v Tencent*. See Supreme People's Court. Resume of Judge Li Zhu. http://ipc.court.gov.cn/zh-cn/news/view-126.html. Accessed 25 March 2025.

[127] See e.g. 李剑 [Li Jian]. 2014. 中国反垄断法实施中的体系冲突和化解 [System conflict and resolution in the implementation of China's anti-monopoly law]. *中国法学 [China Legal Science]* 6: 138–153, 139.

issues in this book. It raises the research aim and the research question to be explored: in which circumstances does the use of trade secrets constitute an abuse of market dominance pursuant to the AML and how can the approach be improved? It outlines and explains the structure of this book. It sets out the significance and scope of this book. As this book is a research project concerning China, this chapter provides a brief introduction to China's anti-monopoly rules so that readers can better understand antitrust analysis in the following chapters. Additionally, this chapter articulates the doctrinal legal method as the primary methodology to be used in this book.

From next chapter, this book will provide substantive analysis on the abuse of market dominance regarding trade secrets. Chapter 2 is going to provide one of the vital concepts of this book: trade secrets.

Chapter 2
Overview of Trade Secrets in China

2.1 Introduction

This book examines the circumstances under which the competition laws prohibiting the abuse of market dominance will apply to trade secrets in China. A trade secret is one of the fundamental concepts in this book. Therefore, this chapter provides an overview of the law on trade secrets, with a particular focus on a Chinese legal framework.

This book mainly focuses on antitrust issues derived from the exploitation of a trade secret. Accordingly, this chapter needs to answer two critical questions. Firstly, what is a trade secret? (how is a trade secret defined legally?) Secondly, what are the characteristics of a trade secret?

This chapter is structured as follows. As discussed earlier, this book uses the US and EU law as comparative experience for China. Section 2.2 analyzes comparative views on trade secrets from the WTO TRIPS agreement as well as the US and EU law. Arguably, influenced by the TRIPS, these two jurisdictions have harmonized their approaches by similarly defining a trade secret,[1] which also influences Chinese legislation. Section 2.3 introduces the legal definition of a trade secret. It firstly analyses the legal system of trade secrets in China, particularly the trade secret framework under the Anti-unfair Competition Law. Subsequently, it examines the three essential requirements for information to be considered as a trade secret in China. Section 2.4 sheds light on the features of a trade secret. It starts by highlighting several categories of trade secrets and illustrating the characteristics of each type of trade secret. It explains why the protection of trade secrets is indefinite, differentiating it from other forms of intellectual property. Lastly, it examines the two main reasons

[1] See Barbe, Andre, and Linton, Katherine. Trade secrets: international trade policy and empirical research. OECD. https://www.oecd.org/sti/144%20-%20OECD%20Trade%20Secrets%202016-8-5.pdf. Accessed 23 March 2025.

P. Wu, *Trade Secrets and Market Dominance*, Contemporary Chinese Civil and Commercial Law, https://doi.org/10.1007/978-981-95-1152-5_2

(self-creation and reverse engineering) that trigger the limited exclusivity of a trade secret. Section 2.5 provides some differences that trade secrets have with more typical intellectual property (patents as an example). Section 2.6 concludes the chapter.

2.2 Comparative Views of Trade Secrets as a Category of Intellectual Property

Professor Mark Lemley described trade secret law as ‘a puzzle’.[2] He argued that ‘no one can seem to agree where trade secret law comes from or how to fit it into the broader framework of legal doctrine.’[3] Different jurisdictions may rely on diverse methods of protecting confidential information. For example, British courts provide the protection afforded to confidential information under the English common law[4] while the US now regards a trade secret as a form of intellectual property now.

As noted in the Introduction, the EU and the US are two jurisdictions that provide comparative experience for China regarding the abuse of market dominance in trade secrets. Hence, this section briefly introduces the legal frameworks of trade secrets in the EU and US. Additionally, the US, EU members and China are all members of the World Trade Organization (WTO) and have obligations to follow requirements of WTO treaties, including the Agreement on Trade-Related Aspects of Intellectual Property Rights (TRIPS). This section introduces some provisions of the TRIPS agreement because the agreement requires its member states to protect trade secrets.

2.2.1 The TRIPS

TRIPS is ‘the most comprehensive multilateral agreement on intellectual property.’[5] TRIPS governs several specific forms of intellectual property, such as copyright, trademarks, geographical indications, industrial designs, patents and undisclosed information. Article 39 of TRIPS is believed to have set out explicit requirements for protection of undisclosed information in public international law for the first time.[6]

---

[2] See Lemley, Mark. 2008. The surprising virtues of treating trade secrets as IP rights. *Stanford Law Review* 62: 311–353, 312.

[3] Ibid.

[4] British courts often use the doctrine of breach of confidence to protect confidential information. Trade secrets are a sub-set of confidential information in a general sense. See Browne, Michael. 2017. United Kingdom in *Abuse of dominant position and globalization & protection and disclosure of trade secrets and know-how,* ed. Pranvera Këllezi, Bruce Kilpatrick, and Pierre Kobel, 605–619, 605. Berlin: Springer.

[5] See Trade-related aspects of intellectual property rights. WTO. https://www.wto.org/english/tratop_e/TRIPS_e/TRIPS_e.htm. Accessed 23 March 2025.

[6] Secretariat, Commonwealth, and Centre du commerce international CNUCED/OMC. 1995. Business guide to the Uruguay round. Commonwealth Secretariat 337. Thanks to the criteria articulated

The neutral term 'undisclosed information' used in TRIPS is due to a common consensus during the negotiations between parties to avoid the correlation of the term to any of legal systems where the expression 'trade secrets', 'know-how' or 'confidential information' may differ.[7] The WTO explains that article 39 of TRIPS protects trade secrets (or know-how).[8]

Article 39 of TRIPS defines a trade secret as information that:

(a) is secret in the sense that it is not, as a body or in the precise configuration and assembly of its components, generally known among or readily accessible to persons within the circles that normally deal with the kind of information in question;
(b) has commercial value because it is secret; and
(c) has been subject to reasonable steps under the circumstances, by the person lawfully in control of the information, to keep it secret.

TRIPS provides nothing further but requires all members to take action to protect trade secrets. As part of the WTO agreements, TRIPS only provides intellectual property protection at a minimum level.[9] This means that members of the WTO may take different approaches to protecting trade secrets so as to meet TRIPS requirements.[10] However, TRIPS substantially influences the protection of trade secrets across the world. For instance, as shown in a report of the International Chamber of Commerce (ICC), definitions of a trade secret are similar across jurisdictions such as the US and the EU, reflecting the criteria of article 39 of TRIPS.[11]

2.2.2 *Comparative Views from the EU*

European countries did not have a uniform standard for trade secret protection prior to 2016. The EU Commission conducted the *Study on Trade Secrets and Confidential Business Information in the Internal Market* in 2013, which claimed that 'the current situation at the EU level is that the legal protection afforded by Member States to

---

in TRIPS, trade secret definitions share many similarities across jurisdictions. See Schultz MF and Lippoldt DC. 2014. Approach to protection of undisclosed information (trade secrets). *OECD Trade Policy Paper* 162.

[7] Unctad-Ictsd, et al. 2005. *Resource book on TRIPS and development.* Cambridge: Cambridge University Press, 521.

[8] See Overview: the TRIPS Agreement. WTO. https://www.wto.org/english/tratop_e/TRIPS_e/intel2_e.htm#tradesecrets. Accessed 23 March 2025.

[9] Cornish, William, and Liddell, Kathleen. 2016. The origins and structure of the trips agreement. In *TRIPS Plus 20,* eds. Hanns Ullrich, Reto Hilty, Matthias Lamping and Josef Drexl, 20. Berlin: Springer.

[10] The WTO explains that the TRIPS agreement does not necessarily require undisclosed information to be treated as a form of property. See WTO. Overview: the TRIPS agreement. https://www.wto.org/english/tratop_e/TRIPS_e/intel2_e.htm#tradesecrets. Accessed 24 March 2025.

[11] Brant, Jennifer and Lohse, Sebastian. 2016. Trade secrets: tools for innovation and collaboration. https://iccwbo.org/publication/trade-secrets-innovation-process/. Accessed 24 March 2025.

trade secrets varies significantly'.[12] For example, jurisdictions such as Germany, Austria, Spain and Poland relied on an anti-unfair competition law to protect trade secrets.[13] By contrast, France, Italy and Portugal used their intellectual property law to achieve the goal of protection.[14] Additionally, the report stated that there was no uniform definition of trade secrets in European countries.[15]

The EU enacted the *Directive on the protection of undisclosed know-how and business information (trade secrets) against their unlawful acquisition, use and disclosure* (Trade Secret Directive) in 2016 so as to achieve a harmonized legal protection of trade secrets across Europe.[16] Member states of the EU had legal obligations to amend their domestic laws to comply with the Trade Secret Directive by 2018.[17]

The Trade Secret Directive recognizes that TRIPS articulates common international standards for trade secret protection and all EU members (and the EU itself) are bound by TRIPS. The Trade Secret Directive provides the same definition of a trade secret as that in TRIPS.[18]

The Trade Secret Directive does not solve the problem of whether a trade secret can act 'as a complement or as an alternative to intellectual property' because there is no consensus in EU countries on this issue.[19] Despite this, the Trade Secret Directive considers a trade secret as an essential asset for 'business competitiveness as well as for research and development, and innovation-related performance.'[20]

This book researches the antitrust intervention in the field of trade secrets. Whether a trade secret is a type of intellectual property remains an issue in the Trade Secret Directive. Yet, the EU competition agencies or courts consider that a trade secret should be treated equally as other forms of intellectual property.[21] For instance, in

---

[12] European Commission. Study on trade secrets and confidential business information in the internal market. https://ec.europa.eu/newsroom/growth/items/48269/. Accessed 24 March 2025.

[13] The German-style of protecting trade secrets influences China's legislation due to the close relationship between German law and Chinese law. China enacted its Anti-unfair Competition Law in 1993 to protect trade secrets. However, Germany has changed its tradition and enacted a standalone trade secret law to meet the requirements of the EU Trade Secret Directive. See 吴佩乘 [Wu Peicheng]. 2019. 欧盟与德国商业秘密立法及对中国的借鉴 [Legislation on trade secrets in the EU and Germany and its implications on China]. 中德法学论坛 *[China–Germany Law Review]* 2:23–35.

[14] Ibid. As the UK is no longer an EU member, this book does not analyse the British model in detail.

[15] Ibid. Despite this, this report argued that most jurisdictions adopted specific requirements to qualify information as a trade secrets, which are similar to conditions set out in the TRIPS agreement.

[16] Niebel, Rembert, Lorenzo de Martinis and Clark, Birgit. 2018. The EU trade secrets directive: All change for trade secret protection in Europe? *Journal of Intellectual Property Law & Practice* 13 (6): 445–457, 446.

[17] Article 19 of the Trade Secret Directive.

[18] Article 2 of the Trade Secret Directive.

[19] Para. (2) of the Trade Secret Directive.

[20] Ibid.

[21] The Trade Secret Directive should not affect the application of competition rules. See para. (38) of the Trade Secret Directive.

the 2004 TTBER[22] which governed the antitrust intervention of technology transfer agreements, the EU Commission considered a trade secret as a form of intellectual property like patents or copyright.[23] Also, in the EU *Microsoft* case,[24] the Court treated trade secret as equivalent to exclusive intellectual property.[25]

2.2.3 Comparative Views from the US

The US relied on common law to protect trade secrets until the Uniform Trade Secrets Act (UTSA). The UTSA is a US suggested model law for states.[26] Most states (48 states[27]) in the US have adopted the UTSA to protect trade secrets. In 2016, the US Congress further introduced the *Defend Trade Secrets Act* (DTSA) to provide trade secret holders with the right to file a civil cause of action to a federal court.[28]

Influenced by TRIPS, the definition of a trade secret in the UTSA is basically the same as that articulated in article 39 of TRIPS.[29] Under the UTSA, a trade secret means information that (1) derives independent economic value; (2) is not generally known to and readily ascertainable by proper means by other persons who can obtain economic value from its disclosure or use; and (3) is the subject of efforts that are reasonable under the circumstances to maintain its secrecy.

In terms of the nature of a trade secret, the US considers it a category of intellectual property. Some inventors choose to protect their inventions by keeping them secret.[30] By providing legal protection for those secrets, trade secret law encourages the creation of inventors and enables inventors to sell information.[31] Therefore, a trade

[22] Commission Regulation No. 772/2004 on the Application of Article 81 (3) of the Treaty to Categories of Technology Transfer Agreements (TTBER).

[23] Article 1 of the 2004 TTBER says that 'intellectual property rights includes industrial property rights, know-how, copyright and neighbouring rights.'

[24] This was a leading antitrust case in the EU where Microsoft's refusal to disclose trade secrets constituted the abuse of market dominance. Chapters 4 and 5 of this book will further analyse this case in detail.

[25] Surblyte, Gintare. 2011. *The refusal to disclose trade secrets as an abuse of market dominance-microsoft and beyond*. Berne: Stämpfli, 17.

[26] Varanini, Emilio. 2017. United States of America. In *Abuse of dominant position and globalization & protection and disclosure of trade secrets and know-how,* eds. Pranvera Këllezi, Bruce Kilpatrick, and Pierre Kobel, 625. Berlin: Springer.

[27] The other two states are Massachusetts and New York which rely on common law to protect trade secrets. See Determann, L., Schmaus, L., and J. Tam. 2017. Trade secret protection measures and new harmonized laws. *Computer Law Review International* 17(6):179–189, 179.

[28] Sandeen, Sharon and Seaman, Christopher. 2017. Toward a federal jurisprudence of trade secret law. *Berkeley Tech. Law Journal* 32: 829–914, 829.

[29] See Section 1 of the UTSA.

[30] See e.g. Lemley, Mark. 2008. The surprising virtues of treating trade secrets as IP rights. *Stanford Law Review* 61(2): 311–353, 313.

[31] Ibid.

secret is a form, 'not of traditional property, but of intellectual property.'[32] Indeed, the US suggested treating trade secrets as the same high level as other intellectual property during the Uruguay Round of negotiations on the WTO TRIPS.[33]

When it comes to antitrust cases involving intellectual property, the US antitrust agencies also recognize a trade secret as a form intellectual property. For instance, in the US *Antitrust Guidelines for the Licensing of Intellectual Property*, the US Department of Justice (DOJ) and the Federal Trade Commission (FTC) consider that antitrust rules should apply in the field of intellectual property, including patents, copyright and trade secrets.

Given the US's role as a super economic power, it is arguable that US views on trade secrets have noticeable influences on China. In January 2020, the US and China achieved a trade agreement[34] (China–US Agreement) to temporarily pause their trade conflicts from 2018. Both countries made compromises during negotiations of the China–US Agreement. Nonetheless, China made critical concessions to accept US requirements around better protection of trade secrets.[35] It is suggested that China now adopts the US approach and deems a trade secret as a type of intellectual property due to the requirements of the China–US Agreement.[36] This is also reflected in China's newly-enacted Civil Code (2020).[37]

---

[32] Ibid.

[33] MTN/GNG/NG11/W/14.

[34] It is known as the 'phase one' deal because the two countries are still discussing other subject matters. For the official version of the agreement, see http://www.mofcom.gov.cn/article/ae/ai/202001/20200102930845.shtml. Accessed 27 March 2025.

[35] Wang Yong. 2019. Interpreting US–China trade war background, negotiations and consequences *China International Strategy Review* 1 (1):111, 114.

[36] Wu Peicheng, and Charlie Xiao-chuan Weng. 2020. Implications of the China–US trade agreement on the civil protection of trade secrets in china: Is it a game changer? *Asia Pacific Law Review* 28 (2):316–336, 335. Additionally, some argue that China has noticeably increased the civil protection of trade secrets after the China–US agreement, such as introducing the US-style punitive damages for the secret holder in a misappropriation case. See ibid. 330–333.

[37] Article 123 of the Civil Code of China provides that 'Intellectual property rights are the exclusive rights of the persons on the following objects according to law:

(1) Works;
(2) Invention, utility model and design;
(3) Trademark;
(4) Geographical indications;
(5) Trade secrets;
(6) Integrated circuit layout design;
(7) New plant varieties;
(8) Other objects prescribed by law.'

2.2.4 *Conclusion*

This section briefly introduces comparative views on trade secrets from the WTO TRIPS, the EU and the US. This section draws the following conclusions: (1) TRIPS sets out a common standard for defining a trade secret from an international normative perspective. A trade secret should be information that (a) is a secret; (b) has commercial value, and (c) is reasonably protected by the secret holder. (2) The EU Trade Secret Directive marked a harmonised protection of trade secrets at the EU-level and adopted the same definition of a trade secret as the TRIPS provisions. The EU competition agencies and courts do not differentiate trade secrets from other forms of intellectual property in antitrust cases. (3) The US definition of a trade secret in the UTSA is also similar to that of TRIPS. The US considers a trade secret as a category of intellectual property, as shown in its *Antitrust Guidelines for the Licensing of Intellectual Property.*

It is clear that the definition of a trade secret is very similar in all of these jurisdictions, which mainly reflects the criteria in TRIPS. Additionally, antitrust agencies in the EU and US usually deem a trade secret to be a form of intellectual property, and they may apply antitrust rules relating to intellectual property to trade secrets.

2.3 The Definition of a Trade Secret in China

The obligation of China to protect trade secrets derived from the TRIPS agreement when China tried to join the WTO from the 1990s.[38] As a result, China's definition of a trade secret is similar to those definitions in the TRIPS agreement, and the US UTSA and EU Trade Secret Directive. This section firstly introduces the framework of trade secret protection under China's *Anti-unfair Competition Law* (AUCL). Subsequently, this section critically examines the three essential requirements of for constituting a trade secret in China. This section will use the comparative experience to explain the three requirements, because definitions of trade secrets on both sides of the Atlantic have become similar in recent years.

---

[38] Becoming a member state of the WTO means that the country (or region) accepts TRIPS simultaneously. See Chow, Daniel, and Thomas Schoenbaum. 2012. *International Trade Law: Problems, Cases, and Materials*. Wolters Kluwer. 589.

2.3.1 Trade Secrets Under the AUCL of China

The AUCL[39] provides the primary legal basis to protect trade secrets in China.[40] The reasons for the establishment of a trade secret protection system in China in the early 1990s can be explained from several perspectives. The enactment of the AUCL, including trade secret provisions, was because of China's efforts to accede to the WTO. Specifically, it was intended to meet the requirements of the TRIPS.[41] In addition, companies and enterprises, regardless of doing international or domestic businesses, required protection from the illegal disclosure of trade secrets to their competitors.[42]

Article 9 of the AUCL (2019) defines a trade secret and prohibits others from the misappropriating trade secrets. The AUCL provides three similar requirements to TRIPS for the establishment of a trade secret:

> Trade secrets referred to in this Law shall mean commercial information such as technical information and business information, which is not known to the public and has commercial value and for which the rights holder has adopted the corresponding confidentiality measures.

It is suggested that there are two distinct theoretical justifications for trade secret protection: intellectual property rights and unfair competition grounded in tort.[43] As discussed earlier, some European countries, such as Germany, relied on anti-unfair competition law to protect trade secrets before the EU Trade Secret Directive. The US consider that a trade secret should be protected as intellectual property.

Generally, after the AUCL was enacted in 1993, China initially accepted the method of protecting trade secrets through European traditions of unfair competition, particularly the German style[44] at the level of legislation. However, China adopted the US-style method and regards a trade secret as intellectual property because of its close economic relationship with the US, particularly after the China–US Agreement

---

[39] China's AUCL was enacted in 1993 and amended in 2017 and 2019 respectively.

[40] Bai, Benjamin, and Da Guoping. 2010. Strategies for trade secrets protection in China. *Nw. J. Tech. & Intell* 9:351–376, 355.

[41] Xiong, Ping, and Philip Griffith. 2014. Protecting trade secrets in China: History and context. *Queen Mary Journal of Intellectual Property* 4 (1):30–56, 51.

[42] Ibid, 31.

[43] Menell, Peter, Lemley, Mark, and Robert Merges. 2018. *Intellectual Property in the New Technological Age 2018: Volume I: Perspectives, Trade Secrets and Patents.* Clause 8 Publishing. 43. It should also be noted that some common law jurisdictions, such as the UK and Australia, rely on 'breach of confidence' law to protect confidential information. However, this protection method has little influence on civil law countries like China.

[44] German 1896 Anti-Unfair Competition Law (also known as 'UWG') is the first statutory unfair competition law globally and influenced many civil law jurisdictions. Provisions regarding trade secrets are enacted in German UWG after 1896. 王博闻 [Wang Bowen]. 2016. 德国反不正竞争法私法属性的历史和理论建构 [The Historical And Theoretical Constructions Of The Private Law Nature Of German Anti-Unfair Competition Law] 竞争政策研究 *[Competition Policy Research]* 4:31–41.

in 2020.[45] For example, China enacted its Civil Code[46] in 2020, which was effective from the new year of 2021. Article 123 of the Civil Code stipulates explicitly that trade secrets are exclusive intellectual property rights.[47]

Recognizing a trade secret as a type of intellectual property, Chinese lawmakers are now considering excluding trade secret protection from the AUCL and preparing for the enactment of a standalone trade secret law.[48] For instance, Professor Yide Ma, a deputy to the National People's Congress (NPC) of China, proposed a draft of trade secret law in May 2020 at the NPC session. This draft is now under review by relevant departments of the NPC.[49]

To conclude, China has recognized that a trade secret belongs to a category of intellectual property in the Chinese Civil Code. Nevertheless, it is still the AUCL that provides the detailed definition of a trade secret and the prohibition of misappropriation of a trade secret.

2.3.2 Requirement of 'Secrecy'

The core requirement of protecting a trade secret is that the information in question is kept secret. In other words, once the information is disclosed to the public,[50] the legal protection of a trade secret vanishes.

A trade secret should be unknown to the public. Notwithstanding this, besides the secret holder, others may know the content of the trade secret as well. For instance, if the secret holder licenses the trade secret to other companies, the licensees are aware of the content of the secret. Therefore, some researchers argue that if the information is kept relatively secret this sufficiently fulfills the 'secrecy' requirement, instead of being kept absolutely secret.[51]

---

[45] Wu Peicheng, and Charlie Xiao-chuan Weng. 2020. Implications of the China–US trade agreement on the civil protection of trade secrets in china: Is it a game changer? *Asia Pacific Law Review* 28 (2):316–336, 335.

[46] Observers believe that the Chinese Civil Code is a milestone towards to the rule of law in China. It intends to secure property, family and personal rights. See Leonte, Andreea, and Valentina Crivat. A civil code for China: A great leap forward for the rule of law. The Diplomat. https://thediplomat.com/2017/03/a-civil-code-for-china-a-great-leap-forward-for-the-rule-of-law/. Accessed 24 March 2025.

[47] The China–US Agreement also considers a trade secret as a form of intellectual property.

[48] Wu Peicheng, and Charlie Xiao-chuan Weng. 2020. Implications of the China–US trade agreement on the civil protection of trade secrets in china: Is it a game changer? *Asia Pacific Law Review* 28 (2):316–336, 333.

[49] Ibid.

[50] For instance, if competitors reverse engineer a product incorporating know-how and disclose the information online, there is no trade secret anymore.

[51] Unctad-Ictsd, et al. 2005. *Resource book on TRIPS and development*. Cambridge University Press. 529.

Comparative experience demonstrates that trade secret law promotes the dissemination of information, rather than prevents it. Professor Lemley argues that undertakings would invest too much in keeping secrets without the legal protection of a trade secret.[52] Trade secret protection is a substitute 'for the physical and contractual restrictions those companies would otherwise impose in an effort to prevent competitors from acquiring their information.'[53] With trade secret protection, a trade secret holder can take advantage of the secret information. For example, as Xiong and Griffith argued, the secret information can be disclosed through contracts or licenses in China.[54]

China's AUCL merely stipulates that a trade secret should be unknown to the public. The SPC further interprets the requirement of secrecy in its judicial interpretation (Trade Secret Interpretation) regarding trade secret infringement.[55] As provided in this judicial interpretation, the information is unknown to the public if it is not generally known by and easily available to the relevant persons within the circles that normally deal with the kind of information.[56] Arguably, this is a reiteration of article 39 (a) of the TRIPS agreement. Additionally, the Trade Secret Interpretation articulates five circumstances where the information should be regarded as public information (instead of a trade secret).[57] The Trade Secret Interpretation does not deem secret information which is licensed to others as public information. Consequently, a secret holder may use its secret information through legal licenses.

---

[52] See Lemley, Mark. 2008. The surprising virtues of treating trade secrets as IP rights. *Stanford Law Review* 62: 311–353, 313.

[53] Ibid.

[54] Ping Xiong, and Philip Griffith. 2014. Protecting trade secrets in China: History and context. *Queen Mary Journal of Intellectual Property* 4 (1):30–56, 47.

[55] It is the *Provisions on Several Issues Concerning the Application of Law in the Trial of Civil Cases Involving Trade Secret Infringement*, which was effective from 12 September 2020.

[56] Ibid article 3.

[57] Article 4 of the Trade Secret Interpretation provides that: 'In any of the following circumstances, the people's court may recognize relevant information as known to the public:

(I) where the information falls within the scope of common sense or industry practice in the field;
(II) where the information only involves the simple combination of dimensions, structures, materials and components of the product in question, and can be directly obtained by relevant persons in the field by observing such product on the market;
(III) where the information has been publicly disclosed on any publication or any other mass medium; or
(IV) where the information has been publicized in form of public report or exhibition, etc.; or
(V) where the information may be obtained by relevant persons in the field through other public channels.'

2.3.3 Requirement of 'Commercial Value'

A trade secret should have commercial value. When the AUCL was enacted in 1993, it required that a trade secret should encompass not only 'economic benefits' but also 'practical utility'. This description triggered debates. It was controversial in academia whether negative secret information (such as the information of a failed experiment) can constitute a trade secret.[58]

From a comparative perspective, Jorda claims that trade secret law should protect negative know-how, e.g., erroneous research approaches or results of failed experiments.[59] One US commentator observed that the results of lengthy and expensive research proving that some industry processes may not work could be valuable to rivals in the market.[60] Noteworthy is that this is different from the requirements of the formation of other intellectual property. For instance, as argued by Surblyte, in contrast to the fact that patent owners can be granted exclusive rights based on the positive effects of the patent specification,[61] a trade secret can have both positive and negative values.

China amended the AUCL twice in 2017 and 2019. The latest version of AUCL requires that a trade secret should possess commercial value instead of 'economic benefits and practical utility', which is consistent with the phrase used in TRIPS. It is suggested that the new definition includes both positive and negative secret information.[62]

2.3.4 Requirement of 'Reasonable Secret-Keeping Precautions'

A trade secret is not a registered intellectual property like patents in China.[63] This means that no national authorities are responsible for granting a trade secret. Instead, a secret holder must take reasonable precautions to protect trade secrets. Nonetheless,

58 韩德宽 [Han Dekuan]. 2012. 商业秘密之实用性浅析 [Analysis on the practicality of trade secrets] 中国专利与商标*[China Patents & Trademarks]* 2:31–32, 32.

59 Jorda, KF. Trade secrets and trade-secret licensing. In *Intellectual property management in health and agricultural innovation: A handbook of best practices,* eds. A. Krattiger, RT. Mahoney and L. Nelsen. MIHR. Oxford.

60 Czapracka, Katarzyna. 2007. Antitrust and trade secrets: The US and the EU approach. *Santa Clara Computer & High Tech. Law Journal* 24:207–273, 222.

61 Surblyte, Gintare. 2011. *The refusal to disclose trade secrets as an abuse of market dominance-microsoft and beyond.* Berne:Stämpfli 23.

62 See e.g. 张鸽, 黄琳琳[Zhang Ge and Huang Linlin]. 2018. 以知识产权管理体系保护企业商业秘密[Protecting trade secrets of enterprises through intellectual property management system]. 上海商学院学报*[Journal of Shanghai Business School]* 49:53–54.

63 Ong, Ryan. 2013. Trade secret enforcement in China: Options and obstacles. *China Business Review* 40 (1):49, 51. This is also the case in the EU and the US.

whether the security precaution taken by the holder is an essential element for the establishment of a trade secret is questionable.

Some courts in the US hold that the struggle to maintain secrecy is evidence to illustrate that the secret is valuable enough for litigation.[64] However, the UTSA explicitly views the efforts to maintain secrecy as the core element of defining a trade secret.[65] The EU Trade Secret Directive also considers reasonable secret-keeping precautions as a requirement of defining a trade secret.[66]

Consistent with international and comparative standards, China's AUCL requires a secret holder to take reasonable measures to protect the secret information. The China–US agreement reaffirmed this essential requirement.[67]

It is notable that 'reasonable' protection measures are sufficient for the requirement of a trade secret. For instance, in *E.I. DuPont v Christopher*,[68] the plaintiff DuPont was in the process of building its factory. A third party hired the defendant Christopher to take aerial photos of the plaintiff's secret process flying over DuPont's plant. The plaintiff sued Christopher for the misappropriation of trade secrets. In this case, the defendant argued that DuPont did not take reasonable precautions to protect the secret process. The court held that there was no requirement for the plaintiff to establish a roof over its unfinished plant. Instead, the plaintiff had taken reasonable measures, such as fencing the construction site, to protect trade secrets. Therefore, DuPont had a legally-defined trade secret.

China's SPC interprets the requirement of reasonable protection measures in detail. Article 5 of the Trade Secret Interpretation requires Chinese courts to identify reasonable secret-keeping precautions on a case-by-case basis. Furthermore, this judicial interpretation identifies six circumstances where the court may consider that the secret holder has taken reasonable precautions to protect trade secrets.[69]

---

[64] Menell, Peter, Lemley, Mark, and Robert Merges. 2018. *Intellectual Property in the New Technological Age 2018: Volume I: Perspectives, Trade Secrets and Patents.* Clause 8 Publishing. 49.

[65] See Section 1 of the UTSA.

[66] Article 2 of the Trade Secret Directive.

[67] Wu Peicheng, and Charlie Xiao-chuan Weng. 2020. Implications of the China–US trade agreement on the civil protection of trade secrets in china: Is it a game changer? *Asia Pacific Law Review* 28 (2):316–336, 324.

[68] See E. I. du Pont deNemours & Co. v. Christopher, 431 F.2d 1012, 1970 U.S. This is a leading trade secret misappropriation case in the US.

[69] Article 6 of the Trade Secret Interpretation provides that 'Under any of the following circumstances, if normal conditions are sufficient to prevent disclosure of a trade secret, the people's court shall hold that the obligee has taken corresponding confidentiality measures:

(I) signing a confidentiality agreement or stipulating the obligation of confidentiality in a contract;
(II) putting forward the confidentiality requirements to employees, former employees, suppliers, clients and visitors, etc. who may have access to or obtain the trade secret in such ways as articles of association, training, rules and systems and written notification;
(III) limiting visitors to the classified factory buildings, workshops or other production places or conducting differentiated management; or

2.3.5 Conclusion

Unlike patents or trademarks that are issued by national authorities and the existence of them can be easily identified, a trade secret is not a registered intellectual property. Consequently, it is important to legally define a trade secret. A trade secret is a form of intellectual property in the Chinese Civil Code. The AUCL is the primary legal source providing the definition of trade secrets and how to protect secret information. A trade secret should be information with secrecy, commercial value and reasonable precautions taken by the secret holder.

2.4 Characteristics of a Trade Secret

The last section defines a trade secret in China by providing three requirements. This section analyses several characteristics of a trade secret based on its legal definition. This section argues that there are diverse types of trade secrets, a trade secret can be protected indefinitely, and the exclusivity of a trade secret is limited. As discussed earlier in the Introduction Chapter, antitrust analysis regarding intellectual property across jurisdictions most commonly focuses on patent cases. Therefore, this section also critically compares the characteristics of a trade secret with those of a patent.

2.4.1 Diverse Categories of Trade Secrets

As stated above, the legal definition of a trade secret is general and flexible, so that it can encompass all types of information that meet the three statutory requirements. Identification of a trade secret, thus, is a dynamic process.[70] Trade secrets were commonly classified into two categories under the 1993 AUCL, namely technical and business information. This technical/business dichotomy arises from German

(IV) differentiating and managing the trade secret and its carriers by such means as marking, classification, isolation, encryption, sealing up for safekeeping and limiting the scope of persons who can reach or obtain such secret;
(V) taking measures such as prohibiting or restricting the use of, visiting, storing or reproducing computer equipment, electronic equipment, network equipment, storage equipment and software, etc. which can be used to access or obtain the trade secret;
(VI) requiring resigned employees to register, return, clear away or destroy the trade secret they have accessed to or acquired as well as the carriers thereof, and to continue to assume the obligation of confidentiality; and
(VII) taking other reasonable confidentiality measures.'

[70] Glick, Mark, Reymann, Lara, and Richard Hoffman. 2002. *Intellectual property damages: Guidelines and analysis*. John Wiley & Sons. 281.

law, which believes that a trade secret consists of industrial and business secrets.[71] However, in addition to technical and business secrets, some new trade secrets are emerging in the digital era.

2.4.1.1 Technical Secrets

Many undertakings choose to put their essential technical assets under the protection of trade secrets, an example of which is Google's search algorithm.[72] Generally, technical secrets contain research and development information, product-related information, and methods of production.[73]

Technical secrets do not need to be patentable.[74] There are two categories of technical secrets. One is not patentable. The other is patentable in fact, but the information or invention holder chooses to keep it secret rather than applying for patent protection.[75] Technical secrets are important for facilitating technology and innovation and may benefit consumers by providing new products or services.[76]

2.4.1.2 Business Secrets

Some may argue that the policy of trade secret protection is to promote innovation.[77] This function mainly refers to a technical secret because it can incentivise secret holders to create more inventions. However, business trade secrets, such as Coca-Cola's recipe and Kentucky Fried Chicken's eleven herbs and spices in the

---

[71] Hoeren, Thomas. 2017. Germany. In *Abuse of dominant position and globalization & protection and disclosure of trade secrets and know-how,* eds. Pranvera Këllezi, Bruce Kilpatrick and Pierre Kobel, 425–453, 428. Berlin: Springer.

[72] Bengtsson, Henrik. 2017. International report. In *Abuse of dominant position and globalization & protection and disclosure of trade secrets and know-how,* eds. Pranvera Këllezi, Bruce Kilpatrick and Pierre Kobel, 291–312, 292. Berlin: Springer.

[73] Kolasa, Magdalena. 2018. *Trade secrets and employee mobility: volume 44: in search of an equilibrium. vol. 44.* Cambridge University Press. 75.

[74] Dessemontet, Fracois. 1998. Protection of trade secrets and confidential information. In *Intellectual property and international trade. The TRIPS Agreement,* eds. Carlos Correa and A. Yusuf, 3. Kluwer Law International, London-Cambridge.

[75] As Pooley argued, all patentable inventions begin as trade secrets. See Pooley, J. 1997. The top ten issues in trade secret law. *Temple Law Review* 70:1181–1190.

[76] Drexl, Josef. 2011. Refusal to grant access to trade secrets as an abuse of market dominance. In *Intellectual Property and Competition Law-New Frontiers,* eds. Steven Anderman and Ariel Ezrachi, 165, 182. Oxford: Oxford University Press.

[77] Crass, Dirk, et al. 2019. Protecting innovation through patents and trade secrets: Evidence for firms with a single innovation. *International Journal of the Economics of Business* 26 (1):117–156, 117.

fried chicken,[78] may not contain elements of technical innovation. The reason why the information can be protected is merely because the holder keeps it a secret. In this scenario, the value of a business trade secret is related to the function of the underlying information instead of the innovation characteristic.[79] For instance, Microsoft's interoperability information of Windows, which is unrelated to the software innovation, is protected as a business secret. It is essential to enter Windows, but Microsoft refuses to disclose the secret information to its competitors in order to prevent other competitors from entering the relevant market.[80] The business secrets enable Microsoft to gain competitive advantages in the software market. As one can see, the categories of business secrets can vary considerably. The commercial value and function of a business secret need to be analyzed on a case-by-case basis.

2.4.1.3 Other Kinds of Secrets

China formerly followed the German tradition, which insists on a technical/business secret dichotomy. The definition of a trade secret in the 2019 AUCL abandons this dichotomy and uses the term 'commercial information' rather than 'technical or business information'.[81]

Most trade secrets can usually be classified into technical secrets or business secrets. In digital areas, however, Graef observes that some types of information, such as commercial datasets, which are difficult to define as a technical or business secret, deserve trade secret protection as well.[82] With the development of artificial intelligence (AI), the elements of AI, such as its training data and learning algorithms, are likely to constitute trade secrets.[83] There is not a black-and-white boundary between traditional trade secrets (technical or business secrets) and these new types.

---

[78] Bengtsson, Henrik. 2017. International report. In *Abuse of Dominant Position and Globalization & Protection and Disclosure of Trade Secrets and Know-How,* eds. Pranvera Këllezi, Bruce Kilpatrick and Pierre Kobel, 291–312, 292. Berlin: Springer.

[79] Drexl, Josef. 2011. Refusal to grant access to trade secrets as an abuse of market dominance. In *Intellectual Property and Competition Law-New Frontiers,* eds. Steven Anderman and Ariel Ezrachi, 165, 182. Oxford: Oxford University Press.

[80] *Microsoft v European Commission* (T-201/04) [2007] ECR II-3601.

[81] Ibid.

[82] Graef, Inge. 2016. Data as essential facility: competition and innovation on online platforms. 143, https://lirias.kuleuven.be/1711644?limo=0. As the definition of a trade secret is very similar across jurisdictions, big data is likely to be protected as a trade secret in China as well.

[83] See Fitzgerald, Nina, Martyn, Eoin, et al. 2021. Got a secret? can you keep it? using trade secrets to protect AI, ACC. https://www.acc.com/resource-library/got-secret-can-you-keep-it-using-trade-secrets-protect-ai. Accessed 25 March 2025.

2.4.1.4 Conclusion

In summary, categories of trade secrets are diverse. From the legal tradition of Germany, a trade secret can be divided into technical and business information. A technical secret containing technological superiority can usually bring competitive advantages to the secret holder, promoting innovation incentives at the same time. Although unrelated to elements of innovation, a business secret can be of great commercial value to secret holder depending on its function. Additionally, new secrets are emerging. All types of information that fulfil the definition of a trade secret deserve the same level of protection, although the role a trade secret plays may vary from case to case. The following chapters explain how different categories of a trade secret impact antitrust analysis. For example, technical secrets may bring about market power due to superior technology.[84] Those secrets without technical elements may also result in market power if the secret information can act as a de facto standard.[85]

2.4.2 Indefinite Term of Protection

A critical feature of a trade secret is the indefinite duration of protection. This feature of a trade secret is different from other forms of intellectual property. An essential objective of protecting intellectual property rights is to encourage the dissemination of ideas and the disclosure of inventions to foster the creative activities of others. Mansell argues that intellectual property system maintains a balance between society's interest in the disclosure of ideas by creating an exclusive right to control and profit from intellectual products.[86] Therefore, the protection of most intellectual property endures for a certain period of time.[87] When the term of protection expires, the intellectual property enters public domain for the service of human beings. For example, the validity period of patent rights for an invention is 20 years in China.[88]

On the contrary, as secrecy is the core element constituting a trade secret, a trade secret's status disappears once it is disclosed in any way. In most circumstances, other people, including competitors and judges, will not know when a trade secret was formed and the exact contents of a trade secret until a misappropriation claim is submitted to the court. Consequently, the law is unable to set out a term of protection

[84] See Chap. 4 of this book.

[85] Ibid.

[86] Mansell, Robin, and Steinmueller, Edward. 1995. Intellectual property rights: The development of information infrastructures for the information society. LSE Research Online. https://www.academia.edu/2697915/Intellectual_property_rights_the_development_of_information_infrastructures_for_the_information_society. Accessed 25 March 2025.

[87] See What are intellectual property rights? https://www.wipo.int/en/web/about-ip. Accessed 25 March 2025.

[88] Article 42 of the Patent Law of China.

for trade secrets in practice. In other words, as long as the holder keeps the information secret, it will gain protection under the trade secret law.

2.4.3 *Limited Exclusivity*

The exclusive right of a trade secret is limited because there are some restrictions on the protection of a trade secret. This means that other competitors are legally entitled to obtain the holder's secret information in certain circumstances.

Different jurisdictions take various approaches to limiting the use of trade secrets according to the local social and economic background. For example, the US trade secret law provides a 'Whistle-blower Protection Clause', which prevents any individual from being liable for the confidential disclosure of a trade secret to a government official or attorney for the purpose of reporting or investigating a suspected violation of law.[89] Under the EU Trade Secret Directive, it is lawful to disclose a trade secret in order to exercise rights of freedom of speech or to protect public interests.[90] All the same, self-creation and reverse engineering are two vital exceptions that do not constitute trade secret misappropriation recognized by China, the US and the EU.[91]

2.4.3.1 Self-Creation

Self-creation is one of the limitations on the exclusivity of a trade secret. There may be multiple holders of the same trade secret if they create the secret separately and independently. For example, divergent undertakings can make the same customer list on the grounds of a similar transaction process. For registered intellectual property such as patents and trademarks, self-creation is not allowed since the contents (e.g. the patent specification or the picture of a brand) have already become public and everyone can imitate them. Nonetheless, due to the secrecy element of a trade secret, others do not know the specific contents of the secret information and thus are allowed to develop the same secret independently as they would be unknowingly doing so. Consequently, Chinese law stipulates that the self-creation of a trade secret should be an exception from the infringement of trade secrets.[92]

---

[89] Determann, L., Schmaus L., and J. Tam. 2016. Trade Secret protection measures and new harmonized laws. *Computer Law Review International*, 17 (6):179–189, 181.

[90] Article 5 of the EU Trade Secret Directive.

[91] E.g. Article 14 of the Trade Secret Interpretation provides that '[I]n case of obtaining the sued infringement information through development and research by itself or reverse engineering, the people's court shall determine that it does not constitute the trade secret infringement as stipulated in Article 9 of the Anti-unfair Competition Law.' See also para. 16 of the EU Trade Secret Directive and Section 1 of the UTSA.

[92] See article 14 of the Trade Secret Interpretation.

2.4.3.2 Reverse Engineering

Reverse engineering is common in areas with technical needs, such as in fields of electronic components, computer programs (software), biological, chemical and organic matters.[93] One can acquire trade secrets through deconstructing a man-made product to reveal its designs, architecture, or to extract knowledge from the product.[94] Lawyers and economists have endorsed reverse engineering as a legitimate way to acquire trade secrets, even though the intention is to manufacture products that will draw consumers away from the manufacturer of the reverse-engineered products.[95] In the US landmark case *Kewanee Oil Co. v. Bicron Corp.*,[96] the US Supreme Court claimed that 'a trade secret law, however, does not offer protection against discovery by fair and honest means, such as ...by so-called reverse engineering'.

Reverse engineering is significant for competition and innovation. It has a positive effect on price competition and on the dissemination of technical secrets that can lead to improved products.[97] The threat of reverse engineering intensifies the competitive pressure for the secret holder, which is an incentive to innovate.[98] As a result, reverse engineering is an important factor influencing the competitive advantages of a trade secret holder.

2.5 Trade Secrets V. Patents

Chapter 1 (Introductory Chapter) has established the 'family resemblance' doctrine to explain trade secrets as opposed to other categories of intellectual property. The trade secret shares noticeable similarities with other intellectual property, enabling this book to apply antitrust experience of other intellectual property to trade secret cases. However, the trade secret is different from other typical intellectual property in some ways. As the patent is a typical form of intellectual property, this section articulates the differences between a trade secret and a patent. The following chapters will consider these differences when analyzing special cases related to trade secrets.

A trade secret and a patent are two forms of intellectual property in China. Nonetheless, they are different in some aspects. The following details some differences between them, particularly in the context of Chinese laws.

---

[93] See Thayer, Ken. 2017. How does reverse engineering work? Engineering360. https://insights.globalspec.com/article/7367/how-does-reverse-engineering-work. Accessed 25 March 2025.

[94] Eilam, Eldad. 2011. *Reversing: Secrets of reverse engineering*. John Wiley & Sons. 3.

[95] Samuelson, Pamela, and Scotchmer, Suzanne. 2001. The law and economics of reverse engineering. *Yale Law Journal* 111:1575–1663, 1577.

[96] Kewanee Oil Co. v. Bicron Corp., 416 U.S. 470 (1974).

[97] Samuelson, Pamela, and Scotchmer, Suzanne. 2001. The law and economics of reverse engineering. *Yale Law Journal* 111:1575–1663, 1590.

[98] Surblytė, Gintarė. 2016. *Enhancing TRIPS: Trade secrets and reverse engineering. TRIPS plus 20.* Berlin:Springer. 752.

Table 2.1 Differences between trade secrets and patents

	Patents	Trade secrets
Registration	Required	Not required
Public disclosure	Yes	No
Duration of protection	Approximately 20 years	Indefinite period
Geographical scope of protection	National	Across jurisdictions

Firstly, a patent is a registered intellectual property. A patentee should apply to the China National Intellectual Property Administration to acquire a patent in China. By contrast, a trade secret is not a registered intellectual property. Any information that meets the three requirements above can constitute a trade secret.

Secondly, the specifications of a patent are disclosed to the public. However, a secret holder keeps its confidential information as a secret, which is unknown to the public.

Thirdly, the Chinese Patent Law gives protection for a fixed period.[99] After the expiration of the patent, it enters the public domain, at which point anyone can imitate it. By contrast, a trade secret can be protected indefinitely as long as the secret holder keeps it confidential.

Lastly, the geographical scope of the protection between patents and trade secrets is different. Because a patentee should apply for a patent, the patent is granted on a national basis.[100] For example, a patent granted by the Chinese authority may not necessarily constitute a patent in the US. Nevertheless, as definitions of a trade secret are becoming similar across nations, a trade secret in one jurisdiction (e.g. Coca-Cola's recipe) is most likely to be protected in other jurisdictions as well.

The following table illustrates the differences between a patent and a trade secret (Table 2.1):

As discussed earlier, this book will borrow antitrust experience related to other forms of intellectual property to trade secret cases due to similarities a trade secret has with other forms of intellectual property like a patent. It is arguable that the differences between a trade secret and a patent may also influence antitrust analysis in specific cases. The following chapters will consider the distinctness when analyzing the abuse of market dominance related to trade secrets.

---

[99] Article 42 of the Patent Law (2020) of China provides that: '[T]he duration of patent rights for an invention shall be 20 years, the duration of patent rights for a utility model shall be 10 years and the duration of patent rights for a design shall be 15 years, commencing from the filing date.'

[100] Brant, Jennifer, and Lohse, Sebastian. Trade secrets: tools for innovation and collaboration. https://innovationcouncil.org/trade-secrets-tools-for-innovation-and-collaboration/. Accessed 25 March 2025.

2.6 Conclusion

This chapter concentrates on the legal framework for trade secrets in China. Through doctrinal analyses, this chapter provides an overview of how a trade secret is defined and featured. Based on the discussions in this chapter, this chapter draws the following conclusions.

Firstly, the WTO TRIPS provides a common standard for trade secret protection. The EU Trade Secret Directive and the US UTSA harmonize the definition of a trade secret following the requirement of TRIPS. Additionally, competition agencies in these two jurisdictions consider a trade secret as a form of intellectual property when dealing with antitrust cases.

Secondly, China protected trade secrets in the 1993 AUCL to fulfil TRIPS requirements. China initially accepted the German tradition in which trade secret misappropriation was purely a question of unfair competition. Nevertheless, influenced by the US, the Chinese Civil Code now considers a trade secret as a category of intellectual property. For now, China mainly relies on the AUCL to provide detailed rules concerning the protection of trade secrets, and lists a trade secret as a type of intellectual property in the Civil Code.

This book adopts a clear three-requirement definition of a trade secret. The secret information that meets the following requirements are trade secrets in China. Secrecy is at the core of this definition. Next, a trade secret should possess commercial value that can bring competitive advantages to its holder. The last requirement is that the secret holder needs to take reasonable measures to protect the secret.

Thirdly, trade secrets have distinct characteristics and diverse categories. From a traditional perspective, a trade secret can be divided into technical information and business information. The former is related to innovation, while the value of the latter depends on its specific functions. Apart from the two categories, other new secrets are emerging with the development of the digital or AI industry. Furthermore, the duration of protection of a trade secret is indefinite as long as the secret holder keeps the information confidential. Additionally, others can obtain the trade secrets of the holder through legitimate methods, such as self-creation and reverse engineering, which would undermine the exclusivity of the trade secret.

Last but not least, a trade secret is different from other categories of intellectual property, such as patents. For instance, a patent is a registered intellectual property while a trade secret is not. The content of a patent is disclosed to the public while the holder keeps a trade secret as confidential information. There is a duration of protection for a patent. The secret holder can protect a trade secret indefinitely. A patent is granted and protected in a certain jurisdiction. However, as definitions of a trade secret come similar in different nations, a trade secret may be protected across jurisdictions. The following chapters will take account of these differences when analyzing the abuse of dominance cases relevant to trade secrets.

This chapter introduces trade secrets as one crucial component of this book. The next chapter presents another core conception of this book: the abuse of market dominance.

Chapter 3
Overview of the Abuse of Market Dominance

3.1 Introduction

The abuse of market dominance is one of the main three anti-competitive practices prohibited in modern competition law.[1] This book is founded on the framework of the abuse of market dominance. Therefore, it is essential for this chapter to provide an overview of laws related to the abuse of dominance. Antitrust laws, as Fox argued, substantially diverge in the area of monopolization/abuse of dominance.[2] This chapter mainly focuses on the abuse of dominance rules in three jurisdictions: the US, the EU and China. The US and the EU are the two primary competition law jurisdictions that have influenced the enforcement of competition law in many countries around the world. Relied on its super economic power, the US rationale for antitrust laws has affected the assessment of competition law in many countries. By contrast, many jurisdictions, particularly those with codified law traditions, have chosen to adopt the competition law of the EU, whose member states are almost all civil law countries.

This chapter is divided into three parts, which discuss the US antitrust law, the EU competition law, and China's anti-monopoly law respectively. Section 3.2 discusses how the US Sherman Act treats cases of monopolization or attempted monopolization (Section 2 of Sherman Act). The section firstly examines changing philosophies (such as Harvard School, Chicago School and Post-Chicago School) that have impacted the enforcement of the US antitrust law after the Second World War. It then analyses how US regulators and courts apply Section 2 of the Sherman Act in practice, mostly

[1] The other two are merger control and anti-competitive agreements.

[2] Fox, Eleanor. 2019. Should China's competition model be exported?: A reply to Wendy Ng. *European Journal of International Law* 30(4): 1431–1440, 1432.

Chapter 3 contains some material from Wu Peicheng. 2021. How does China prohibit the abuse of market dominance? A comparative analysis with the US and EU approaches. *Journal of Law and Economy of China* 1: 4–16.

P. Wu, *Trade Secrets and Market Dominance*, Contemporary Chinese Civil and Commercial Law, https://doi.org/10.1007/978-981-95-1152-5_3

guided by the Chicago School, the current dominant antitrust thinking. Section 3.3 examines the application of article 102 of the TFEU in Europe. This section begins with assessment of German Ordoliberalism, a legal theory affecting the establishment and application of article 102 of the EU competition law. It then evaluates the wording and conditions of the application of article 102 in specific cases. This section also sheds light on a change in moving from the traditional form-based approach to the US-style effects-based approach in the application of article 102. The next section, Sect. 3.4, reviews Chinese legal practice in regard to the anti-monopoly law. The first part of the section provides the conditions for determining the abuse of dominance in the anti-monopoly law, the framework and provisions of which are analogous to those of the EU competition law. Subsequently, this section introduces a landmark case—*Qihoo v. Tencent*—which exemplifies the application of competition law in cases of abuse of dominance. The attitudes towards whether a form—or effects-based approach prevails in China were different before and after this landmark case. This section also scrutinizes the application of the abuse of dominance in China after the *Qihoo v. Tencent* case. The last part (Sect. 3.5) presents the conclusion.

3.2 Lessons from US Antitrust Law

Comparative competition law[3] scholars, such as David Gerber, state that the US antitrust community considers its regime the 'father' of modern competition law owing to its great influence on the rest of the world.[4] Section 2 of the US Sherman Antitrust Act is one of the earliest statutory provisions prohibiting unilateral anti-competitive conduct all over the world. However, Section 2 of the Act, like other provisions in the Sherman Act, is a general prohibition, leaving interpretations of the wording to courts. Economic theories play an essential role when US courts handle antitrust cases. Thus, changes in economic theory in the antitrust field may trigger different approaches to antitrust cases. In light of this, this section first analyses various economic theories in the US which ground and may affect the application of the Sherman Act. It then concentrates on the current approach to the application of Section 2 prohibiting monopolization and attempted monopolization in certain cases.

[3] Different jurisdictions refer to competition law as various names. For example, it is called antitrust law in the US, competition law in the EU, and anti-monopoly law in China.

[4] Gerber, David. 2019. Comparative competition law. In *The Oxford handbook of comparative law*, eds. Mathias Reimann and Reinhard Zimmermann, 1169, 1175. Second edition. Oxford: Oxford University Press. The US antitrust law was almost the first competition law worldwide.

3.2.1 *Philosophies of Unilateral Anti-competitive Practices in the US*

3.2.1.1 Harvard School

The wording of the US Sherman Act is quite simple. As noted by antitrust scholars, the Act was aimed at combating industrial trusts, high concentration and abuses of market power, and maintaining an open market in the enactment of the Act in 1890.[5] It regulated industrialists who were 'building business empires at the expense of farmers, buyers and other small players and were undermining the vision of the social good'.[6] However, the approach to antitrust thinking has always been closely tied to prevailing economic theory in the US.

By the middle of the twentieth century (after the Second World War), the Harvard structuralist School of thought dominated antitrust thinking in the US. Initially, Harvard University scholars, like Edward Mason[7] and Joe Bain,[8] introduced the Structure–Conduct–Performance (S–C–P) paradigm. They believed the S–C–P paradigm complied with the industrial organization theory. It was their views that the structure of a certain market influences an undertaking's conduct, which, in turn, determines a firm's market performance (such as efficiency and technical progress).[9] Under this assumption, Harvard economists argued that a highly concentrated structure will result in poor market performance, reduced output and extremely high prices.[10] In summary, market structure regulation was the core element of antitrust law inspired by Harvard School of thought. Secondly, it has been argued that Harvard School should seek 'the closest available working approximation' to perfect competition, defined as 'workable competition'.[11] Additionally, Bain, in his influential book, attached much importance to barriers to entry and claimed barriers for new undertakings can be easily controlled by dominant firms.[12]

In the 1950s and 1960s, antitrust authorities and then the US Supreme Court (the so-called 'Warren Court'[13]) were convinced by the Harvard structuralist School. As

---

[5] See Fox, Eleanor. 2013. Against goals. *Fordham Law Review* 81: 2157–2161.

[6] Fox, Eleanor, and Deborah Healey. 2013. When the state harms competition-The role for competition law. *Antitrust Law Journal* 79: 769–820.

[7] Mason, Edward. 1964. *Economic concentration and the monopoly problem.* New York: Atheneum.

[8] Bain, Joe. 1956. *Barriers to new competition: Their character and consequences in manufacturing industries.* Cambridge: Harvard University Press.

[9] Healey, Deborah. 2020. The ambit of competition law: Comments on its goals. In *Research handbook on models and methods of competition law,* eds. D. Healey, M. Jacobs, and R. Smith, 12–37. Cheltenham: Edward Elgar.

[10] Ibid.

[11] Clark, J. M. Toward a concept of workable competition. *The American Economic Review* 30: 241–256.

[12] Bain, Joe S. 1956. *Barriers to new competition: The character and consequences in manufacturing industries,* 1–42, 114–143. Cambridge: Harvard University Press.

[13] The 'Warren Court' is the name given to the US Supreme Court when Justice Earl Warren was the Chief Justice between 1953 and 1969.

a result, the court tended to take an interventionist antitrust approach and preferred structural rather than behavioral remedies.

3.2.1.2 Chicago School

Economists and lawyers at the University of Chicago (known as Chicago School) criticized the Harvard School strongly on the basis of its perceived over-regulation. This approach is regarded by economists like George Stigler, as having replaced the dominant antitrust thinking of Harvard School, with its concerns of corruption of government.[14] Demsetz distrusted the 'S–C–P' paradigm because the market structure can change rapidly as a more efficient firm tends to become large.[15] In contrast to attitudes of the Warren Court, which held that antitrust policy can include fairness and equity goals, the Chicago School argued the sole objective of competition law should be to promote economic efficiency.[16] Chicagoans also believed enterprises in the market are rational profit-maxi-misers and the market can be self-corrected without government intervention.[17] To summarize, Chicago School favors a laissez-faire approach, considering economic efficiency as the exclusive purpose of competition law.

The Chicago School uses the consumer welfare standard, which relies on price theory in assessing anti-competitive effects. One important reason that the Chicago School dominated US antitrust thinking from 1980s was the doctrine met the popularity of President Ronald Reagan's 'leave business alone' reforms.[18] Therefore, US antitrust regulators and courts gradually departed from the Harvard School and embraced Chicago School, moving to a 'law-and-economics' approach. They found the Chicago School's exclusive aim to enhance economic efficiency was rather more measurable in practice. In most cases, courts would adopt the maximization of consumer welfare, as postulated by Chicago scholars,[19] as the exclusive goal of

---

[14] Appelbaum, Binyamin. 2019. *The economists' hour: false prophets, free markets, and the fracture of society,* 139; Healey, Deborah. 2020. The ambit of competition law: comments on its goals. In *Research handbook on models and methods of competition law,* eds. D. Healey, M. Jacobs, and R. Smith, 12–37, Cheltenham: Edward Elgar.

[15] Demsetz, Harold. 1973. Industry structure, market rivalry, and public policy. *The Journal of Law and Economics* 16: 1–9, 1.

[16] Healey, Deborah. 2020. The ambit of competition law: comments on its goals. In *Research handbook on models and methods of competition law,* eds. D. Healey, M. Jacobs, and R. Smith, 12–37, Cheltenham: Edward Elgar.

[17] Hovenkamp, Herbert. The Harvard and Chicago Schools and the dominant firm. In *How the Chicago School overshot the mark the effect of conservative economic analysis on U.S. antitrust,* ed. Robert Pitofsky, 110, Oxford: Oxford University Press.

[18] Gerber, David. 2019. Comparative competition law. In *The Oxford handbook of comparative law,* eds.

Mathias Reimann, and Reinhard Zimmermann, 1169, 1175. Second edition. Oxford: Oxford University Press.

[19] Bork, Robert. 1978. *The antitrust paradox: A policy at war with itself, 426.* New York: Basic Books.

antitrust law. In other words, the standard for determining an anti-competitive practice was to assess whether such a practice could reduce output and raise prices. Influenced by the Chicago School, it has been suggested that the US antitrust lawyers often 'disparage the concept of abuse of a dominant position'[20] because the concept is 'too vague and potentially too restrictive'.[21] Another implication of the Chicago School is that US courts, particularly the Supreme Court, are more likely to apply the rule of reason to assess the economic impacts instead of the per se illegal rule in antitrust cases.[22]

3.2.1.3 Criticisms on the Chicago School

There are some criticisms of the Chicago School. Eleanor Fox argued that: 'Law is not economics…The basic difference between Chicagoans and traditionalists is a difference of vision about what kind of society we are and should strive to be…'.[23] Dworkin even criticized Judge Posner for promoting purely 'protestant' political values, questioning the Chicago School: 'Is wealth a value?'[24] Others, often called the Post-Chicago School, were more sceptical about the market itself and the self-correctived function of market failures. For instance, Hovenkamp considered the Chicago School as a simplified assumption because 'markets are much more varied and complex than Chicago theories were willing to admit.'[25] In terms of the abuse of dominance, Evans challenged the Chicago School's 'impossibility theorems' (which claim that undertakings with substantial market power are unlikely to conduct unilateral anti-competitive practices) using game theory.[26] In practice, markets do not rapidly self-correct, and so firms could illegally exploit market imperfections to generate inefficiency even in a competitive market. However, Post-Chicagoans only put forward questions but does not provide any reliable answers, making it of limited practical utility.[27]

Furthermore, the consumer welfare standard itself, as Eleanor Fox stated, is not a unified theory. She also questioned whether it really exists ('There is no such

---

[20] Gerber, David. 2019. Comparative competition law. In *The Oxford handbook of comparative law*, eds. Mathias Reimann, and Reinhard Zimmermann, 1169, 1175. Second edition. Oxford: Oxford University Press.

[21] Ibid.

[22] See United States v. Arnold, Schwinn & Co., 388 U.S. 365 (1967); United States Steel Corp. v. Fortner Enterprises, Inc., 429 U.S. 610 (1977); State Oil Co. v. Khan, 522 U.S. 3 (1997).

[23] Fox, Eleanor, and Lawrence Sullivan. 1987. Antitrust–retrospective and prospective: Where are we coming from—where are we going. *NYU Law Review* 62: 936–988, 936.

[24] Dworkin, Ronald. 1980. Is wealth a value? *The Journal of Legal Studies* 9:191–226, 211–212.

[25] Hovenkamp, Herbert. 2001. Post-Chicago antitrust: A review and critique. *Columbia Business Law Review 2001*: 257–268, 268.

[26] Evans, David, and A. Jorge Padilla. 2005. Designing antitrust rules for assessing unilateral practices: A neo-Chicago approach. *The University of Chicago Law Review* 72(1): 73–98, 74

[27] Crane, Daniel. 2009. Chicago, post-Chicago, and neo-Chicago. *The University of Chicago Law Review* 76:1911–1933, 1911.

thing.').[28] Josef Drexl also believed the consumer-welfare approach relies on 'collective' consumer interests but ignores the fact that consumers may have colliding interests.[29] Harry First took a more compromised approach saying that antitrust should neither be divorced from economics nor democratic concerns (cf. individual choices).[30]

Despite these criticisms of the Chicago School, it still dominates the US antitrust enforcement. In fact, recent discussions in the US primarily focus on the most appropriate efficiency and welfare standards.[31]

3.2.2 Section 2 of the Sherman Act: Monopolization and Attempted Monopolization

From the wording of Section 2, the Sherman Act prohibits monopolization, attempts to monopolize and conspiracy to monopolize.[32] Nonetheless, the US antitrust community agrees that prohibition of conspiracy has 'never enjoyed the distinctive status held by monopolization and attempt'.[33] Accordingly, this Sect. 3.2.2 of this book emphasize the established and attempted monopolization.

3.2.2.1 Monopolization

The Concept of 'Monopolization' Under US Antitrust Law

Section 2 of the US Sherman Act considers that it is illegal for any individuals to 'monopolize, or attempt to monopolize, or combine or conspire with any other person or persons, to monopolize any part of the trade or commerce among the several States, or with foreign nations…'.

---

[28] Interview with Eleanor M Fox, *CPI Talks* (7 November 2019).

[29] See Drexl, Josef. 2011. Chapter 17: On the (a)political character of the economic approach to competition law. In *Competition policy and the economic approach: Foundations and limitations,* eds. Josef Drexl, Wolfgang Kerber, and Rupprecht Podszun, 316. Cheltenham: Edward Elgar Publishing.

[30] First, Harry. 2019. American express, the rule of reason, and the goals of antitrust. *Nebraska Law Review* 98: 319–344, 344.

[31] For example, traditional Chicagoans like Bork claim that antitrust policy should be understood as the maximization of consumer welfare. See Bork, Robert. 1978. *The antitrust paradox: A policy at war with itself,* 426. New York: Basic Books. Others favour a total welfare standard. See e.g. Kaplow, Louis. 2012. On the choice of welfare standards in competition law. In *The goals of competition law,* ed. Daniel Zimmer, 3ff. Cheltenham: Edward Elgar.

[32] Section 2 of the Sherman Act provides that 'Every person who shall monopolize, or attempt to monopolize, or combine or conspire with any other persons, to monopolize any part of the trade or commerce among the several States, or with foreign nations, shall be deemed guilty of a felony…'.

[33] Hovenkamp, Herbert. 2016. *Federal antitrust policy: The law of competition and its practice,* 378, 5th ed. St. Paul, MN: West Academic Publishing.

The terse statutory language leaves an unanswered question: what is monopolization under the Sherman Act? At its heart are the goals of monopolization law in the US. It has been suggested that Section 2 shares the same essential goals as other provisions of the Sherman Act.[34] That is, the US antitrust law intends to facilitate the market economy and maximize the wealth and economic growth of the society.[35]

In terms of the monopolization law, Section 2 of the Sherman Act accomplishes the above objectives by preventing the acquisition or maintenance of monopoly power[36] through improper means.[37] By prohibiting these monopolistic conduct, Section 2 protects a competitive market which provides undertakings with incentives to boost economic growth.[38]

It can be noted that the term 'monopolization is about two elements: firstly whether the firm acquire or maintain 'monopoly power', and secondly whether the firm pursues for the monopoly power through 'improper means'. Arguably, the first element stands at the core of monopolization law. Undertakings with ill-gotten monopoly power may lead to higher prices and lower prices,[39] which falls into the scope of antitrust intervention that the Chicago School supports.

Trinko[40] was a landmark US Supreme Court case which dealt with the monopolization dispute. It remains a good case-law today. Chapter 5 of this book, which analyses some abusive practices in relations to trade secrets, will assess the *Trinko* case in detail. This chapter provides details about the *Trinko* judgement to reveal how the US Supreme Court describes and treats monopoly/monopolization. This case dealt with the refusal by a dominant telecommunications exchange carrier, Verizon, to grant a competitive exchange carrier access to its network infrastructure.

Justice Scalia discussed the relationship between monopoly and a free market in *Trinko.* In his opinion, monopoly power itself and the ability to charge monopoly prices are important driving forces of the free-market system:

> The opportunity to charge monopoly prices—at least for a short period—is what attracts "business acumen" in the first place; it induces risk taking that produces innovation and economic growth. To safeguard the incentive to innovate, the possession of monopoly power will not be found unlawful unless it is accompanied by an element of anti-competitive conduct.

---

[34] The US Department of Justice. 2022. Competition and monopoly: Single-firm conduct under Section 2 of the Sherman Act. https://www.justice.gov/atr/competition-and-monopoly-single-firm-conduct-under-section-2-sherman-act-chapter-1. Accessed 23 March 2025.

[35] Ibid.

[36] This book discusses the market power issue in Chap. 4. In short, monopoly power is a large amount of market power a dominant firm may possess.

[37] The US Department of Justice. 2022. Competition and monopoly: Single-firm conduct under Section 2 of the Sherman Act. https://www.justice.gov/atr/competition-and-monopoly-single-firm-conduct-under-section-2-sherman-act-chapter-1. Accessed 23 March 2025.

[38] Ibid.

[39] Ibid. See also Gavil, Andrew. 2004. Exclusionary distribution strategies by dominant firms: Striking a better balance. *Antitrust Law Journal* 72: 3–81, 33.

[40] Verizon Communications v. Law Offices of Curtis V. Trinko, LLP, often shortened to Verizon v. Trinko, 540 U.S. 398 (2004).

The *Trinko* case remains good law in the US as the Supreme Court has not overruled it.[41] However, the US Congress, another branch of the US government, has recently revisited the history of antitrust law and revealed some different attitudes towards the monopolization law in digital era. A US Congress report[42] argued that courts have noticeably misinterpreted the monopolization law for decades.[43] It argued that the US courts established very strict legal standards that makes it difficult for the plaintiffs to prove monopolization.[44] The report said that many business practices conducted by digital platforms are harmful to fair competition, but may be difficult to fit within the existing monopolization law interpreted by the US courts.[45] By criticizing the Chicago School focusing on economic efficiency as the exclusive goal of antitrust laws, the report argued that the US antitrust laws should protect consumers as well as 'workers, entrepreneurs, independent businesses, open markets, a fair economy, and democratic ideals.'[46]

In summary, the US monopolization law (Section 2 of Sherman Act) shares the same goals as the antitrust framework, aiming at preventing harms to economic efficiency. Although the term 'monopolization' is closely related to concerns of monopoly power, the US Supreme Court has held that it has economic advantages. The US monopolization law makes it unlawful to acquire or maintain monopoly power by illegal means. Despite the fact that there are some different opinions on the application of the monopolization law between the courts and Congress, the Supreme Court *Trinko* decision remains a good doctrine in the case-law jurisdiction.

---

[41] It should be noted that the US *Microsoft* was another leading case regarding Section 2 of the Sherman Act. See Microsoft Corp. v. United States (DC Cir. 2001).

[42] In 2019, the Committee on the Judiciary of the US House of Representatives initiated an antitrust investigation against the US giant tech companies and issued a report. See House Committee on the Judiciary. Antitrust investigation of the rise and use of market power online and the adequacy of existing antitrust laws and current enforcement levels. https://democrats-judiciary.house.gov/issues/issue/?IssueID=14921. Accessed 23 March 2025.

[43] Ibid. 395–396.

[44] Ibid.

[45] Ibid.

[46] Ibid. 392. It is notable that the Biden Administration issued the 'Executive Order on Promoting Competition in the American Economy' in July 2021. The executive order followed the Congress Report against digital platforms, claiming that the Biden Administration will combat the abuses of market power and the harmful effects of monopoly and monopsony. See The White House. Executive order on promoting competition in the American economy. https://bidenwhitehouse.archives.gov/briefing-room/presidential-actions/2021/07/09/executive-order-on-promoting-competition-in-the-american-economy/. Accessed 23 March 2025.

The Establishment of a Monopolization in the US

Monopolization in Section 2 of the Sherman Act refers to active practices[47] by a dominant firm in the relevant market that are worthy of condemnation. However, this section does not provide much on how these practices are identified. Justice Brandeis believed that Section 2 of the Act serves to protect against '[T]he Curse of Bigness'.[48] The provisions of Section 2 are rather general prohibitions. Therefore, it is the court's role to interpret the elements constituting a monopolization. The US Supreme Court once held a 'no fault' approach when the Harvard School prevailed, claiming in *Griffith* that monopoly power itself constitutes an evil stance.[49] After the 1960s, the US Supreme Court changed its position and concluded in *Grinnell* that there exist two elements of illicit monopolization: '(1) the possession of monopoly power in the relevant market and (2) the wilful acquisition or maintenance of that power as distinguished from growth or development as a consequence of a superior product, business acumen, or historic accident.'[50] Hovenkamp points out that a defendant's conduct falls into the scope of monopolization if the defendant (1) has 'monopoly power' and (2) has exercised the power.[51] Such exercise of market power may also be defined as 'exclusionary' conduct.

Merely having monopoly power is legal. Although Schumpeter and Arrow had debates on whether market power or competition provides incentive for innovation, it is generally believed that both market power and competition contribute to technical advancement.[52] Firms, including those with substantial market power, are encouraged to compete in markets even through aggressive means. Although a dominant firm may be conducting exclusionary practices, this does not necessarily mean that such conduct is illegal. Hovenkamp argues the existing US case law has set the standard of banned exclusionary practices as those that '(1) are reasonably able to generate, increase and maintain substantial market power by deterring competitors; and (2) either (2a) are not beneficial to consumers at all, or (2b) are needless for the particular consumer benefits claimed for them, or (2c) lead to disproportionate losses to any resulting advantages.'[53] These criteria imply that the assessment of completed monopolization is based on its economic impact on consumers. Some commentators have also suggested a so-called 'sliding approach' to define the relationship

[47] The wording 'monopolize suggests an active conduct. Stroux, Sigrid. US and EC oligopoly control. Vol. 14. Kluwer Law International BV, 2004, 58.

[48] Brandeis, Louis, Osmond K. Fraenkel, and Clarence M. Lewis. 1965. *The curse of bigness*. New York: Kennikat Press.

[49] United States v. Griffith Corp., 334 U.S. 100 (1948).

[50] United States v. Grinnell Corp., 384 U.S. 563 (1966).

[51] Hovenkamp, Herbert. 2016. *Federal antitrust policy: The law of competition and its practice*, 355, 5th ed. St. Paul, MN: West Academic Publishing.

[52] Baker, Jonathan. 2007. Beyond Schumpeter vs. Arrow: How antitrust fosters innovation. *Antitrust Law Journal* 74(3): 575–602, 575.

[53] Hovenkamp, Herbert. 2016. *Federal antitrust policy: The law of competition and its practice*, 5th ed. 356. St. Paul, MN: West Academic Publishing.

between monopoly power and exclusionary conduct.[54] That is, a company with greater market power is more likely to take advantage of relatively minor behaviors to restrict competition and vice versa.

3.2.2.2 Attempted Monopolization

Aside from substantive monopolization, Section 2 also forbids attempted monopolization, which is unusual in civil law jurisdictions. Justice Holmes, one of the founders of US common law system, introduced the common law conception of attempt to Section 2. Based on Holmes's judgement in Swift & Co.,[55] it is now generally accepted that a plaintiff should prove the following elements for an attempted breach: (1) specific intent to control prices or eliminate competition[56]; (2) anti-competitive practices in pursuit of illegal objectives; and (3) a dangerous probability of success.[57]

It should be noted that the conditions of an attempted breach should be stricter than that of substantive monopolization; otherwise any unfair business practices could fall within the scope of attempt. As a result, some limitations are necessary in the application of the attempt statue. For example, most courts are of the view that the intent of merely vanquishing rivals does not suffice and that the intent to accomplish monopoly power should be involved.[58] Because it is hard to define 'attempt' in some cases, Hovenkamp claims the law prohibiting attempt to monopolize is one of the most complex antitrust violations in the US.[59]

---

[54] Ibid, 359.

[55] Swift & Co. v. United States, 196 U.S. 375 (1905).

[56] While the Supreme Court in *Aspen* claimed that the intent is relevant to both attempted and completed monopolization, most case law upheld a monopolization breach does not require the intent.

[57] Hovenkamp, Herbert. 2016. *Federal antitrust policy: The law of competition and its practice*, 5th ed. 370. St. Paul, MN: West Academic Publishing.

[58] See e.g. 668 F. 2d 1014—William Inglis Sons Baking Co v. Itt Continental Baking Company Inc William.

[59] Hovenkamp, Herbert. 2016. *Federal antitrust policy: The law of competition and its practice*, 5th ed., 369. St. Paul, MN: West Academic Publishing.

3.2.3 Lessons from EU Competition Law

3.2.4 Philosophy of EU Law of the Abuse of Dominance

3.2.4.1 Overview of Ordoliberalism

In the EU, Ordoliberal thinking is the predominant philosophy that guides the establishment and application of law prohibiting the abuse of market dominance. As Möschel argued, Ordoliberal thinking supported an 'economic constitution' where competition and economic freedom are incorporated into the law, so that there is neither unconstrained private power nor destructive government power (e.g. Hitler) in the market.[60] The Ordoliberal School stems from German economists and lawyers at the University of Freiburg during the Nazi occupation.[61] When European countries decided to become united after the 1950s, ordoliberalism was introduced in the theoretical foundations of the European Union (EU), particularly in the competition law and policy. Ordoliberals believe that competition law is aimed at protecting the competitive process (freedom of competition), keeping the market competitive.[62] Many competition lawyers and courts apply Ordoliberal thinking today, particularly in the German-speaking world.[63]

3.2.4.2 Ordoliberalism and the Abuse of Market Dominance

Ordoliberal thinking, especially the conception of the freedom of competition, affects the doctrine of the abuse of market dominance in the EU. Ordoliberals, such as Mestmacker, argued 'competition as a process is advantageous to consumers'.[64] They view competition as a dynamic process in which the producers can decide what to produce on their own and consumers have the chance to choose between products. Behrens argued consumers cannot attain benefits only if there is residual pressure of competition (a competitive market).[65] As a consequence, Ordoliberals

---

[60] Möschel, Wernhard. 1989. Competition policy from an ordo point of view. In *German neo-liberals and the social market economy*, 142. London: Palgrave Macmillan.

[61] The leading representatives of the Ordoliberals were Walter Eucken, Franzbohm and Hans Grossmann-Doerth. See Jones, Alison, BE, Sufrin, and Niamh Dunne. 2019. *EU competition law: Text, cases, and materials,* 7th ed. 27–28. Oxford: Oxford University Press.

[62] Quoting: 方小敏 [Fang Xiaomin]. 2010. *竞争法视野中的欧洲法律统一[Unifications of European laws from the perspective of competition law].* 北京: 中国大百科全书出版社 [Beijing: Encyclopedia of China Publishing House] 185.

[63] Drexl, Josef. 2011. *Competition policy and the economic approach: Foundations and limitations*, 325–326. Cheltenham: Edward Elgar Publishing.

[64] Mestmacker, Ernst-Joachim. 1972. Concentration and competition in the EEC. *Journal of World Trade Law* 6: 615–647, 641.

[65] Behrens, Peter. 2018. The ordoliberal concept of 'abuse' of a dominant position and its impact on Article 102 TFEU. In *Abusive practices in competition law,* 11. Cheltenham: Edward Elgar Publishing.

do not focus only on economic efficiency. They also care whether the competitive process itself is impeded, such as whether high barriers to entry exist in the relevant market.

The European Court of Justice (ECJ)[66] read ordoliberal thinking into its interpretations on Article 102 of TFEU (former Article 86 of Rome Treaty[67] and Article 82 of EC Treaty[68]), which prohibits the abuse of a dominant position, and developed a legal theory—the 'special responsibility' of a dominant firm. As is clearly stated in Article 3(3) TFEU, one of the aims of establishing the EU is to achieve an "internal market". The "internal market" is further interpreted as "a system ensuring that competition is not distorted."[69] Behrens argues that this approach in TFEU reflects the ordoliberal's approach to competition.[70] The ECJ then affirmed in the *Michelin* case[71] that a dominant firm 'has a special responsibility not to allow its conduct to impair genuine undistorted competition on the common market.' This means that it is necessary to impose an obligation for dominant firms to act "as if" they were in a fully competitive market.[72]

3.2.5 *Article 102 of TFEU: Prohibition of the Abuse of a Dominant Position*

Article 102 of the TFEU provides that:

> Any abuse by one or more undertakings of a dominant position within the internal market or in a substantial part of it shall be prohibited as incompatible with the internal market insofar as it may affect trade between Members States. Such abuse may, in particular, consist in:

(a) directly or indirectly imposing unfair purchase or selling prices or other unfair trading conditions;
(b) limiting production, markets or technical development to the prejudice of consumers;

---

[66] The Court of Justice of the EU consists of ECJ and General Court (GC), which are responsible for interpreting the law, enforcing the law, annulling EU legal acts, ensuring the EU takes action and sanctioning EU institutions. See Court of Justice of the European Union. *European Union.* https://europa.eu/european-union/about-eu/institutions-bodies/court-justice_en. Accessed 23 March 2025.

[67] The Treaty of Rome established the European Economic Community in 1957. The current law is set out in the Treaty on the Functioning of the European Union.

[68] Treaty establishing the European Community (Consolidated version 2002).

[69] See Treaty on European Union and the Treaty on the Functioning of the European Union (Protocol (No. 27) on the Internal Market and Competition).

[70] Behrens, Peter. 2018. The ordoliberal concept of 'abuse' of a dominant position and its impact on Article 102 TFEU. In *Abusive practices in competition law,* 10. Cheltenham: Edward Elgar Publishing.

[71] *NV Nederlandsche Banden-Industrie Michelin v Commission* (Case 322/81) [1983] ECR 3461, para.57.

[72] Gormsen, Liza Lovdahl. 2010. *A principled approach to abuse of dominance in European competition law,* 45–47. Cambridge: Cambridge University Press.

(c) applying dissimilar conditions to equivalent transactions with other trading parties, thereby placing them at a competitive disadvantage;
(d) making the conclusion of contracts subject to acceptance by the other parties of supplementary obligations which, by their nature or according to commercial usage, have no connection with the subject of such contracts.

Article 102 is the law forbidding a firm from abusing its dominant position. However, TFEU does not provide further explanation of its relevant essential components, such as what are the criteria for dominance. These interpretations rest on the judicial practices of EU courts and the Commission. This chapter provides brief analysis of the concepts of 'dominance' (the dominant position) and 'abuse' under the EU competition law. Chapters 4 and 5 will make deeper assessments on the EU experience regarding market dominance and abusive practices.

The concept of the dominant position (dominance):

While the statutory language of the TFEU leaves the term 'dominant position' undefined, modern EU antitrust literature often revisits the landmark *United Brands*[73] case for a definition of dominance. The ECJ held that:

> The dominant position...relates to a position of economic strength enjoyed by an undertaking which enables it to prevent effective competition being maintained on the relevant market by affording it the power to behave to an appreciable extent independently of its competitors, customers and ultimately of its consumers.

Therefore, the traditional concept of 'dominance' refers to the ability of a firm to act independently from its rivals and consumers, and hence is not restrained by the competitive process.[74] However, it is difficult to measure the 'independence' a company may possess. The European Commission, as the European competition authority, relates 'independence' to the degree of 'market power' from an economic point of view. The Commission regards that 'an undertaking which is capable of profitably increasing prices above the competitive level for a significant period of time does not face sufficiently effective competitive constraints and can thus generally be regarded as dominant'.[75]

The concept of abuse:

It has been generally considered that the ECJ provided its jurisprudence on 'abuse' in the *Hoffmann La-Roche* case.[76] The ECJ held that an abuse can affect the structure of a market and has the effect of weakening the degree of competition.[77]

---

[73] Case 27/76 United Brands v Commission [1978] ECR 207, para. 65.

[74] Kaczorowska-Ireland, Alina. 2016. *European Union Law*, 931. London: Routledge.

[75] Commission Communication (EC) of 24 February 2009 on Guidance on the Commission's Enforcement Priorities in Applying Article 82 of the EC Treaty to Abusive Exclusionary Conduct by Dominant Undertakings [2009] OJ C 45, para. 11.

[76] Case 85/76 Hoffmann-La Roche & Co. AG v Commission [1979] ECR 461.

[77] Ibid.

The above cases remain effective in EU case law today. The European Commission often cites the *United Brands* and *Hoffmann La-Roche* to explain the principle of the abuse of a dominant position in its recent decisions.[78]

In short, abuses are practices conducted by a dominant firm that may harm competition and consumers. The provision gives a list of certain prohibited acts, but the list is not exhaustive serving merely as examples.[79] The competition agency and courts may examine whether a practice conducted by a dominant company constitute an abuse on a case-by-case basis.

Pursuant to the TFEU and its jurisprudence developed by the EU courts, the party alleging an infringement of article 102 must prove the following requirements:

(a) the alleged party is in a dominant position (in the relevant market), (b) there exist abuses; and (c) the abuse has an effect on inter-State trade.[80] As Gormsen points out, while article 102 has not been changed since the time of the Treaty of Rome, the EU legal environment alters rapidly.

3.2.6 Has the EU Accepted an Effects-Based Approach?

3.2.6.1 Introducing an Effects-Based Approach to Article 102

Case law of EU courts has shown the preference for a formalistic approach to Article 102 (previous Article 86 of the Treaty of Rome and Article 82 of the EC Treaty) instead of assessment of actual economic effects ('effects-based approach).[81] However, there has been a continuous 'modernization of EU competition law since the 1990s. The modernization efforts in Europe were largely influenced by the law-and-economics movement and Chicago School which sees enhancing efficiency as the exclusive goal of competition law on the other side of the Atlantic. In the EU, the modernized effects-based approach, also known as more economic approach, was introduced firstly to vertical restraints, then merger control and cartels, but there nevertheless remains a question as to whether the effects-based approach can apply to the law prohibiting the abuse of dominance (Article 102).[82]

The European Commission is the main driving force to read the effects-based approach into the interpretation of article 102, tracking the similar path to that of

[78] See e.g. Case AT. 40099, *Google Android* Decision of 18 July 2018, para.431; Case AT. 3974, *Google Search (Shopping)* Decision of 27 June 2017, para. 264.

[79] Jones, Alison, Sufrin, Brenda and Niamh Dunne. 2019. *EU competition law: text, cases, and materials,* 279. 7th ed. Oxford: Oxford University Press.

[80] Jones, Alison, Sufrin, Brenda and Niamh Dunne. 2019. *EU competition law: text, cases, and materials,* 290. 7th ed. Oxford: Oxford University Press.

[81] Geradin, Damienand, and Nicolas Petit. 2010. Judicial review in European Union competition law: A quantitative and qualitative assessment. *Tilburg Law School Research Paper,* 39.

[82] Gerber, David. 2014. Searching for a modernized voice: Economics, institutions, and predictability in European competition law. *Fordham International Law Journal* 37(5):1421–1450, 1435–1436.

article 101 and mergers. In 2005, the Directorate-General (DG) for Competition of the Commission released a Discussion Paper which stated that enhancing consumer welfare is the ultimate goal of article 82 of the EC Treaty (now Article 102 TFEU).[83] The Discussion Paper was an informal document of the Commission for public discussions. In 2009, the European Commission issued a Guidance Paper concerning the application of Article 82 (now Article 102 TFEU), which prohibits the abuse of dominance.[84] The Guidance Paper adopted a more economic approach rather than a form-based approach.[85] According to the Guidance Paper, the Commission will accept the 'as efficient competitor-test' (AEC-test) to determine if the competitors are prevented from the market because they are less efficient than the dominant firm.[86]

3.2.6.2 Hesitant Attitudes Towards an Effects-Based Approach

Despite the Guidance Paper that clearly sets out an economic effects-based approach, EU courts sometimes challenge this approach. The Guidance Paper is not a secondary legal source.[87] It is persuasive but not legally binding.[88] The EU courts take a more conservative approach to departing from their own established jurisprudence which reflects Ordoliberalism. In many cases, the EU courts would take factors other than economic efficiency into account when analyzing whether the underlying company has conducted abuses or not. For example, the Court stressed in the *Deutsche Telekom* case that "equality of opportunity was not observed on the relevant market and, therefore, that a system of undistorted competition was not assured".[89] However, in the recent *Intel* case,[90] it is worth noting that the ECJ approved the Commission's effects-based approach and claimed that enterprises have no obligations to protect less efficient competitors from leaving the market.[91]

---

[83] DG Competition Discussion Paper on the Application of Article 82 of the Treaty to Exclusionary Abuses para 4. https://ec.europa.eu/competition/antitrust/art82/discpaper2005.pdf. Accessed 23 March 2025.

[84] Commission Communication (EC) of 24 February 2009 on Guidance on the Commission's Enforcement Priorities in Applying Article 82 of the EC Treaty to Abusive Exclusionary Conduct by Dominant Undertakings [2009] OJ C 45.

[85] Witt, Anne. 2010. The commission's guidance paper on abusive exclusionary conduct-more radical than it appears? *European Law Review* 35: 214–235, 214.

[86] Behrens, Peter. 2018. The Ordoliberal concept of 'abuse' of a dominant position and its impact on Article 102 TFEU. *Abusive Practices in Competition Law*, 15. Cheltenham: Edward Elgar Publishing.

[87] EU laws can be divided into primary sources (such as the TFEU) and secondary sources (such as Directives or Regulations promogulated by the EU Parliament or Commission). Secondary sources must follow the rules of primary sources.

[88] In the Guidance Paper, the Commission clarifies it is not intended to be a statement of the law. See Guidance Paper, para. 3.

[89] *Deutsche Telekom AG v European Commission* (C-280/08) [2010] ECR 09555, para. 240.

[90] *Intel Corporation Inc v. European Commission* [2017] (Case-C-413/14 P).

[91] Despite this, it is still too early to conclude the ECJ has abandoned its form-based approach because it also clarified the test can be applied only 'in the cases where the undertaking concerned

Despite these controversies, the effects-based approach has more or less influenced the application of Article 102 TFEU, particularly in the competition enforcement of the European Commission. Accordingly, this book may refer to the important document of EU Guidance Paper when necessary in the following chapters.

3.2.7 *Approach to the Abuse of Market Dominance in China*

3.2.8 *Provisions of Abuse of Market Dominance in the Anti-monopoly Law*

When China decided to implement the 'reform and opening-up' policy in the 1980s, many economic-related laws, including competition rules on the abuse of market dominance, were transplanted from Europe.[92] In 2007, in order to address potential practices that may restrict competition, China enacted the Anti-Monopoly Law[93] ('AML'), Chapter 3 of which regulates prohibited unilateral conduct. The 2022 AML remains stable.

The structure of the AML provisions is quite similar to that of article 102 of the TFEU in terms of unilateral practices. The AML states in the 'General Principles' that it prohibits an undertaking from abusing a dominant market position.[94] More specifically, Chapter 3 of the AML specifies the framework which addresses the abuse of a dominant market position, with article 22 being the fundamental provision and both articles 23 and 24 further explaining some of the concepts.

The AML defines a dominant market position (dominance) as the ability to control prices, quantities or any other trade conditions in the relevant market, or to obstruct market entry.[95] Arguably, this definition of dominance is similar to the EU 'independence' standard of dominance, which focuses on the ability of a company to act freely in the market. Also similar to the EU tradition, Chinese competition authorities often relate the dominance to the concept of 'market power' in order to have a better assessment.[96]

---

submits […], on the basis of supporting evidence, that its conduct was not capable of restricting competition and, in particular, of producing the alleged foreclosure effects'.

[92] Hou Liyang. 2015. The influence of EU and US legal theory on competition law in China: Divergence and convergence. https://ssrn.com/abstract=2586859. Accessed 23 March 2025.

[93] Competition law has different names in various jurisdictions. For instance, it is called antitrust law in the US, competition law in the EU and anti-monopoly law in China. In some other countries, such as France, competition rules are in the commercial code. China's AML was promulgated in 2007 and in effect from 1 August, 2008.

[94] Article 7 of the AML.

[95] Article 22 of the AML.

[96] Chapter 4 will discuss methods of measuring market power that Chinese competition authorities may use.

Inspired by the traditions of the EU competition law, article 22 of the AML also provides an inclusive list of prohibited conduct with a catch-all provision. Most Chinese competition law scholars agree that market dominance itself is not illegal in the market. For example, as Xiaoye Wang argues, a company is eligible to achieve dominance under government authorization,[97] or through making technology and efficiency advancement, or through illegal practices. However, it is difficult or even impossible for an undertaking to attain market power through illegal conduct if competition rules work well. As a consequence, a dominant market position acquired in a competition rules-based market is basically legal.[98] According to article 22, a court or competition agency may find a company abusing market dominance if (1) the company employs market dominance in the relevant market and (2) the company has abused such dominance to restrict competition. Also listed in article 22 are six detailed abusive practices, which are divided into exploitative and exclusionary conduct. In addition to the listed behaviors, there is also a catch-all provision in article 22, which stipulates that other abusive practices can be identified as well.

The precondition of determining the abuse of dominance is that the undertaking must be dominant in a relevant market. Therefore, articles 23 and 24 are concerned with how to determine a dominant market position under the AML. A distinction between the EU competition law and the AML is that article 24 contains presumptive thresholds for dominance based on market shares, whereas the TFEU does not.[99] This is because the AML made reference to the German Act against Restraints of Competition (ARC) in its enactment.[100] The AML also allows the alleged dominant undertaking to rebut the market share presumption by other evidence. The lawmakers of the AML explained that the reason for such a presumption is to achieve legal certainty.[101] The presumption clause, in theory, shifts the burden of proof. For example, if a plaintiff manages to prove the dominance of an enterprise merely through evidence of huge market share, it would be the accused party's burden of proof to rebut such presumption pursuant to article 24. Notwithstanding, this doctrinal analysis of article 24 has never been favoured by either Chinese academia or courts. An empirical research conducted by Mezzanotte and Hou found that between 2008 and 2013 there were few cases in which market share presumption was the only decisive element in the

[97] For instance, only those companies which have the authorization of the central government in China can produce and sell tobacco.

[98] 王晓晔 [Wang Xiaoye]. 2011. *反垄断法 [Chinese Anti-Monopoly Law]*. 北京: 法律出版社 [Beijing: Law Press China], 192–193.

[99] Dominance is presumed in article 24 where: the relevant market share of one company consists of one half or more of the relevant market; the joint market share of two companies as a whole accounts for two thirds or more in the relevant market; or the aggregate market share of three companies as a whole accounts for three quarters or more of the relevant market.

[100] The German ARC presumes a company with more than 40% market share in a relevant market as a dominant undertaking. See Hartmann-Ru¨ppel, Marco. *Abuse of dominant position and globalization & protection and disclosure of trade secrets and know-how*. eds.'Germany' in Pranvera Këllezi, Bruce Kilpatrick and Pierre Kobel, 109–120. Cham: Springer.

[101] 曹康泰 [Cao Kangtai]. 2006. 关于《中华人民共和国反垄断法 (草案)》的说明 [Statement on the Anti-Monopoly law (Draft)]. http://www.npc.gov.cn/zgrdw/wxzl/gongbao/2007-10/09/content_5374671.htm. Accessed 23 March 2025.

identification of dominance in China.[102] Xianlin Wang argues that market share sometimes is not always reliable because other elements like barrier to market entry or product substitution could be decisive in certain cases.[103] Likewise, the SPC held in the *Qihoo v. Tencent*[104] and reiterated in the *Xushuqing v. Tencent*[105] that market share is a relatively crude and potentially misleading indicator for evaluating dominance, particularly in the internet-based sector. It can be argued that these attitudes are reasonable and comply with article 24, in which more considerations are enumerated when defining the market dominance.

3.2.9 Enforcement of the AML in China: Qihoo V. Tencent as a Landmark Case

The most controversial issue when dealing with cases of the abuse of dominance in China, which is similar to the EU, is determining whether unilateral conduct assessment is form-based or effects-based. The AML does not state positively whether an economic anti-competitive effect is essential, particularly for those unilateral practices that are already listed. Emch's research shows that, before 2014, neither competition agencies nor courts considered the evidence of anti-competitive effects as a requirement.[106]

In 2014, the SPC, China's top court, finally faced these issues in its first case regarding the abuse of market dominance—*Qihoo v. Tencent*.[107] The case is quite influential not only because it was adjudicated directly by the SPC but also for the

[102] Mezzanotte, Félix, and Hou Liyang. 2015. The role of presumptions of market dominance in civil litigation in China. *Journal of Antitrust Enforcement* 3:i108–i131.

[103] 王先林 [Wang Xianlin]. 2018. *竞争法学 [Chinese competition law]*. 北京: 中国人民大学出版社 [Beijing: Press of Renmin University of China], 243.

[104] 北京奇虎科技有限公司诉腾讯科技 (深圳) 有限公司, 深圳市腾讯计算机系统有限公司滥用市场支配地位纠纷案 [Beijing Qihoo Technology v Shenzhen Tencent Technology—Abuse of Market Dominance Case], 最高人民法院 [Supreme People's Court], 2013民三终字第4号 [Economic Judgement No. 3], 8 October 2014.

[105] 徐书青诉深圳市腾讯计算机系统有限公司滥用市场支配地位纠纷案 [Xushuqing v Shenzhen Tencent Technology—Abuse of Market Dominance Case], 最高人民法院 [Supreme People's Court], (2017) 最高法民申 4955 号 [SPC Economic Judgement No. 4955], 14 September 2018.

[106] Emch, Adrian. 2016. Effects analysis in abuse of dominance cases in China-Is Qihoo 360 v Tencent a game-changer. *Competition Law International* 12: 11–31, 12.

[107] In fact, it is the first case with respect to anti-monopoly issues adjudicated by the SPC.

reason that it is a Guidance Case (No. 78),[108] which makes the judgement binding for lower courts. The facts and ruling were as follows[109]:

Qihoo (the plaintiff) was the market leader in the area of security software in China. 'QQ' was the flagship product of Tencent (the defendant) offering an instant messaging (IM) service. Tencent sent a public letter to its users on 3 November, 2010, requesting them to stop running QQ on computers which had Qihoo's 360 (security software) installed. Just a day later, Qihoo announced that the two software applications were compatible with each other. In September 2010, Tencent offered QQ IM software and QQ Software Management as an online package without a prompt notice to its users. Tencent then issued a notice that the current version of QQ Software Management and its security software, QQ Doctor would be automatically updated to QQ Computer Housekeeper. Tencent's requirements for abandoning Qihoo's service and using its own package were said to constitute exclusive dealing and tying. For these reasons, Qihoo filed a lawsuit against Tencent for the abuse of market dominance by the conduct of exclusive dealing[110] and tying. The SPC dismissed the case by upholding that Tencent did not hold a dominant market position in the relevant market and that its practices did not impede competition.

The SPC highlighted and analyzed the effects of these practices in this judgement. The court clarified that it is essential to assess the potential positive and adverse effects of alleged unilateral conduct on consumers and competition when determining whether the practice of a dominant firm breaches the AML. For example, when the SPC judged whether Tencent's 'from-two-choose-one'[111] policy constituted an abuse of dominance, the court emphasized the effects on consumer welfare, competition as such and the intention of Tencent. The court pointed out that the AML does not care about the interests of individual undertakings but priorities whether a healthy competition framework is distorted or deterred. Furthermore, the SPC affirmed that a dominant firm can justify its behaviour, with justifications being distinct from the requirement of economic effects.[112]

[108] As a civil law jurisdiction, judicial cases in China, even though those judged by the SPC, are not binding for other courts. However, the Guidance Cases which are selected by the SPC have the legal binding effects on other courts. Article 7 of *Rules of the Supreme People's Court on Guidance Cases* provides that '[P]eople's courts of all levels shall carry out trials of similar cases with reference to the guidance cases issued by the Supreme People's Court.'

[109] World Intellectual Property Organization (WIPO) and SPC (2019) *WIPO Collection of Leading Judgment on Intellectual Property Rights: People's Republic of China (2011–2018)*, 113–121. WIPO: Geneva; SPC: Beijing.

[110] Article 22 (4) which prohibits exclusive dealing is often referred in China as the restrictive trade practice.

[111] This term is regularly used in China. It means that the Tencent requires the users to choose to use the service provided by the Tencent and its competitors.

[112] The SPC judgement did not specify justifications that Tencent may provide for the court. In Chinese judicial practices, the alleged dominant firm may often justify its practice by arguing that the practice complies with public interests. See 王先林 [Wang Xianlin]. 2018. *竞争法学 [Chinese competition law]*. 北京: 中国人民大学出版社 [Beijing: Press of Renmin University of China], 247–248.

Another hotly-debated issue that arose in the Qihoo case is whether a market definition is indispensable when assessing market dominance. Traditionally, the Chinese courts, as Justice Liu of the SPC claims, define a relevant market first in an abuse of dominance case.[113] The State Council's Guidelines on market definition also state that the market definition should be the first step of a competition agency when investigating the abuse of dominance cases.[114] However, some US scholars, particularly economists, always argue that where 'direct' evidence of market power exists, market definition is not essential.[115] The US attitude influenced Chinese judges in the Qihoo case. Judge Zhu, one of the panel members in the Qihoo case, argued in his article that if market power can be inferred from the firms' behaviors, it is unnecessary to define what the relevant market is.[116] Therefore, in the Qihoo case, the SPC upheld that if there exists direct evidence to assess market power (dominance) and anti-competitive effects, market definition is not required (although the SPC defined the relevant markets in this case). Wang (Xiaoye) has criticized this ruling as she believes that defining a relevant market is indispensable in cases of abuse of dominance, unless the market is directly controlled by the government.[117] There may be direct evidence that can reflect market power in economic theory. Nevertheless, such direct evidence, which is mainly based on the presumption of a company pricing its product freely, is really hard to obtain in legal practice. In many cases, neither the competition agency nor the plaintiff can calculate the marginal cost of a product precisely, making it difficult to determine whether the selling price is reasonable. Accordingly, this book argues that market definition is still necessary in most abuse of dominance cases; although this book will discuss any circumstances where direct evidence arises theoretically.

---

[113] 刘贵祥 [Liu Guixiang]. 2016. 滥用市场支配地位理论的司法考量 [How can courts handle cases of the abuse of market dominance]. *中国法学 [China Legal Science]* 5: 260–280, 260.

[114] Article 2 of Guidelines of the Anti-monopoly Commission of the State Council on the Definition of a Relevant Market.

[115] Hovenkamp, Herbert. 2016. *Federal antitrust policy: The law of competition and its practice*, 358. Fifth edition. Minnesota: West Academic Publishing.

[116] 朱理[Zhu Li]. 2015. 互联网领域竞争行为的法律边界：挑战与司法回应[Legal boundaries of competition in Internet area: Challenges and responses]. *竞争政策研究[Competition Policy Research]* 7: 11–19, 17

[117] 王晓晔 [Wang Xiaoye]. 2018. 论相关市场界定在滥用行为案件中的地位和作用 [Functions of market definition in cases of the abuse of market dominance]. *现代法学 [Modern Law Science]* 3: 57–69, 65; 王先林 [Wang Xianlin]. 2014. 3Q 垄断纠纷案终审判决的行业意义与法律影响 [Meanings and legal effects of Qihoo v Tencent]. *中国审判 [China Trial]* 11: 78–80, 79.

3.2.10 Post-Qihoo V. Tencent: Effects-Based Approach

Unlike the position in vertical restraints[118] whereby there are many debates on whether the effects-based approach should apply,[119] the SPC seems to provide a very definite answer that in determining abuse of dominance behaviour should be analyzed on the basis of its pro- and anti-competitive effects. After the Qihoo case, the SPC reiterated the effects-based approach in the *Xushuqing v. Tencent*. Although these cases are civil competition cases, the attitudes of China's top court do affect the competition agency in its administrative procedure. In 2019, the SAMR issued an administrative order,[120] article 21 of which states that the SAMR will consider the following four conditions when determining the abuse of market dominance: (1) the undertaking is dominating the market; (2) the undertaking has undertaken abusive practices; (3) the undertaking has no legitimate justifications; and (4) acts of the dominant firm have an effect of restricting competition. Accordingly, Chinese courts and competition agencies have now reached a consensus on the effects-based approach in cases of abuse of dominance after the landmark Qihoo case.

However, the Qihoo case was not an end. The SPC's ruling did not specify the benchmark for assessing anti-competitive effect.[121] Unlike Chicago School or the 'more economic approach' set out in the EU Guidance Paper, the SPC, in different cases, has concentrated on various effects, which are not limited to consumer welfare. For example, the SPC focused on the impact on consumer welfare, the intention of Tencent and competition as such in the Qihoo case, to the choice of consumers in a tying case (*Wu v. Shaanxi Broadcast & TV Network*),[122] and to other rivals in the *Yingding Corp. v. Sinopec Group.*[123] These cases demonstrated the substance of the effects-based approach, and that the meaning of 'effects' in Chinese legal practice is different from (at least not the same as) that favoured by the US and EU (Commission), but similar to what the ECJ holds now. In short, apart from the effect of economic efficiency, the SPC may consider all types of effects of the conduct. Additionally, the available justifications enable the courts to focus not just on economic efficiency in an abuse case. The SPC upheld in the *Xushuqing v. Tencent* that if a refusal to deal is under the requirement of other laws (advertisement law), such

---

118 Article 18 of the AML prohibits vertical monopoly agreements.

119 吴佩乘 [Wu Peicheng]. 2018. 反垄断法中纵向垄断协议的解释学澄清 [Clarifications of RPM in China's anti-monopoly law]. *知识产权 [Intellectual Property]* 11: 44–51.

120 See Interim Provisions on Prohibition of the Abuse of Market Dominance. The administrative order is binding for competition agency but not for courts.

121 Emch, Adrian. 2016. Effects analysis in abuse of dominance cases in China-Is Qihoo 360 v Tencent a game-changer. *Competition Law International* 12: 11–31, 24.

122 World Intellectual Property Organization (WIPO) and SPC (2019) *WIPO Collection of Leading Judgment on Intellectual Property Rights: People's Republic of China (2011–2018)*, 121–122. WIPO: Geneva; SPC: Beijing.

123 云南盈鼎生物能源股份有限公司，中国石化销售有限公司云南石油分公司拒绝交易纠纷 [Yunnan Ying Ding v Sinopec Group—Refusal to Deal Dispute Case], 最高人民法院 [Supreme People's Court], (2017) 最高法民申 5063 号 [Economic No. 5063], 11 November 2019.

conduct can be justified.[124] Ding concluded that the justification clause for the abuse of dominance, which is not enacted clearly like article 15 for monopoly agreements, contains a broad range of elements.[125] The AML imported the framework of abuse of dominance from traditional EU competition law, yet the enforcement in China is now greatly affected by the US effects-based approach. However, considering that the social and political backgrounds of China do not support laissez faire economics, it is quite difficult to imagine that China will accept the US Chicago School in its entirety. In view of these reasons, as Xiaoye Wang argued, although competition policy pursues enhancing efficiency and consumer welfare, the direct goal of competition law, at least in China, is to promote free competition and economic democracy.[126] Arguably, in terms of the abuse of dominance, Chinese courts will continue to consider economic results as well as other potential effects on a case-by-case basis.

3.3 Conclusion

Many jurisdictions have their own laws prohibiting the abuse of market dominance. These laws may share some similarities but can vary in many different aspects. There is little doubt that the US and the EU are the two major competition law jurisdictions that have influenced competition frameworks in both developed and developing countries. Comparatively, China's codified competition law is relatively young as it was established from 2008.

The US community views antitrust law as a branch of economics. Economic thinking, however, is evolving and not static. The Harvard School dominated the US antitrust thinking after the Second World War and held a market structure-based interventionism. The Chicago School, which was considered to be laissez-faire, criticized the Harvard Structuralist School. It believes that the exclusive goal of antitrust is to protect consumer welfare. From the 1980s, the Chicago School gradually replaced the Harvard School as the dominant antitrust thinking. This explains why antitrust enforcement in the US changed from interventionism to a more cautioned approach, which in essence follows the laissez-faire doctrine. Nevertheless, the Chicago School

---

124 王先林, 吴佩乘 [Wang Xianlin and Wu Peicheng]. 滥用市场支配地位案例评析 [Assessment of Cases of the Abuse of Market Dominance in China]. *中国竞争法律与政策研究报告 2018–2019 年 [Report on Competition Law and Policy of China 2018–2019].*

125 丁茂中[Ding Maozhong]. 2020. 我国《反垄断法》的修订路径. [Analysis on revisions of China's anti-monopoly law]. *法学[Law Science]* 5: 133–150: 139

126 Professor Wang Xiaoye claimed this view in her preface for Professor Fang Xiaomin's book, in which Fang discussed the relationship between law and economics of competition law in Europe. See 方小敏 [Fang Xiaomin]. 2010. *竞争法视野中的欧洲法律统一[Unifications of European laws from the perspective of competition law].* 北京: 中国大百科全书出版社 [Beijing: Encyclopedia of China Publishing House] 2. As Professor Fox noted, the US antitrust was the economic democracy of markets before the twenty-first century. It means that the competition authorities should prevent exclusions and intimidation of small companies and battle with economic concentration. See Fox, Eleanor. 2018. Competition and democracy. OECD Report DAF/COMP/GF (2017)5. https://one.oecd.org/document/DAF/COMP/GF(2017)5/en/pdf. Accessed 23 March 2025.

is not perfect. Many of its critics argue that the assumptions of Chicago economists do not necessarily comply with the conditions of modern markets, and that its consumer welfare standard is too narrow. In view of these concerns, whether US courts and regulators will revise their Chicago-style antitrust enforcement remains a question going into the future. Section 2 of the Sherman Act, which prohibits monopolization and attempted monopolization, is quite simple in terms of its wording. The interpretations of its application rest on the courts. The antitrust law does not prohibit the possession of market power, but it condemns the wilful acquisition or maintenance of such power, i.e. illegal exclusionary conduct. Influenced by the Chicago School, the assessment of whether an exclusionary practice is anti-competitive or not is only based on the impact on consumer welfare. In addition to monopolization, the Sherman Act also prohibits attempted monopolization. An attempted breach needs evidence of the specific intent to restrict competition, anti-competitive practices for illegal purposes, and a dangerous probability of success.

The EU competition law emerged during the integration of European states after the Second World War. The EU competition law framework, particular its provisions against the abuse of market dominance (article 102 of TFEU now), were substantially influenced by German Ordoliberal thinking. Ordoliberals trusted the rule of law more than mere economic theories. They believed the competition process deserved protection. In other words, they held that even though an alleged abusive practice will benefit consumer welfare (outcomes), it can be prohibited because it could impede competition (process). The EU courts, guided by Ordoliberal thinking, argued that the dominant firm in the market has a 'special responsibility'. Hence, it required a dominant firm not to conduct certain practices even if other non-dominant firms can engage in the same. Similar to the US Sherman Act, Article 102 of TFEU does not condemn a dominant position but it condemns illegal abusive practices. However, in addition to exclusionary practices, article 102 also prohibits exploitative abuses (such as excessive pricing), whereas US antitrust law allows such practices. With the influence of US economic-oriented antitrust thinking, the EU is undertaking a reform in competition law to take a more economic approach. As for merger control and monopoly agreements, the EU has adopted an effects-based approach. Although the European Commission published a Guidance Paper to express its effects-based attitude towards laws of abuse of market dominance, the EU courts are reluctant to depart from the existing case-law. The adoption of the effects-based approach in laws against the abuse of dominance is an irreversible trend. The EU courts will take this approach into consideration when handling cases. The question is, to what extent will the EU courts apply the effects-based approach, or in other words, whether the EU courts will recognize the protection of consumer welfare as the exclusive goal of article 102 as is the case in the US. Given the fact that the EU competition law is not just shaped by economic thinking, it is more likely that EU courts will take consumer welfare into a consideration.

There are similarities and differences between US monopolization law and EU laws regarding the abuse of dominance. In short, as argued by Eleanor Fox, most completed monopolization conduct under the Sherman Act constitutes the abuse of market dominance in the EU.[127] However, the EU competition law prohibits exploitative abuses but does not prohibit attempted monopolization. Additionally, as argued by Cheng, the European Commission has accepted the more economic approach similar to the US counterparts, while the EU courts does not necessarily share the pure effects-based approach of consumer welfare standards in the US.[128]

Laws against the abuse of dominance in China learn from both the EU and US models. The AML framework has been inspired by the EU competition law, which is based on dominance. Provisions in the AML are more prescriptive than those in article 102 TFEU as they provide factors to be assessed in determining dominance, including a detailed market share presumption. Additionally, after the SPC's ruling in the *Qihoo v. Tencent*, an abuse must exhibit the effects of restricting competition in China. However, China's approach to assessment of such effects considers other elements apart from consumer welfare. Since a defendant can justify its practices in many ways, Chinese courts will survey the effects of certain practices on consumer welfare, other competitors, and choices of consumers or competition as such, depending on the particular case. Arguably, China will not accept the US-style consumer-welfare standard as the sole requirement of the examination of an anti-competitive practice, but will determine whether it breaches the law on a case-by-case basis.

Chapter 3 provides an overview of the framework of the abuse of market dominance law. As discussed in this Chapter, when assessing whether a firm has abused market dominance, a court or the competition agency usually determines whether the firm is in a dominant position in a relevant market, and then identifies whether the firm has conducted abusive practices that would restrict competition. In the following Chapters, Chap. 4 will discuss market dominance in trade secrets, while Chap. 5 will examine some abusive practices relating to trade secrets.

---

[127] Fox, Eleanor. 2014. Monopolization and abuse of dominance: Why Europe is different. *The Antitrust Bulletin* 59 (1): 129–152, 150.

[128] Cheng, Thomas. 2012. Convergence and its discontents: A reconsideration of the merits of convergence of global competition law. *Chicago Journal of International Law* 12 (2): 433–490.

Chapter 4
Market Dominance Concerning Trade Secrets

4.1 Introduction

Chapters 2 and 3 set out two fundamental concepts of this book, namely trade secrets and the abuse of market dominance. In Chap. 4, this book delves into how Chinese competition agencies and courts may identify the abuse of dominance related to trade secrets in specific cases.

The assessment of abuse of dominance law in Chap. 3 illustrates that there are usually two steps to find a company breaching the law: firstly the accused firm should have market dominance and, secondly, the firm has abused such dominance. In order to determine whether a company has market dominance in trade secrets, it is necessary to examine which market the accused party could dominate, i.e. to define a relevant market.

This Chapter, thus, is divided into two parts, which analyse how to define a market with respect to trade secrets (Sect. 4.2), and how to assess market dominance in trade secrets (Sect. 4.3). Section 4.2 starts with the significance of defining a relevant market (Sect. 4.2.1). It then analyses the methods of defining a relevant market associated with trade secrets from three dimensions, namely the product market (Sect. 4.2.2), the technology market (Sect. 4.2.3), and the geographic market (Sect. 4.2.4). Section 4.3 mainly discusses how to assess market dominance involving trade secrets. It first examines the relationship between market dominance and market power in Sect. 4.3.1. In Sect. 4.3.2, this book looks into whether the exclusivity of a trade secret equates to market power in competition law. Sections 4.3.3 and 4.3.4 further discuss market-share hypothesis in trade secret cases and whether secret information could act as barriers to entry, which are two indications of a company's market power that competition authorities may scrutinize in trade secret cases. This Chapter concludes in Sect. 4.4.

P. Wu, *Trade Secrets and Market Dominance*, Contemporary Chinese Civil and Commercial Law, https://doi.org/10.1007/978-981-95-1152-5_4

4.2 Market Definition Concerning Trade Secrets

4.2.1 Why is It Essential to Define a Relevant Market in Abuse of Dominance Cases?

As discussed in Chap. 3, the pre-condition of finding a firm of engaging in the abuse of market dominance is that the company holds a position of market dominance in the relevant market. According to competition law, a company with market dominance possesses a very specific degree of market power.[1] In detail, the concept of 'market dominance' in the EU and China can be basically equated to that of 'substantial market power' or 'monopoly power' in US monopolization cases. Market power can be regarded as the ability of an undertaking to price above marginal cost in the short term, and above-average total costs in the long term.[2] Market power can enable undertakings to charge prices above the competitive level and reduce output, thus giving rise to undermining consumer welfare.

The commonly utilized approach to determine market power is to initially identify a relevant market, and then assess the indicators that could determine the degree of market power in that market (e.g. market shares, entry barriers and potential competition).[3] It should be noted that competition does not occur in a vacuum. Any undertaking must compete with others in a (or some) market(s).[4] Market definition is indispensable in assessing abuse of market dominance and merger control in most jurisdictions.[5] The purpose of defining a relevant market is to determine which of the products (or service) are close substitutes for the product (or service) in question, for which the company can exert competitive restraints on its competitors' practices.

---

[1] For example, the EU Commission argues that 'the assessment of whether an undertaking is in a dominant position and of the degree of market power it holds is the first step in the application of Article 82 (now Article 102 TFEU'. See para 9 of the Guidance Paper.

[2] W., Carlton, Dennis and Perloff M. Jeffrey. 2005. *Modern industrial organization.* Pearson/ Addison Wesley. 4th ed., 642.

[3] Many economists advocate a direct approach to assess market power without defining a relevant market first. Such approach is called Lerner index, which measures the difference between the prevailing price and marginal cost. See Lerner, AP. 1934. The concept of monopoly and the measurement of monopoly power. *The Review of Economic Studies* 1 (3):1. The higher the deviation between price and marginal cost, the higher the market power of the company. The most straightforward formulation of the Lerner index is: $L = (P-MC)/P$. See Bergh, Roger van den, Peter D Camesasca, and Andrea Giannaccari. 2017. *Comparative Competition Law and Economics.* Edward Elgar Publishing. 128–129; Vickers, John. 2006. Market power in competition cases. *European Competition Journal* 2(sup1):3–143, 4–6. However, Wang (Xiaoye) argues that it is, in essence, rather laborious to calculate the marginal cost precisely, thus making it difficult to assess the deviation between the standards of measurement. See 王晓晔 [Wang Xiaoye]. 2018. 论相关市场界定在滥用行为案件中的地位和作用 [The function and status of market definition in abuse of market dominance cases]. 现代法学 *[Modern Law Science]* 3:57–69, 65.

[4] Marshall, Alfred. 2009. *Principles of economics.* 8th edition. Cosimo, Inc.

[5] It is worth noting that the E.U. competition law provides a block exemption based on market share thresholds for monopoly agreements under article 101 TFEU. Therefore, it is also necessary to define a relevant market in monopoly agreement cases in the E.U.

It is only if a relevant market is properly defined that the competition agency or the court can identify whether the accused party possesses market dominance in that market.

Thus, a test is introduced to examine a relevant market—the 'substitutability (interchangeability)' test.[6] Chinese courts and competition authorities require the market definition as the first step in most cases of market dominance abuse. To provide a legal certainty about the market definition, the Anti-monopoly Commission of China's State Council published Guidelines (hereafter 'Guidelines') for market definition in 2009.[7] As noted by Liyang Hou, these Guidelines were 'exactly transplanted from the EU'.[8] According to economic theory, a company's market power is confined to demand substitution and supply substitution.[9] The Guidelines highlight that demand substitution is the primary method to define a relevant market. If in specific antitrust cases the supply substitution may play the same critical role in confining market power as demand substitution does, competition agency shall consider supply substitution as well.[10]

The concept of a 'relevant market' not only exists in the antitrust law, but also occurs in trade secret law (from a broader sense, intellectual property law). Mark Lemley and Mark McKenna have pointed out that intellectual property law relies on market definition in a more ad hoc manner.[11] For example, when awarding damages in cases of trade secret infringement, the court usually takes market definition into account, so as to determine the grounds on which the infringing products would cause the secret holder to lose sales. Even if a court determines the existence of a trade secret infringement as the plaintiff claims, the defendant does not necessarily have to compensate the secret owner if the defendant does not compete with the plaintiff within the same market and does not lead to any losses for the plaintiff.[12] In other words, market definition in trade secret law is aimed at determining whether the infringing party will bring about actual losses for the secret owner.

On this basis, market definition in trade secret law is different from that discussed in this book as a component of antitrust analysis. Market definition in the trade secret

---

[6] Jones, Alison, Sufrin, BE, and Niamh Dunne. 2019. *EU competition law: Text, cases, and materials*. 7th ed. Oxford University Press. 101.

[7] Anti-monopoly Commission of the State Council of China, Guidelines for the Definition of Relevant Markets (2009). Article 12 of the AML provides that the Anti-Monopoly Commission of the State Council of China is responsible for enacting and issuing anti-monopoly guidelines.

[8] Hou pointed out that the Chinese Guidelines introduced the provisions from the E.U. Notice on the definition of the relevant market for Community competition law (hereafter 'Notice'). See Hou Liyang. 2015. The influence of E.U. and U.S. legal theory on competition law in China: Divergence and convergence. https://ssrn.com/abstract=2586859. Accessed 25 March 2025.

[9] Van den Bergh, Roger, D. Camesasca, Peter, and Andrea Giannaccari. 2017. *Comparative competition law and economics*. Cheltenham: Edward Elgar Publishing. 129.

[10] Article 4 of the Guidelines.

[11] A. Lemley, Mark, and Mark P. McKenna. 2012. Is Pepsi really a substitute for coke? market definition in antitrust and IP. *Georgetown Law Journal* 100(6):2055–2118, 2058.

[12] In that case, the plaintiff is still eligible to obtain injunctions to prevent the defendant from using trade secrets.

law and competition law play distinct roles. In detail, market definition in antitrust analysis serves as a tool to assess market power of an undertaking. It determines whether a company has the ability to price above marginal cost in daily transactions. Market definition in trade secret law is usually unrelated to the market power of a company, but is related to calculating damages for the trade secret owner in misappropriation litigation. This means that only if there exists a trade secret infringement would the court analyse a relevant market to determine the amount of damages for the injured secret owner. Although this book is about trade secrets, the objective of defining a relevant market in this book is to examine whether a trade secret can provide the owner with sufficient market power. Therefore, the market definition analysis in this book follows the antitrust framework instead of the trade secret law.

As previously stated, the premise for determining the abuse of dominance is that the party employs market dominance in a particular market. In terms of the abuse of market dominance relating to trade secrets, it is also essential to follow the traditional approach of competition agencies and courts to define a relevant market. However, it is sometimes necessary to bear in mind that it is nearly impossible to identify a 'perfect' relevant market that involves all competitive constraints on the supplier's products. In practice, a court or competition authority needs to rely on materials it can acquire from the investigated firm and the market to define a relevant market. The court and competition agency are likely to define a 'good' relevant market based on accurate evidence, or define a 'poor' market founded on less authentic evidence.

The following sections will discuss the considerations required to be taken into when defining a market from a product, technology, and geographic dimension, respectively. In this regard, the subsequent analysis can serve as a 'route' rather than a final 'destination' on defining a relevant market concerning trade secrets (Fig. 4.1).

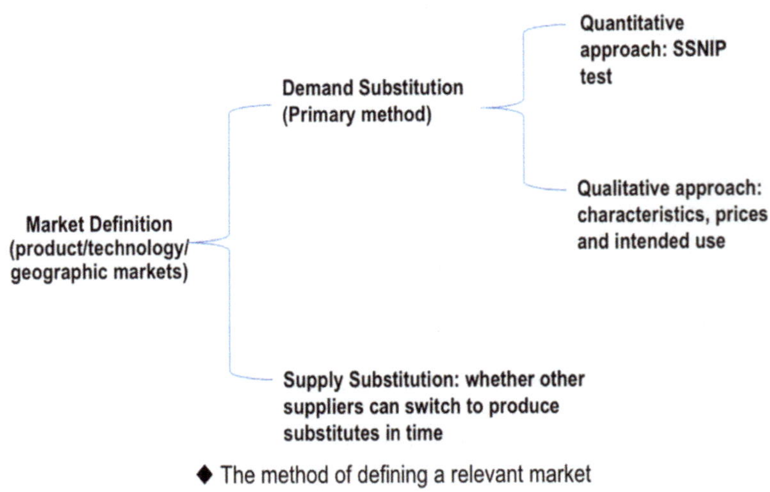

Fig. 4.1 The method of defining a relevant market

4.2.2 Trade Secrets and the Product Market

The approach to defining a relevant market traditionally considers two dimensions, namely the product[13] market and the geographic market. These considerations can be dated back to numerous leading cases in the US and the EU.[14] China's AML follows this approach and provides that:

> The relevant market referred to in this Law shall mean the scope of products and territorial scope in which an undertaking engages in competition in respect of certain products or services within a stipulated period.[15]

Concerning the product market, the US Court has held that if two products are 'reasonably interchangeable', they fall under in the same market.[16] Following the standard of 'reasonably interchangeable', the ECJ, in the classic competition case of *United Brands*,[17] defined the relevant product market as a market comprising all those products and/ or services that are deemed interchangeable or substitutable by the consumer owing to the products' characteristics, prices, and intended use. If a product encompasses sufficient and perfect substitutes, the manufacturer of that product cannot employ surplus market power in that consumers can switch to other close substitutes if the producer charges monopoly prices or reduces output.

In regard to the product market concerning trade secrets, the assessment also needs to adhere to the substitution test. Regarding trade secrets, there could exist two categories of 'products'. One of them is physical products involving trade secrets (e.g. a car in which the part is protected as a secret technology). Another product is trade secrets as such. As a classification of intellectual property, the secret owner is entitled to sell, license or transfer its secret information for monetary gains. Consequently, from a broader prospective of the product market, trade secrets and trade secret products can serve as types of a 'product'. In most circumstances, a transaction related to trade secrets involves the transfer or license of technology, it can be assessed in Sect. 4.2.3 where a technology product is addressed. This part will primarily discuss trade secret products that may constitute a relevant market.

4.2.2.1 Demand Substitution

Whether consumers will purchase goods (or services) or not is the most critical competitive pressure for a firm in the market. As a result, most competition agencies

---

[13] The term 'product' in this book refers to both product.

[14] Van den Bergh, Roger, D. Camesasca, Peter, and Andrea Giannaccari. 2017. *Comparative competition law and economics*. Cheltenham: Edward Elgar Publishing. 132.

[15] Article 12 of the AML.

[16] See Queen City Pizza, Inc. v. Domino's Pizza, Inc, 124 F.3d 430, 436 (3 Cir., rd 1997) ("The outer boundaries of a product market are determined by the reasonable interchangeability of use or the cross-elasticity of demand between the product itself and substitutes for it.").

[17] Case 27/76 United Brands v Commission [1978] ECR 207.

and courts concentrate on the demand-side substitution when defining a relevant market.[18] Demand substitution identifies the product that consumers may consider to be a close substitute for the trade secret product. However, consumers have different opinions and preferences for products. The demand substitution test is not concerned with an individual customer's views, but the behaviors of consumers as a whole.

In order to assess demand substitution, there are two kinds of criteria: the quantitative test and qualitative standards.

The quantitative test based on econometric analysis is often called SSNIP ('Small but Significant Non-transitory Increase in Price') test. It is the most commonly used quantitative method to assess demand substitution. Joe Bain defined a relevant market as a group of products with high cross-price elasticizes with one another, but low cross-price elasticizes with products outside the market.[19] The cross-price elasticity measures how much the demand for product A increases as the price of product B increases. If the price boost in product B results in an increase in demand for product A, this demonstrates that products A and B are in the same relevant market.[20] The cross-elasticity of demand, thus, can be seen as a signal of the degree of 'interchange-ability'. Many competition agencies worldwide use the SSNIP test to measure cross-elasticity of demand in order to define a relevant market.[21] To be more specific, a court will define a market involving trade secret products by inquiring whether a small but significant non-transitory increase in price (usually 5–10%) above the marginal cost will lead customers to switch from one trade secret product to another.[22] The relevant product market is the smallest set of products for which the defendant would find

[18] For example, the E.U. Notice provides that '[F]rom an economic point of view, for the definition of the relevant market, demand substitution constitutes the most immediate and effective disciplinary force on the suppliers of a given product, in particular about their pricing decisions.' See para 13 of the Notice. Article 4 of China's Guidelines also says: 'the definition of a relevant market shall mainly be based on the analysis of substitution of consumers' demands.'

[19] S Bain, Joe. 1951. Relation of profit rate to industry concentration: American manufacturing. *The Quarterly Journal of Economics* 65(3):1936–1940.

[20] Jones, Alison, Sufrin, BE, and Niamh Dunne. 2019. *EU competition law: Text, cases, and materials.* 7th ed. Oxford University Press, 6. The cross-price elasticity of demand was fist applied in the case *Times-Picayune* adjudicated by the US Supreme Court. See Times-Picayune v United States, 345 U.S. 594 (1953).

[21] The SSNIP test was pioneered in the 1982 U.S. Horizontal Merger Guidelines. See now 2010 U.S. Horizontal Merger Guidelines, https://www.justice.gov/atr/horizontal-merger-guidelines-08192010. Accessed 25 March 2025. The E.U. Notice and China's Guidelines both introduce the SSNIP test to help define a relevant market. See article 4.2 of the E.U. Notice and Chap. 4 of China's Guidelines.

[22] To provide a specific example, the SSNIP test is as follows: 'a small (5–10%) rise in the price of widgets is assumed. It is then asked whether this price increase would cause widget customers to purchase blodgets, or to purchase widgets from another area, to such an extent that the price rise is unprofitable. If the answer is yes, then blodgets and/or widgets from the other area form part of the same market. The test is then repeated for that bigger bundle of products until the point is reached when the price rise would be profitable.' See Jones, Alison, Sufrin, BE, and Niamh Dunne. 2019. *EU competition law: Text, cases, and materials.* 7th ed. Oxford University Press, 105–106.

it profitable to increase prices by 5–10%.[23] In other words, all the products that the customers switch to under the pressure of a price rise are in the same product market.

However, whether the SSNIP test can be applied to trade secret products, or to what extent the test is accurate, remains a question. On the one hand, the SSNIP test may trigger the so-called 'cellophane fallacy,' which was first found in the US *Du Pont* case. The SSNIP test's problem is that it is difficult to determine whether consumers treat those 'substitutes for the trade secret products' under competitive prices, or already a monopoly price. The SSNIP test is much more reliable in merger control cases,[24] as the pre-merger undertakings are less likely to have had sufficient market power in most circumstances, guaranteeing that the prices used by the competition authority to assess are at competitive level. However, the test may not work well in the abuse of market dominance cases. In the monopolization (abuse of dominance) cases, 'computing the defendant's marginal cost and determining what the cross-elasticity of demand would be at the competitive price is impossible.'[25] In an abuse of dominance case, if we use the actual market price as a reference price to conduct the SSNIP test, the high cross-price elasticizes may not reflect the degree of interchangeability (or that trade secret products are in the same market), but indicates the undertaking has been abusing market dominance.

On the other hand, having argued that the Chicago school (and the SSNIP test it favors) is founded on price theory (see Chap. 3), the precondition of using SSNIP test to measure a relevant market is that price is the primary (or even, exclusive) variable that influences the choice of consumers. This assumption is workable in many traditional industries. For example, supposing that the company of Coca-Cola, the formula of which is a trade secret, increases the price of the product, consumers may switch to other close substitute drinks, such as Pepsi and Sprite. The SSNIP test can precisely identify whether Coca-Cola, Pepsi, and Sprite are in the same product market.

Notwithstanding this, a price-related test may be futile in high-technology industries when price is not the decisive element on which consumers choose products. Lemley and McKenna argue that intellectual property-based product differentiation and brand loyalty are so important that consumers are hardly influenced by price increases.[26] This argument can also be applied to trade secret products, particularly products involving technical secrets. As Long claimed, the high-technology field (e.g. communication and software domains) could lock consumers into certain

---

23 Van den Bergh, Roger, D. Camesasca, Peter, and Andrea Giannaccari. 2017. *Comparative competition law and economics*. Edward Elgar Publishing, 143.

24 王晓晔 [Wang Xiaoye]. 2018. 市场界定在反垄断并购审查中的地位和作用 [The function and status of market definition in merger control cases]. 中外法学 *[Peking University Law Journal]* 5:1324–1338, 1330.

25 Hovenkamp, Herbert. 2016. *Federal antitrust policy: The law of competition and its practice*. Fifth edition. West Academic Publishing, 170.

26 A. Lemley, Mark, and P. McKenna, Mark. 2012. Is Pepsi really a substitute for coke? market definition in antitrust and IP. *Georgetown Law Journal* 100(6):2055–2118, 2057.

products (lock-in effects).[27] An example regarding smartphones, which consists of many patents and technical secrets, can be used to explain this. Apple's iPhones have gained much popularity in Chinese communities, especially among the young. Because of the economic and political tensions between the US and China since 2018, the Trump administration ordered US firms to stop doing business with WeChat (an instant message software designed by the Chinese giant Tencent), threatening that Apple would abandon WeChat in its iPhone products. Many have noted that WeChat is more than a universal chat app for Chinese communities, but 'the primary means of staying in touch with friends and family'.[28] Although the ban is not in effect, empirical research shows that 95% of Chinese iPhone users would instead give up iPhones if Apple cannot provide WeChat anymore.[29] A similar situation also arises as Chinese consumers may prefer those smartphones adapted to 5G networks. As most metropolitan areas in China are connected to 5G, consumers prefer to choose expensive 5G smartphones to cheaper but 3/4 G phones. These examples demonstrate that price may not be the primary and decisive variable for consumers to purchase in high-technology industries. As Wang Xiaoye argues, in circumstances where competition among undertakings mostly relies on innovation, quality, and technology rather than price and quantity, it is difficult to apply the SSNIP test directly.[30]

In order to address these problems, some measures should be taken to apply the SSNIP test effectively in abuse of dominance cases regarding trade secrets. Firstly, in all abuse of dominance cases, including cases concerning trade secrets, the initial reference price selected for the SSNIP test should be a price at the competitive level, instead of choosing a current prevailing price.[31] Secondly, it is worth noting that SSNIP test serves as an econometric tool and as a conceptual framework at the same time. Despite the fact that consumers are not sensitive to prices in the high-technology sectors, the quality of the product can replace the position of the price here. In other words, as suggested by Gebicka and Heinemann, courts can adopt a qualitative test that examines whether customers would switch to another firm's product if the market

---

[27] 龙柯宇 [Long Keyu]. 2016. 滥用知识产权市场支配地位的反垄断规制研究 *[The anti-monopoly regulation on the abuse of the dominant market position of intellectual property rights]*. 华中科技大学出版社 [HUST Press], 111.

[28] Feng Zhaoyin, and Joshua Cheetham. 2020. Trump WeChat ban "an unwelcome signal" for Chinese community. BBC. https://www.bbc.com/news/world-asia-china-53686507. Accessed 25 March 2025.

[29] Clover, Juli. 2020. 95% of Chinese users surveyed would rather give up their IPhones than lose WeChat. MacRumors. https://www.macrumors.com/2020/08/13/china-iphone-users-prefer-wechat/. Accessed 25 March 2025.

[30] 王晓晔, 张素伦 [Wang Xiaoye, and Zhang Sulun]. 2013. SSNIP测试法运用于互联网行业的思考 [Thoughts of how SSNIP test can be applied in Internet-based Sector]. 法制日报 [Legal Daily], September 18.

[31] See article 11 of China's Guidelines. The selection of a competitive price is a matter of fact and needs a thorough economic analysis. Some scholars even argue that 'if determining the competitive price was easy, we would not need to conduct any other test.' See D. Geradin, A. Layne-Farrar, and N. Petit. 2012. *EU competition law and economics*. Oxford University Press, 185–186.

leader faced a small but significant non-transitory decrease in the quality (hereafter 'SSNDQ') of the product.[32]

Apart from the quantitative test, the competition authorities may use qualitative methods for market definition as well. The competition agency may assess the characteristics, prices and the intended use of the products[33] in order to measure close substitutes of the underlying products. As stated, in the abuse of market dominance cases including cases related to trade secrets, the quantitative SSNIP test may fail to define a product market. The competition agencies or courts have to use qualitative approach to analyse the characteristics and functionality to help identify whether different products are in the same market. For example, in a US antitrust case (*CVD v. Raytheon*),[34] the founders of the plaintiff (CVD Company) were former employees of the defendant (*Raytheon*) which produced zinc selenide or zinc sulfide for sale. The defendant claimed that the manufacturing process was protected as a trade secret. After the formation of CVD, Raytheon argued that CVD misappropriated its secret process information. However, CVD believed that Raytheon's claim of trade secrets was made in bad faith and constituted monopolization and it filed an antitrust lawsuit. In this case, the court defined two separate relevant markets—markets of zinc selenide and zinc sulfide—according to their special intended uses. This was because of the special intended use of ZnSe and ZnS for the reason that they were 'the only suitable materials for certain demanding optical uses'.[35] The European Commission also held in the landmark *Microsoft* case, about the refusal to license trade secrets (in this case, interface information of the Windows system), that in terms of the features and functionality 'there are no products…[which] exercise sufficient competitive pressure on work server operating systems such that they should be included in the same relevant market'.[36] The Commission also considered the price differences and held that basic workgroup server systems and higher-level operating systems should be in distinct markets because it would be 'extremely cost-inefficient' for a customer to buy a much more expensive system merely to fulfil basic needs.[37] However, the qualitative method cannot guarantee a precise product market every time and could

[32] Heinemann, Andreas, and Aleksandra Gebicka. 2014. Social media and competition law. *World Competition* 37: 149–172. In the Qihoo v Tencent case, the SPC also overturned the SSNIP test and adopted an SSNDQ test to define a relevant market. See World Intellectual Property Organization (WIPO) and SPC (2019) *WIPO collection of leading judgment on intellectual property rights: People's Republic of China (2011–2018)*, 112. WIPO: Geneva; SPC: Beijing.

[33] Para 7 of the E.U. Notice provides that '[A] relevant product market comprises all those products and/ or services which are regarded as interchangeable or substitutable by the consumer, by reason of the products' characteristics, their prices and their intended use.'

[34] CVD, Inc. v. Raytheon Co., 769 F.2d 842, 850–51 (1st Cir. 1985).

[35] In detail, 'zinc sulfide is the only suitable material for use in 8–12 micron "forward looking infrared" windows on missiles and jet aircraft. Zinc selenide is the only suitable material for windows in high energy carbon dioxide lasers.' Ibid.

[36] Case T-201/04, Microsoft Corp. v Commission of the European Communities, para. 486.

[37] Comp/37.792, Microsoft [2007] O.J. L 32/23, para. 376.

lead to a narrower product market.[38] As discussed above, both qualitative and quantitative methods have their drawbacks when defining a relevant market. Therefore, the competition authorities and courts may use these two methods concurrently to analyse the relevant market on a case-by-case basis, including in cases involving trade secrets.

4.2.2.2 Supply Substitution

The method of supply-side substitution can act as a supplement for the demand-side substitution to define a relevant market.[39] Both consumers and suppliers can impose dramatic competitive constraints on the firm under investigation. If a producer of one product can rapidly switch to the manufacture of specific trade secret products, these products may be categorized under the same market. One may confuse the conception of supply substitution with that of potential competition. The U.S. 1992 Horizontal Merger Guidelines[40] for the first time defined potential competition. The supplier can suffer competitive pressure from both supply-side substitution and potential competition. The difference is that the conception of potential competition requires more time and cost (to borrow the U.S. Guidelines' words, more 'switching cost') of the potential competitors to enter the market. In other words, if a manufacturer of one product can enter the market to produce a similar trade secret product in a short period without incurring high costs, it should be analyzed at the stage of market definition as a supply-side substitution.[41] By contrast, the potential competition should be considered at the next stage when assessing market power (market dominance) as it is related to the barrier of market entry. Moreover, the SSNIP test can be applied to the assessment of supply substitution by identifying whether the increase of price (5–10%) will be rendered unprofitable by other suppliers moving to manufacture particular trade secrets products.[42] The limitations and improvement of the SSNIP test, as discussed, are also applicable.

---

[38] Many commentators mentioned the EU *United Brands* case to indicate a qualitative approach entirely dependent on (differences in) product characteristics can give rise to a much narrower market. In this case, the ECJ defined a market for bananas, based on the banana's characteristics (such as taste, softness, seedlessness) which could particular suitable for specific groups (the old and very young). Nevertheless, commentators argue that in cases where there does not exist price discrimination, it is unwise to examine consumer's demand based on certain groups of consumers. In this case, a wider market for fresh fruit was supposed to be defined. See Van den Bergh, Roger, D. Camesasca, Peter, and Andrea Giannaccari. 2017. *Comparative competition law and economics*. Cheltenham: Edward Elgar Publishing, 134.

[39] For instance, the European Commission lost the Continental Can case (Case 6/72, E.U.:C:1973:22) before the EU court because the Commission merely relied on demand substitution and ignored the supply substitution to define a market.

[40] See Section 3 of the 1992 Horizontal Merger Guidelines.

[41] See Jones, Alison, Sufrin, BE, and Niamh Dunne. 2019. *EU competition law: Text, cases, and materials*. 7th ed. Oxford University Press, 114.

[42] Niels, G. The SSNIP test: Some common misconceptions. *Competition Law Journal* 3 (4):267.

4.2.2.3 Should Infringing Products Be Included in the Relevant Market?

Generally, trade secret products can be divided into two categories: (1) products involving secret information authorized by the secret owner and (2) products in which information is misappropriated from the secret owner. The former are legal products while the latter includes illegal (infringing) products as per the trade secret law. Chapter 2 of this book has discussed the potential misappropriation of trade secrets in China from the perspective of trade secret law. Many western companies, such as Corning, DuPont, Eli Lilly, and General Motors, have alleged that they experienced misappropriation of trade secrets in China.[43] When Chinese competition agencies are required to define a relevant market related to trade secrets, they are likely to confront whether the infringing products (products that involve trade secrets misappropriated from the secret owner) should be included in the relevant product market.

Arguably, whether the product is legally manufactured is a matter of intellectual property law, but is not relevant to the market definition as to antitrust. The key point is whether infringing products can impose much competitive pressure on products of the company under investigation. As Lin (Ping) argues, if the infringing products can lead to sufficient competitive restraints on the underlying product, these infringing products need to be included in the relevant market for antitrust analysis.[44]

In addition to some traditional methods discussed that can help define a market, there are some other elements that the competition agency or a court may take into account in cases where infringing products exist. Whether the consumers can tell the differences between legally produced products and infringing products may make a difference to the market definition.[45] A reasonable consumer would choose legally manufactured products rather than purchase those goods at the risk of infringing another's intellectual property rights. In cases where it is difficult for consumers to distinguish legal products and infringing products, consumers are likely to regard these products as close substitutes, and thus include them in the same relevant market. By contrast, if consumers are able to distinguish legal products from infringing products, competition agencies will not include these infringing products in the same product market of legal products. For example, if A misappropriates Apple Company's secret information and produces a kind of mobile phones which look just the same as Apple's iPhones. However, because Apple has applied 'iPhone' as a trademark which is protected by intellectual property laws, A cannot name its products as 'iPhones' and has to call it 'aPhones'. In this regard, even if aPhones

---

[43] Office of the United States Trade Representative Executive Office of the President. 2018. Findings of the investigation into china's acts, policies, and practices related to technology transfer, intellectual property, and innovation under Section 301 of the trade act of 1974. https://ustr.gov/sites/default/files/enforcement/301Investigations/301%20Draft%20Exec%20Summary%203.22.ustrfinal.pdf. Accessed 25 March 2025.

[44] 林平 [Lin Ping]. 2019. 假冒/盗版情况下的市场界定 [Market definition in passing off/ piracy]. In 反垄断法的相关市场界定及其技术方法 *[Market definition in the anti-monopoly law and its technical methods], ed.* 王晓晔 [Wang Xiaoye], 268. 法律出版社 [Law Press China].

[45] Ibid.

seem similar to iPhones, a reasonable consumer will not confuse these products with each other by distinguishing the trademark.

In other cases, whether legal products and infringing products are in the same market depends on the ability of the secret owner to prohibit infringing products and move them out of the market promptly. In spite of the fact that consumers cannot tell the difference between legal products and infringing products, if the secret owner is able to prevent the infringement through an effective judicial process, such as obtaining an immediate injunction (as discussed in Chap. 2), infringing products could be swept out of the market quickly. In this regard, it would be unnecessary for a competition agency to include infringing products in the same market as legal products.

4.2.3 Trade Secrets and the Technology Market

Compared with traditional commodities, one highlighted feature of a trade secret (as a type of intellectual property) is that both products involving trade secrets and trade secrets themselves can be marketed. As discussed in Chap. 2, the secret owner can license or transfer its trade secrets to others. Usually, a technology license is concerned with technical secrets, rather than business secrets. Nevertheless, it does not necessarily mean that a technology market merely involves technical secrets. The primary reason for the separation of the technology market from the product market is that trade secrets transactions can be independent of transactions of trade secret products. Therefore, this section, which mainly discusses the technology market definition, will consider both technical and business secret information. For example, in the Microsoft case, the interface information of Windows, was a business secret, and was an essential asset for Microsoft's competitors.[46] This book adopts the conception of the 'technology market'. The technology market is related to all types of trade secrets that can be marketed and is not limited to technical secrets.

The US *Antitrust Guidelines for the Licensing of Intellectual Property*[47] (hereafter 'US IP Guidelines') for the first time clarify the definition of a technology market:

> Technology markets consist of the intellectual property that is licensed and its close substitutes—that is, the technologies or goods that are close enough substitutes to constrain significantly the exercise of market power with respect to the intellectual property that is licensed. When rights to intellectual property are marketed separately from the products in which they are used, the Agencies may analyze the competitive effects of a licensing arrangement in a technology market.[48]

[46] Case T-201/04, Microsoft Corp. v Commission of the European Communities.

[47] The US Department of Justice and Federal Trade Commission issued the US IP Guidelines in 1995 and amended them in 2017. The latest version can be found at: https://www.ftc.gov/system/files/documents/public_statements/1049793/ip_guidelines_2017.pdf.

[48] Section 3.2.2 of the US IP Guidelines.

Similar to the US approach, China's State Council enacted the *Anti-monopoly Guidelines in the Field of Intellectual Property*[49] (hereafter 'China's IP Guidelines'), article 4 of which provides the legal definition of a technology market. As the Guidelines state, a relevant technology market consists of a set of technologies that can be interchangeable with each other from the perspective of demand-side. This demonstrates that the assessment of a technology market, in principle, is the same as that of a traditional product market. The methods as discussed above regarding the means of analyzing the interchangeability, such as the SSNIP quantitative test and qualitative standards based on characteristics, price and intended use, can be applied to define a technology market as well. However, arguably, there are unique considerations when defining a relevant technology market as to trade secrets.

The application of the SSNIP test must have a baseline price for a trade secret license. In order to conduct the SSNIP test to determine a technology market, the competition agency needs to identify the baseline price of specific trade secret licenses, and then increase the price to examine whether customers will switch to other technologies. The baseline price is the license royalties in a trade secret license transaction. It is easier to identify the royalty fees in non-technical secret licenses (e.g. licenses of a customer list or typical formula).

Nevertheless, it is difficult for the competition agency to determine the license royalties in high-technology-based industries. For instance, there could exist a wide range of technical know-how and patents in an iPhone. A technical secret can cover merely a small fraction of a multi-component product. The competition agency is unlikely to obtain the value (price) of the technical secret directly because only the price of the whole product (an iPhone) is available. In these circumstances, the competition agency has to adopt an indirect approach to calculate the price of a secret: to assess the proportion of the value of the secret in the whole product.[50] The situation is much more complicated when cross-licenses of technologies exist. A cross-license agreement enables two or more parties to grant one another the rights to use the technical know-how/patents which each owns. As WIPO has argued, the cross-license benefits competition as parties can concentrate on exploiting technologies without having to worry about infringement.[51] The problem of defining a relevant market here is that if the parties decided to cross-license their technical secrets to each other, the parties may not need to pay royalties. In other words, the baseline price for a SSNIP test does not exist. In order to address this issue, the competition agency may have to abandon the quantitative price-related method and introduce the qualitative standards.

---

[49] The Guidelines were enacted on the 4th of January, 2019. The Guidelines are for the competition agencies and courts for references. The Guidelines themselves are not legally binding as laws and judicial interpretations in China. The Guidelines can be found at: https://mp.weixin.qq.com/s/I0NLXIr77_G-RLMG2XIpkg.

[50] 王晓晔 [Wang Xiaoye]. 2019. 反垄断法的相关市场界定及其技术方法 *[Market definition in the anti-monopoly law and its technical methods]*. 法律出版社 [Law Press China], 174.

[51] WIPO. 2015. Successful technology licensing. *IP Assets Management Series* 50.

In addition, network effects may influence technology market definition involving trade secrets. As Josef Drexl explained, competition policy can be applied to intellectual property because 'network effects lead to intellectual property de facto standards and exclude competitors from market access.'[52] Network effects can occur in cases where trade secrets are involved. Using the iPhone as an example once again: If customers in a certain jurisdiction are much more accustomed to Apple Pay (assuming the software of Apple Pay consists of a trade secret) rather than to cash or credit cards when shopping, they will be reluctant to turn to other close substitutes, even if other smartphones are technically more advanced. In this regard, the technology of trade secrets that have strong network effects may efficiently lock customers into an independent technology market.[53] As China's IP Guidelines state, the competition agency must consider the possibility and switching costs of customers to choose another technology when defining a relevant technology market.[54]

In addition to the analysis above, an emerging area may affect trade secret transactions. As discussed in Chap. 2, companies can use big data to compete with others. A company can keep big data it collects as a type of trade secrets.[55] For example, in the US *HiQ v LinkedIn*[56] case, LinkedIn was a US-based professional networking website where job seekers can pose their profiles. HiQ relied on the LinkedIn's data containing the occupation profiles of millions of users to develop its two products: Keeper (a software that can indicate the possibility of employees that are likely to be poached by competitors) and Skill Mapper (a software that can show the abilities and expertise of employees). The data of each profile of a user in LinkedIn is in the public domain, and thus is not a trade secret of LinkedIn. However, the collected data of many profiles of all types of persons' information may be deemed a trade secret.[57] In this case, LinkedIn refused to continue to license the collection of data to HiQ. HiQ argued that LinkedIn's refusal to deal constituted monopolization. The court defined two markets in this case: the professional networking market (the upstream market) and the data analytics market (the downstream market). LinkedIn was a dominant firm in the upstream market while HiQ was doing business in the downstream market. Through LinkedIn's refusal to license the collection of data which

[52] Drexl, Josef. 2008. The relationship between the legal exclusivity and economic market power. links and limits. In *Intellectual property, market power and the public interest*, eds. Inge Govaere, and Hanns Ullrich, 32. College of Europe Studies, 8 Lang, Brüssel.

[53] Wang (Xianlin) also argues that the price increase will not enable customers to switch to other technology when the network effects happen. Therefore, the SSNIP test could be inaccurate. See 王先林 [Wang Xianlin]. 2016. 知识产权领域反垄断中相关市场界定的特殊问题 [The special problem of anti-monopoly market definition in the field of intellectual property]. 价格理论与实践 *[Price Theory and Practice]* 2:49–53, 51.

[54] Article 4 of China's IP Guidelines.

[55] Not every kind of big serves as trade secrets. If the firm takes precautions to keep big data as a secret and the big data has commercial value, the big date the firm has is a trade secret.

[56] HiQ Labs, Inc. v. LinkedIn Corp., 485 F. Supp. 3d 1137 (N.D. Cal. 2020).

[57] Whether it is a trade secret depends on the way LinkedIn keeps the data. If LinkedIn keeps the collection of data a secret, it is a trade secret. In this case, neither the parties nor the court discussed whether the collected data constituted a trade secret. As a result, technically speaking, this was not an antitrust case involving trade secrets.

was essential to do business in the downstream market, HiQ could not survive. The court held against LinkedIn as it breached antitrust doctrines. It can be inferred from this case that undertakings in the current commercial realities can take advantage of data information, as a unique type of information, to compete.

The competition agency may analyse characteristics of data to define a relevant market. It is worth noting that online data and offline data might be different. For example, supermarkets and online-platforms (e.g. Amazon, eBay and Alibaba) can both collect expense tracker information of customers. The difference is that offline supermarkets can only collect data on what the customers purchase, while the online platforms can also collect information of what the customers have chosen before check-out.[58] Some competition agencies, as stated in a report of the French and German authorities, thus believe that offline and online data are not interchangeable substitutes in the assessment of market definition.[59]

4.2.4 Trade Secrets and the Geographic Market

The market includes a geographic as well as a product/ technology dimension. Even though different suppliers can produce similar (or identical) products, it does not necessarily mean that these products are in the same market. For example, customers will not consider a mirror in a US Wal-Mart store as a close substitute of that in a Chinese supermarket. It would cost too much for a consumer to travel to China just for a mirror.

As the EU Notice provides, a geographic market consists of an area 'in which the conditions of competition are sufficiently homogeneous.'[60] Competition agencies can use the SSNIP test to identify a geographic market as they do in a product/ technology market as well.[61] When it comes to products or technologies involving trade secrets, whether or not the geographic product is global, national or local relies on several factors. During a transaction of products containing trade secrets, the competition agency needs to consider factors such as the cost of transport and the nature of the product.[62] Nevertheless, if it is regarding transactions of technology (know-how, data, etc.), the cost of transport would be less important for the reason that technology as such is intangible. Supposing free trade can prevail worldwide, the geographic market as to technology transactions should be a global one. Conversely,

---

[58] A. Shelanski, Howard. 2013. Information, innovation and competition policy for the internet. *University of Pennsylvania Law Review* 161 (6):1663–1705, 1679.

[59] French Autorité de la concurrence and the German Bundeskartellamt. Competition law and data. Bundeskartellamt. https://www.bundeskartellamt.de/SharedDocs/Publikation/DE/Berichte/Big%20Data%20Papier.html. Accessed 25 March 2025.

[60] EU Notice, para 8.

[61] See supra 30 (An example illustrating how SSNIP test can be applied to determine a geographic market).

[62] See Jones, Alison, Sufrin, BE, and Niamh Dunne. 2019. *EU competition law: Text, cases, and materials*. 7th ed. Oxford: Oxford University Press, 122.

the ideal 'global' market may not happen due to legal regulation. Different jurisdictions may impose restrictions on technology license or transfer, including technical know-how or data transaction across nations.[63] The technologically-advanced countries are more likely to confine technology exportation because of national security concerns, sanctions on certain countries or protectionism. Therefore, competition agencies need to define a geographic market related to trade secrets on a case-by-case basis.

4.3 Trade Secrets and Market Dominance

4.3.1 Market Power and Market Dominance

As discussed, competition law prohibits a company, which is in a dominant position in the relevant market, from abusing its position. After identifying a relevant market, it is necessary to determine whether a firm remains dominant.

Technically speaking, economists examine the degree of 'market power' to assess the market position of an undertaking. As argued by Josef Drexl, every company in the market economy, ranging from the smallest and weakest company, exerts at least some market power.[64] This is owing to the fact that any undertaking which intends to survive in the market needs to attract customers and sell products. Those without market power cannot survive and will be eliminated by their competitors in the market. By contrast, usually only one firm can assert market dominance in a relevant market. Unlike the legislation of the EU TFEU and US Sherman Act which do not set out a clear definition, China's AML defines market dominance as:

> Market dominance referred to in this Law shall mean that an undertaking is able to control the prices, quantities or any other terms of transaction in the relevant market or is able to obstruct and affect the entry of other undertakings into the relevant market.[65]

The concept of market dominance is closely associated with that of market power. Most competition lawyers agree that market dominance translates to a very significant amount of market power, namely substantial market power,[66] and may use the

---

[63] For instance, China lists 53 technologies that are prohibited to export. See http://www.gov.cn/zhengce/zhengceku/2020-08/29/5538299/files/135c5cdd6baa46a986ac5e51a1a49ac3.pdf. Accessed 25 March 2025.

[64] Drexl, Josef. 2008. The relationship between the legal exclusivity and economic market power. links and limits. In *Intellectual property, market power and the public interest*, eds. Inge Govaere, and Hanns Ullrich, 15. College of Europe Studies, 8 Lang, Brüssel.

[65] Article 22 of the AML. Similarly, the ECJ believes that a company has market dominance because it has 'the power behave to an appreciable extent independently of its competitors, customers and ultimately of its consumers'. See United Brands v Commission (1978) Case 27/76, para. 65.

[66] The International Competition Network (ICN) did research on competition policy in many jurisdictions worldwide and argues that '[T]he concept of dominance pursuant to unilateral conduct laws is generally equivalent to the possession of substantial market power'. See ICN Unilateral

wording 'market dominance' and 'substantial market power' interchangeably in literature. In China, 'substantial market power' (or 'monopoly power' in the US context) is basically the same as market dominance under the Chinese law.[67] Arguably, the terms are fundamentally the same. The economic term 'market power' focuses on the pricing ability of an undertaking, while the legal concept 'market dominance' enables a firm to 'control' a market. The incentive of a firm to control markets is, still, to gain monopoly profits. Following the traditional competition law approach, this book does not differentiate market dominance from substantial market power.

4.3.2 *The Exclusivity of a Trade Secret and the Establishment of Market Dominance*

The relationship of a trade secret to monopoly in competition law is important in the context of this book. Many commentators and scholars regard intellectual property rights as a type of 'monopoly rights'.[68] This could be on account of the origin of the modern patent law being called 'Statute of Monopolies (1623)' in England. However, 'monopoly rights' in the intellectual property law are different from the concept of monopoly in the competition law.

Under the competition law, the key question in this book is that whether or not an exclusive right can confer substantial market power on the holder of a trade secret. In fact, a 'monopoly right' refers to as an 'exclusive right'. Intellectual property law defines the exclusive rights of proprietors.[69] A trade secret, as a type of intellectual property from the perspective of this book, also has exclusivity. This means a secret holder can prevent others from accessing the trade secret without the holder's

---

Conduct Working Group. 2015. Dominance/substantial market power analysis pursuant to unilateral conduct laws. https://centrocedec.files.wordpress.com/2015/07/rp-for-dominance_substantial-market-power-analysis-2008.pdf. Accessed 28 March 2025.

[67] 王晓晔 [Wang Xiaoye]. 2019. 反垄断法的相关市场界定及其技术方法 *[Market definition in the anti-monopoly law and its technical methods]*. 法律出版社 [Law Press China], 79–80. However, a few Chinese competition scholars argue that the term 'market dominance' is broader than 'market power' because a dominant firm can conduct many anti-competitive practices other than pricing above the marginal cost. See e.g. 郝俊淇 [Hao Junqi]. 2020. 市场支配地位与实质性市场势力之辨析 [Assessment of market dominance and substantial market power]. 当代法学 *[Contemporary Law Review]* 3:141–150.

[68] See e.g. Duffy, John. 2005. Intellectual property as natural monopoly: Toward a general theory of partial property rights. https://docslib.org/download/7166024/intellectual-property-as-natural-monopoly-toward-a-general-theory-of-partial-property-rights. Accessed 25 March 2025; Andersen, Birgitte. 2003. Intellectual property right" or "intellectual monopoly privilege": Which one should patent analysts focus on? *Conferência Internacional Sobre Sistemas De Inovação E Estratégias De Desenvolvimento Para O Terceiro Milênio.* https://www.researchgate.net/publication/242117169_%27Intellectual_Property_Right%27_Or_%27Intellectual_Monopoly_Privilege%27_Which_One_Should_Patent_Analysts_Focus_On. Accessed 25 March 2025.

[69] George, Alexandra. 2012. *Constructing intellectual property.* Cambridge University Press, 146.

authorization, and can file litigation against anyone who misappropriates the secret.[70] Notwithstanding this, as discussed in Chap. 2, the exclusivity of a trade secret may be limited because others can legally obtain a trade secret through reverse-engineering and self-discovering.

What is the relationship between the (limited) exclusivity of a trade secret and market power? Nowadays, competition agencies all over the world, from western jurisdictions to China, believe that exclusive rights as such do not necessarily translate to market dominance of a firm. For example, the US IP Guidelines state that: '[T]he Agencies will not presume that a patent, copyright, or a trade secret necessarily confers market power upon its owner.'[71] The secret owner can only forbid competitors from manufacturing or selling specific products embodying the owner's trade secret. If there is just one product incorporating a trade secret in the market that could meet the consumers' requirement, the secret holder can control this relevant market through exclusively managing the trade secret. However, in most circumstances, this assumption does not prevail. In a relevant market where there are two or more products that can attract consumers, even though the secret holder can control specific product embodying trade secrets, consumers are able to choose other close substitutes. As a result, the secret holder is unlikely to increase the price for the reason of competitive pressure of other close substitutes. In other words, the secret holder cannot gain sufficient market power in the relevant market merely due to the exclusivity of a trade secret. In reference to this practice, a commentator describes this scenario as the fact that an exclusive right prevents 'competition by imitation', instead of 'competition by substitution'.[72]

Does the exclusivity of a trade secret actually have no impact on the market power of the secret holder? The answer is unclear and will depend on the particular case. The analysis above is based on the demand side which examines whether consumers are bound to purchase the secret holder's products. By contrast, the supply side may tell a different story at times, particularly in cases where a trade secret becomes 'essential'. The exclusive intellectual property right can restrict market entry and potential competition. For example, if a patent is embodied in an industry standard in the relevant market, any potential competitors who are willing to enter the market need to obtain the license of the patent from the patentee.[73] In this regard, the patent which is essential to the market can confer market power upon the patentee.

---

[70] Details are presented in Chap. 2.

[71] Para. 2.2 of the US IP Guidelines. Article 2 of Chinese IP Guidelines also stipulates that the agency will not presume that an undertaking has market dominance merely because it has intellectual property.

[72] Drexl, Josef. 2008. The relationship between the legal exclusivity and economic market power. links and limits. In *Intellectual property, market power and the public interest*, eds. Inge Govaere, and Hanns Ullrich, 16. College of Europe Studies, 8 Lang, Brüssel. See also Surblyte, Gintare. 2011. *The refusal to disclose trade secrets as an abuse of market dominance-microsoft and beyond.* Berne:Stämpfli, 201.

[73] See e.g. Broadcom Corp. v. Qualcomm, 543 F.3d 683.

A trade secret can be essential in selective cases. The following is an example that can illustrate the 'essentiality' that a trade secret may possess.[74] For example, a paint producer may develop a manufacturing process that can enhance the durability of the paint compared to its competitors. Customers are more likely to pay a premium price for a product which can last longer, if no one else can match the superior quality. The manufacturing process can be a trade secret provided that the owner keeps the secrecy.[75] If it is crucial to produce a better paint through the secret process, the trade secret in question becomes an essential asset for potential competitors to enter the market. In this regard, if the secret holder chooses not to disclose the process to competitors, the superior grade of paint, which appeals to a vast majority of customers, will enable the secret holder to increase prices, without worrying about competitive constraints. In other words, the exclusivity of the trade secret brings market power.

In that case the trade secret acts as a 'standard' just like a patent. The difference is that a trade secret cannot be a formal standard. A formal industry standard can be enacted by either regional or international standardization organizations.[76] These standards which often incorporate patents (also known as Standard-Essential Patents or SEPs) are made public. Any potential entrants to the market know the exact contents of a standard and can negotiate with patentees on the conditions of a SEP license. Conversely, it is impossible for standardization organizations to introduce a trade secret as a formal standard because of the core element of a trade secret (secrecy).[77] Despite this, a trade secret can act as a de facto standard. In the above example, if the paint manufactured through a better process is so appealing that other paints are unable to impose sufficient competitive pressure, the superior quality paint defines a relevant market.[78] In this relevant market, any undertakings which are willing to produce the better product must acquire the manufacturing process under the protection of trade secret law. In this regard, the secret process becomes a de facto standard, and confers market power on the secret holder in this market. The

---

[74] The framework of this example is proposed by Professor Herbert Hovenkamp. However, in Hovenkamp's example, the underlying intellectual property is a patent. See Hovenkamp, Herbert. 2016. *Federal antitrust policy: the law of competition and its practice.* Fifth edition. St. Paul, Minnesota: West Academic Publishing, 186.

[75] For instance, the plaintiff in the CVD case argued that its manufacturing process constituted a trade secret. See CVD, Inc. v. Raytheon Co., 769 F.2d 842, 850–51 (1st Cir. 1985).

[76] For instance, the Chinese Standardization Administration sets out industry standards in China. The International Organization for Standardization (ISO) is an international-level standardization organization.

[77] For example, Mark Lemley describes secrecy is 'a central part of what makes trade secret law work'. See Lemley, Mark. 2008. The surprising virtues of treating trade secrets as IP rights. *Stanford Law Review* 61(2):311–353, 342.

[78] See Hovenkamp, Herbert. 2016. *Federal antitrust policy: The law of competition and its practice.* Fifth edition. St. Paul, Minnesota: West Academic Publishing, 186. ('If, as a result, the paint manufacturer can reduce the output of the better paint and raise its price for a substantial length of time, the better paint defines a relevant market.').

function of a trade secret as a de facto standard[79] existed in the EU *Microsoft* case, which is further explained in Sect. 4.3.4.

Consequently, it can be concluded that (1) the exclusivity of a trade secret, in principle, does not equate to market power in the competition law; (2) in most circumstances, the exclusivity of a trade secret cannot bring about substantial market power to the secret holder; and (3) in cases where a trade secret becomes a de facto standard and essential, the exclusivity may confer market power.

4.3.3 Market-Share Hypothesis

In most abuse of market dominance cases, competition agencies or courts worldwide are able to deduce some form of convincing data for the ease of determining market power of a company. For example, in the famous case *Hoffmann-La Roche*,[80] the ECJ held that very large shares for some time are in themselves, and save in exceptional circumstances, evidence of the existence of a dominant position.[81]

Some jurisdictions set various criteria on how market shares can indicate the market dominance of a firm. For instance, some courts in the US believed that 70% share is sufficient.[82] The ECJ in the *AKZO* case[83] argued that a market share of 50% could be regarded as a 'very high market share' set out in *Hoffmann-La Roche*. Evidently, Chinese lawmakers introduced the standard of EU competition law to the AML. Article 24 of the AML provides a presumption of a dominant position of a firm if the undertaking has over 50% market share in the relevant market. The market share hypothesis can be applied to market power relating to trade secrets as well. Assuming that the owner of a certain trade secret product possesses more than 50% market share in the relevant market, China's AML will supposedly presume the owner as a dominant firm, although the presumption is rebuttable.

Nevertheless, it should always be borne in mind that market share is an important but not decisive indicator of market power. An undertaking with a 100% market share may not hold substantial market power. For instance, it is likely that a trade secret owner will acquire 100% market share because of the superiority of the trade secret product. However, if the trade secret product can be easily reverse engineered, other competitors can acquire the trade secret and participate in competition promptly.

---

[79] Josef Drexl and Gintare Surblyte also point out that a trade secret which serves as de facto standard can confer market power. See Drexl, Josef. 2011. Refusal to grant access to trade secrets as an abuse of market dominance. In *Intellectual property and competition law-new frontiers,* eds. Steven Anderman, and Ariel Ezrachi, 182. Oxford University Press; Surblyte, Gintare. 2011. *The refusal to disclose trade secrets as an abuse of market dominance-microsoft and beyond*. Berne: Stämpfli, 148.

[80] *Hoffmann—La Roche v Commission* Case 85/76 [1979] ECR 461.

[81] Ibid, para. 41. The ECJ also recognized that the 'importance (of market share) varies from market to market'. See Ibid, para. 40.

[82] See e.g. United States v Paramount Pictures, Inc., 334 U.S. 131, 68 S. Ct. 915 (1948).

[83] Case-C-62/86, AKZO EU: C: 1991: 286, para. 60.

Therefore, some argue that market share does not highlight 'whether the undertaking is vulnerable to market entry'.[84] Market share hypothesis is also static. In some markets where dynamic competition is involved, such as cases including high-technology or digital data,[85] even quasi-monopolies are 'under permanent threat from innovating competitors and they are only able to retain their top spot if they continue to innovate'.[86] In other words, merely possessing a high percentage market share in these markets does not guarantee sufficient market power of a firm.

There is also a problem when it comes to the market share presumption relevant to trade secrets in China. The market share analysis in China's AML focuses on percentage only, and does not examine how long it may last. In the EU *Hoffmann-La Roche* case, the ECJ held that 'very large shares' should exist for 'some time'.[87] Furthermore, the ECJ interpreted that "some time" should be considered 'a long period'.[88] This requirement makes sense. A secret holder may uphold little market power if the trade secret product can be readily reverse engineered, even though the holder can have many market shares temporarily. Some may suggest that the stable and high market share should last over than 5 years in order to identify sufficient market power.[89]

Chinese lawmakers and competition agencies (or courts) must address these problems in abuse of dominance cases involving trade secrets. As stated above, the market-share presumption has its problems. As examined in Chap. 3, although the market-share presumption in China's AML is rebuttable, it will, in principle, increase the burden of proof for the accused party.[90] The criterion of 50% market share should be a rough estimation, instead of a presumption. For instance, even if the EU competition case law sets out a 50% market share benchmark, the lowest market share at which a firm was determined dominant by the ECJ was 39.7%.[91] The above analysis has indicated that the threshold of amount of market share to identify market dominance associated with trade secrets could vary depending on different abusive practices. Therefore, it would be necessary for the competition agencies or courts to abandon the traditional 50% share presumption and take into account market share as one of the important indicators of market dominance in cases involving trade secrets. In addition, Chinese competition agencies and courts should examine not only the percentage of shares, but also the time-frame that particular percentage can exist.

---

[84] See Jones, Alison, Sufrin, BE, and Niamh Dunne. 2019. *EU competition law: Text, cases, and materials*. 7th ed. Oxford: Oxford University Press, 331. The difficulty of reverse engineering a trade secret acts as a kind of entry barrier which is discussed next.

[85] As discussed in Sect. 4.2.3, technical know-how and business can be types of a trade secret.

[86] Ahlborn, Christian, Evans, David, and A. Jorge Padilla. 2001. Competition policy in the new economy:Is European competition law up to the challenge? *European Competition Law Review* 22 (5): 156–167, 162.

[87] *Hoffmann—La Roche v Commission* Case 85/76 [1979] ECR 461, para. 41.

[88] Case C-457/10 P, AstraZeneca EU:C:2012:770, para. 176.

[89] V. Rose, and D. Bailey. 2013. *European union law of competition*. 7th edn. Oxford: Oxford University Press, 10.026.

[90] See Sect. 3.4.1 of Chap. 3.

[91] Case T-219/99, *British Airways* EU:T:2003: 343.

Agencies can determine the duration of the time on a case-by-case basis. If high shares can disappear shortly, it means that market shares may not be an appropriate indication of market power.

4.3.4 Barriers to Entry

The market share of a firm can be 'a useful first'[92] but not decisive indication of market power. The market-share hypothesis only indicates the competitiveness of the undertaking it used to have but fails to explain the market power it will possess.[93] A company cannot charge monopoly profits in a market if numerous other firms can enter the market and compete freely. Therefore, whether a firm is in a dominant position relies on its vulnerability to other entrants to the market. This makes 'barriers to entry' a fundamental concept in the assessment of market power. Robert Bork describes that: 'the concept of barriers to entry is crucial to antitrust debate…The ubiquity and potency of the concept are undeniable.'[94]

Joe Bain, the leading scholar of Harvard School, provided the classic description of 'barriers to entry' which is now often quoted in competition law practices on the both sides of the Atlantic[95] that:

> the extent to which, in the long run, established firms can elevate their selling prices above the minimal average costs of production and distribution…without inducing potential entrants to enter the industry.[96]

The OECD Roundtable report of 2005[97] summarized diverse types of market barriers from the perspective of competition law, such as sunk costs, economies of scale, high capital costs, vertical integration, and strategic behaviour by incumbents. This book examines several kinds of market barriers that may be relevant to abuse of dominance cases with respect to trade secrets.

---

[92] See para. 13 of the EU Guidance Paper.

[93] See 王晓晔 [Wang Xiaoye]. 2018. 论相关市场界定在滥用行为案件中的地位和作用 [The function and status of market definition in abuse of market dominance cases]. 现代法学 *[Modern Law Science]* 3:57–69, 62.

[94] H Bork, Robert. 1978. *The antitrust paradox: A policy at war with itself.* Basic Books. 310–311.

[95] Jones, Alison, Sufrin, BE, and Niamh Dunne. 2019. *EU competition law: Text, cases, and materials.* 7th ed. Oxford University Press, 127.

[96] Bain, Joe. 1968. *Industrial organization.* 2d edn. Wiley. 242.

[97] DAF/COMP (2005) 42, OECD Policy Roundtable on barriers to entry.

4.3.4.1 Legal and Regulatory Barriers: Trade Secret Protection

Although the WTO has been diligently working to promote international free trade over years,[98] completely free trade from country to country does not exist. Every jurisdiction is able to impose its own laws, rules and restrictions on domestic market entry. Among all of these legal and regulatory barriers, intellectual property rights may act as the most material entry barrier.[99] The protection of trade secrets, as a type of intellectual property, can constitute an entry barrier.

Chapter 2 of this book has examined the increasing protection of trade secrets in China. If China (or other jurisdictions) does not protect trade secrets at all, any individual may misappropriate a trade secret without legal recourse. Even if the holder has kept the valuable information a secret, the information could be disclosed easily to the holder's competitors. Consequently, the secret holder is unable to hold sufficient market power arising from the secret information. Furthermore, the secret holder's current market power could be jeopardized as a result of lack of trade secret protection.

By contrast, the more a jurisdiction protects trade secrets, the higher entry barrier a secret holder is likely to establish. For example, a trade secret may be such essential information (probably as a de facto standard in the relevant market) that other competitors have to obtain it in order to enter the market. As discussed in Chap. 2, China has shifted from protecting trade secrets from an unfair competition approach to an intellectual property approach. Under the unfair competition approach, the secret holder may only sue the competitors who misappropriate the secret information, but cannot sue employees who steal the secret. In other words, the secret holder is still exposed to a high risk of disclosure of the secret information. As secrecy is the core requirement of constituting a trade secret, any disclosure will make the secret (and the de facto standard) disappear, and destroy the secret holder's market dominance. The intellectual property approach enables the secret holder to protect secret information from being disclosed by anyone, including both competitors and employees.

4.3.4.2 Lack of Access to Key Secret Information

It is difficult for potential competitors to enter a market if they lack access to key property. Such critical input could be tangible property (e.g. gypsum[100]), SEPs, big

[98] The WTO aims at 'lowering trade barriers' and is sometimes described as a 'free trade' institution. See Principles of the trading system. WTO. https://www.wto.org/english/thewto_e/whatis_e/tif_e/fact2_e.htm. Accessed 25 March 2025.

[99] Jones, Alison, Sufrin, BE, and Niamh Dunne. 2019. *EU competition law: Text, cases, and materials.* 7th ed. Oxford: Oxford University Press, 131.

[100] BPB Industries [1989] OJ L10/50, para. 120.

data[101] or a trade secret. The EU *Microsoft* case[102] is a prime example that illustrates why lack of specific trade secret information can act as a barrier to entry for new participants.

A competitor of Microsoft, Sun Microsystems, accused Microsoft of abuse of market dominance in 1998 for refusal to disclose secret interface information to competitors. During the investigation, the EU Commission defined two relevant markets in this case: the client PC operating systems market (the upstream market) and the workgroup server operating systems market (the downstream market).[103] The Commission first identified Microsoft was in an 'overwhelming dominant position' in the client PC operating systems,[104] with more than 90% market share. In this regard, some argue that Windows acted as 'a de facto standard operating product for client PCs'.[105] Microsoft was the owner of 'interface (or interoperability) information' which was kept as a trade secret and was necessary for software providers to obtain in order to enable their products to operate with the system (e.g. Windows). Microsoft had provided the interface information free of charge for the producer of workgroup operating systems to interoperate with Windows for many years. Josef Drexl argued that this was the Microsoft's strategy 'to tip the market and to promote the establishment of Windows as the de facto standard'.[106] After Microsoft itself entered the workgroup server operating system market, it refused to supply the interface information to other competitors. Without the secret information, other rivals, such as Sun in this case, were unable to provide their own workgroup server operating systems that could connect to Windows. Microsoft leveraged the secret information to exclude competitors from the relevant market.

The EU *Microsoft* case showed that interface information, which was a trade secret of Microsoft, became essential and a de facto standard technology for new entrants to enter the market. However, unlike patents which can be a technology standard owing

---

[101] See e.g. Mahnke, Robert. 2015. Big data as a barrier to entry. *Antitrust Chronicle* 5; Graef, Inge. 2015. Market definition and market power in data: The case of online platforms. *World Competition* 38 (4).

[102] Comp/37.792, Microsoft [2007] O.J. L 32/23; Case T-201/04, Microsoft Corp. v Commission of the European Communities.

[103] The EU Microsoft case was a refusal to deal case. In most refusal to deal cases, EU Commission often defines one upstream market (the raw material market) and one downstream market (the derivatives market). If a company is dominant in the upstream market, its refusal to deal with customers in the downstream market could eliminate competition in the downstream market, and thus constitute the abuse of market dominance. See Jones, Alison, Sufrin, BE, and Niamh Dunne. 2019. *EU competition law: text, cases, and materials*. 7th ed. Oxford: Oxford University Press, 486.

[104] Microsoft's client PC operating system is its well-known Windows system.

[105] Surblyte, Gintare. 2011. *The refusal to disclose trade secrets as an abuse of market dominance-microsoft and beyond*. Berne: Stämpfli, 8.

[106] Drexl, Josef. 2011. Refusal to grant access to trade secrets as an abuse of market dominance. In *Intellectual property and competition law-new frontiers, eds.* Steven Anderman, and Ariel Ezrachi, 182. Oxford: Oxford University Press.

to advancements in technology, Josef Drexl points out that the reason the interface information became essential was merely due to vital information being maintained as a secret, and because of Windows's popularity.[107] The European Commission's empirical research also supported this argument. The Commission's customer surveys indicated that customers would rather choose competitors' systems than Microsoft's, however, customers showed more concerns over the incompatibility (with Windows) of software provided by other companies. Therefore, the lack of access to key secret information could morph itself into a barrier to entry.

Additionally, the difficulty of reverse-engineering and self-invention of a trade secret will influence the essentiality of a trade secret. Microsoft did defend itself before the EU Commission by stating that Sun could get access to the secret information through reverse-engineering. However, the Commission found that reverse-engineering of the interface information required 'considerable efforts with uncertain chances of success'.[108] Assuming that new entrants can easily reverse engineer the secret information of Microsoft, or invent independently the same secret information, Microsoft's interface information will no longer act as a barrier to entry.

A vast majority of consumers, regardless of jurisdiction, are still used to Microsoft's PC services. As a transnational corporation, Microsoft's behaviors also gave rise to competition concerns in China. In 2013, some companies accused Microsoft of refusal to supply interoperability information to connect to Windows or Office systems. Currently, the Chinese competition agency is investigating these potential competition problems.[109] There are no more details available since the case is still under investigation.[110] Nevertheless, the Chinese situation reflects significant similarities to the EU *Microsoft* case. As a result, Chinese competition authorities may learn from the EU experience on how secret information can be a barrier to entry.

4.3.4.3 Superior Technology

The incumbent's superior technology can act as a barrier for new entrants. From time to time, superior technology is referred to as the 'structural advantage' of an incumbent in the relevant market.[111] The issue of whether a trade secret can act as superior technology depends on the extent of innovation it possesses. If the incumbent has a secret technology that is superior to the technology of other competitors, potential entrants and would-be entrants may find it difficult to compete successfully against

---

[107] Ibid.

[108] Comp/37.792, Microsoft [2007] O.J. L 32/23, para. 685.

[109] The SAIC is now deeply investigating microsoft's competition issues. 2014. State Council of China. http://www.gov.cn/xinwen/2014-08/26/content_2739925.htm. Accessed 25 March 2025.

[110] It has taken quite a few years for the Chinese competition agency to investigate Microsoft. However, due to some political reasons, particular the US-China tensions, Chinese government has not published the final decision till now.

[111] See Jones, Alison, Sufrin, BE, and Niamh Dunne. 2019. *EU competition law: Text, cases, and materials*. 7th ed. Oxford: Oxford University Press, 347.

the incumbent in this market. Accordingly, as Josef Drexl concluded, a trade secret may contain vital innovation that is particularly valued by consumers, and confers substantial competitive advantages for an incumbent firm.[112]

4.4 Conclusion

The premise of applying the law of abuse of market dominance is that the company under investigation has market dominance. This Chapter focuses on ways of determining the dominant position of a firm in the case of abuse of market dominance in trade secrets. In order to identify the market dominance of an undertaking, the competition agency and the court generally define a relevant market first and then examine the indicators in that market that could show the degree of market power of the firm. As a result, this Chapter is divided into two parts: market definition in trade secrets and indicators showing the market dominance in trade secrets.

The competition agency and the court must identify the relevant product and the relevant geographic market when it comes to trade secret products. In cases where a trade secret acts as a commodity in the transaction, the agency and the court need to define the technology market and the geographic market. The objective of defining a relevant market is to identify close substitutes of the certain product/technology/area. In order to assess the degree of substitution, there are two main approaches: the quantitative approach based on SSNIP test and the qualitative standards based on characteristics, price and intended use.

The SSNIP test may not work well in some cases of abuse of market dominance related to trade secrets. In some high-tech industries, consumers are not sensitive to price changes. In this regard, competition agencies need to adjust the SSNIP test (e.g. to a SSNDQ test) or accept the qualitative approach. In cases of licenses of trade secrets, if it is difficult to calculate the royalty fees or whether there are network effects, competition agencies should not unduly rely on the SSNIP test and need to determine the factors affecting the consumer's opinions on close substitutes. This book suggests that Chinese competition agencies and courts should use both quantitative and qualitative methods to define a market in abuse of dominance cases in trade secret on a case-by-case basis.

This book examines the relationship between trade secrets and market dominance. Firstly, the exclusivity of a trade secret does not necessarily bring about market power to the secret owner. In cases where a trade secret becomes 'essential' for new entrants to enter a market, the exclusivity will lead to market power. Secondly, market share is a crucial but not decisive indication of the market power of a company. Market-share hypothesis can be used in cases of abuse of market dominance in trade secrets as well. Nevertheless, the competition agency must also examine barriers to entry and the

[112] Drexl, Josef. 2011. Refusal to grant access to trade secrets as an abuse of market dominance. In *Intellectual property and competition law-new frontiers, eds.* Steven Anderman, and Ariel Ezrachi, 182. Oxford: Oxford University Press.

influences of innovation when necessary. Lastly, this book discusses circumstances in which trade secrets can be entry barriers and enhance market power. The protection of trade secrets by national authorities can develop into a legal and regulatory barrier. Lack of access to the trade secret is another entry barrier. Additionally, the incumbent company can establish a barrier to entry provided that its secret technology is much superior to the potential entrants'.

To sum up, this chapter focuses on whether a company can have dominance in the market arising from trade secrets. Only if the firm is in a dominant position may there be an abuse of dominance. This book will further examine specific abusive practices related to trade secrets that a dominant company can engage in in the next chapter (Chap. 5).

Chapter 5
Abusive Practices in Trade Secrets

5.1 Introduction

This book analyses the abuse of market dominance relating to trade secrets in China. While Chaps. 2 and 3 provided the legal frameworks of trade secret protection and the abuse of market dominance, Chap. 4 focused on the establishment of market dominance as to trade secrets. Chapter 5 will now consider several abusive practices that a dominant undertaking may engage in using its trade secrets, as to list them all would be impossible.[1]

It has been suggested previously that China's anti-monopoly legislation and enforcement are noticeably influenced by the EU competition law and the US antitrust law. Since China has little experience in dealing with relevant abusive practices with respect to trade secrets, this Chapter analyses comparative lessons from the US and the EU. Through decoding comparative experience, this Chapter also provides suggestions for anti-monopoly practices of Chinese competition authorities.

This Chapter is divided into 5 sections, assessing three selected abusive practices regarding trade secrets. As examined in Chap. 2 of this book, a trade secret, like other forms of intellectual property, can be licensed. As the refusal to supply is a type of potential abusive practices under the competition law, Sect. 5.2 analyses the refusal to disclose trade secrets as a sub-category of the refusal to supply. According to Chap. 2, a secret holder is in principle entitled to file lawsuits for misappropriation of its trade secret. However, if the secret holder litigates in bad faith, such litigation may constitute the abuse of market dominance and this conduct is discussed in Sect. 5.3. During a license of intellectual property, a dominant company may compel the licensee to accept terms including that any challenge to the validity of intellectual property is prohibited. Such non-challenge clauses may raise antitrust concerns and

[1] As discussed earlier in Chap. 3, the EU competition law and China's AML lists some abusive practices that a dominant firm may conduct. However, there exists catch-all provisions which means the lists are not exhaustive.

P. Wu, *Trade Secrets and Market Dominance*, Contemporary Chinese Civil and Commercial Law, https://doi.org/10.1007/978-981-95-1152-5_5

are analyzed in the context of trade secrets (see Sect. 5.4). The last section (see Sect. 5.5) presents the conclusion to Chap. 5.

5.2 Refusal to Disclose Trade Secrets

5.2.1 Introduction

The abuse of market dominance occurs when a dominant firm undertakes abusive practices. This section will further assess some abusive practices related to trade secrets a dominant undertaking may engage in.

In principle, the holder of a trade secret can freely exploit its secret information through licensing or transferring the information. This means that the holder can refuse to disclose trade secrets to others. However, under some circumstances, a refusal to disclose trade secrets (or a refusal to deal in a broader sense) may be a type of abusive practice prohibited by competition law.

Section 5.2 is divided into three parts. Section 5.2.2 discusses some legal practices concerning the refusal to disclose trade secrets in China. It begins with assessment of refusal to deal in the AML and the development of the so-called 'essential facilities' doctrine in China (see Sect. 5.2.2.1). It then appraises provisions of the refusal to license IPRs in China (see Sect. 5.2.2.2). It considers a case study of *Hytera v Motorola*,[2] the only case in China involving the refusal to disclose trade secrets (see Sect. 5.2.2.3). Section 5.2.3 provides comparative lessons from the US and the EU. The US part delves into the development of the refusal to deal law and essential facilities doctrine, concentrating on the landmark Supreme Court decision in the *Trinko* case (see Sect. 5.2.3.1). The EU part focuses on case law concerning the refusal to supply (or license) and studies the famous *Microsoft* case regarding the refusal to disclose trade secrets (see Sect. 5.2.3.2). Section 5.2.4 intends to provide suggestions for Chinese competition agencies and courts as to how they can handle cases related to the refusal to disclose trade secrets, which might constitute the abuse of market dominance under the AML. It first argues that the EU approach might be the better option for China (see Sect. 5.2.4.1), and proposes several suggestions for dealing with cases involving the refusal to disclose trade secrets in China (see Sect. 5.2.4.2). The last part (see Sect. 5.2.5) concludes that China should learn from the EU case-law to establish a clear criterion for analyzing cases of the refusal to disclose trade secrets under the AML.

---

[2] 海能达与摩托罗拉滥用市场支配地位纠纷案 [Hytera v Motorola—Disputes of the Abuse of Market Dominance], 北京知识产权法院 [Beijing Intellectual Property Court, People's Republic of China], 北京知识产权法院 (2017) 京73民初1671号 [Economic Appeal No. 1671], 31 December 2019.

5.2.2 *Refusal to Disclose Trade Secrets in China*

5.2.2.1 Refusal to Deal in the AML and the Essential Facilities Doctrine

Companies usually have the right to choose with whom they are willing to deal. In other words, they are entitled to refuse to deal. This reflects the two fundamental principles of commercial law, namely the freedom of contract and the exclusivity of property.[3] Nevertheless, this does not mean that one is absolutely allowed to exercise the freedom to deal. These rights are limited by reasonable regulation, and it is generally assumed that competition law, which promotes efficiency, innovation and consumer welfare, is a part of such reasonable regulation.[4]

China's AML prohibits the abuse of market dominance.[5] Article 22 lists several abusive practices that might result in anti-competitive consequences, one of which is the refusal to deal with others without justification. However, this provision does not specify in which circumstances a refusal to deal is illegal under the AML.

In 2018, the Supreme People's Court (SPC) for the first time adjudicated a case Xu v Tencent,[6] in relation to the refusal to deal. WeChat, which was invented by the Tencent company, is a popular (probably the most popular) instant messaging software in China. Individuals can upload stickers (also known as 'internet memes') they have produced to the WeChat platform for public use, as long as they comply with WeChat's policy. Shuqing Xu was a WeChat user and requested to upload some stickers he had designed to the platform. However, Tencent refused Xu's request. Xu thus claimed that Tencent had abused its market dominance in refusing to deal with him.

In this case, the SPC reiterated that the premise of finding an illegal refusal to deal is that the defendant was a dominant firm in the relevant market. The SPC held that Tencent was not in a dominant position in the market as insufficient evidence was produced by Xu.[7] Despite this, the SPC analyzed the alleged refusal to deal practice in this case. In the view of the SPC, a court should consider the following issues in a refusal to deal case: (1) whether the defendant refuses to deal if it would deal with others on similar conditions; (2) whether the refusal would substantially restrict

[3] Hou Liyang argues that the obligation to deal is in principle contrary to these two principles. See Hou Liyang. 2012. The essential facilities doctrine—what was wrong in Microsoft? *IIC international review of intellectual property and competition law* 43(4): 251–271.

[4] Fox, Eleanor. 2006. Monopolization, abuse of dominance, and refusal to license intellectual property to competitors: Do Antitrust duties help or hurt competition and innovation? How do we know? In *European competition law annual* 2005, 633–634. Oxford: Hart Publishing.

[5] Articles 7 and 22 of the AML.

[6] 徐书青与腾讯滥用市场支配地位纠纷案 [Xu Shuqing v Tencent—Disputes of the Abuse of Market Dominance], 最高人民法院 [Supreme People's Court], (2017) 最高法民申 4955 号 [Economic Appeal No. 4955], 14 September 2018.

[7] In this case, Tencent did not possess sufficient market share in the relevant market. The plaintiff (Xu) neither provided any other evidence to show the dominant position of Tencent. Therefore, the SPC held that Tencent was not in a dominant position in the relevant market.

competition in the relevant market and harm consumers; and (3) whether the refusal can be justified.[8]

The SPC believed that in the current circumstances the alleged refusal to deal was not illegal under the AML for the following reasons. Firstly, the WeChat policy clearly prohibited any stickers which contained advertisements. Those stickers uploaded by Xu included promotional information about Xu's law firm, which violated the non-advertising policy of WeChat. The SPC concluded that Tencent was unlikely to deal with anyone if its stickers contained advertisements. Second, the SPC held that a single refusal to deal with Xu would not have any negative impact on competition. If Xu would design another set of stickers in compliance with WeChat's policy, they could compete with stickers of other competitors.

The 'Tencent test', to some extent, interprets the refusal to deal law under the AML. It indicates that not every refusal conducted by a dominant company will constitute the abuse of dominance, and that the legality of a refusal to deal should be assessed on the basis of an effects-based approach rather than a form-based approach. At the same time, the Tencent test is still a general interpretation as it does not provide details on how to assess the possible anti-competitive effects resulting from a refusal to deal.

Soon after China's new and uniform competition agency (SAMR) was established in 2018, the agency published the *Interim Provisions on Prohibition of the Abuse of Market Dominance*, which detail the refusal to deal law. Article 16 of the Interim Provisions provides several circumstances where the competition authority may declare a refusal to deal illegal. It is worth noting that SAMR introduces the concept of an 'essential facility' when it comes to determining whether a refusal to supply property could be a type of an illegal refusal to deal.[9] SAMR explains some considerations when defining an 'essential facility', such as the feasibility of investing reasonably to otherwise develop or construct the facilities in question, and the reliance of trading partners on such facilities in order to carry out their production and business operation effectively.[10]

The 'essential facilities' doctrine, which originated from US antitrust law and was also developed in the EU competition law,[11] is a highly disputed concept in the competition law domain. The essential facilities doctrine means that the proprietor of an 'essential' facility may be mandated to share the property with rivals,[12] where the proprietor's refusal to supply constitutes an abuse of dominance. SAMR has

---

[8] See 王先林, 吴佩乘 [Wang Xianlin and Wu Peicheng]. 2019. 滥用市场支配地位案例评析. [Assessment of cases of the abuse of market dominance]. *中国竞争法律与政策研究报告2018-2019年 [Report on competition law and policy of China 2018–2019]*. 北京:中国商务出版社 [Beijing: China Commerce and Trade Press], 126.

[9] According to Article 16 of the I*nterim Provisions on Prohibition of the Abuse of Market Dominance*, a refusal to let their trading partners in the production and business activities to use their essential facilities with reasonable conditions is listed as a possible anti-competitive refusal to deal.

[10] Article 16 of the Interim Provisions on Prohibition of the Abuse of Market Dominance.

[11] This book will review the essential facilities doctrine in the US and the EU in Sect. 5.2.3.

[12] OECD. The essential facilities concept. OECD Competition Policy. https://www.oecd.org/competition/abuse/1920021.pdf. Accessed March 25, 2025.

never applied the essential facilities doctrine in a specific case, yet the release of the above provisions is an indication that China is likely to take the concept of essential facilities into account in cases pertaining to the refusal to deal.

5.2.2.2 Refusal to License Intellectual Property Rights

A refusal to license intellectual property rights (hereafter 'IPRs') is a subset of the refusal to deal. Besides the *Hytera v Motorola* case, which will be discussed in the next section, there are no cases involving a refusal to license IPRs under the AML in China. Even so, this does not imply that Chinese competition agencies and courts do not recognize the possible anti-competitive effects of a refusal to license IPRs.

In 2015 the then Chinese competition authority[13] issued the *Provisions on Prohibiting the Abuse of Intellectual Property Rights to Exclude and Restrict Competition*, a document that focuses on potential anti-competitive practices resulting from the exercise of IPRs. This document clearly states that intellectual property may constitute an 'essential facility', and it forbids a dominant firm from refusing to license 'essential' intellectual property to other competitors on reasonable terms.[14] This indicates that the Chinese competition agency is likely to apply the 'essential facilities' doctrine in the intellectual property domain in follow-on cases.

Nevertheless, it is worth noting that the above provisions were enacted by the competition agency, and according to the legislative procedure in China,[15] they are not necessarily binding for Chinese courts. According to the AML, the central government of the PRC (also known as the 'State Council') is responsible for establishing an Anti-monopoly Commission, one of whose duties is to publish anti-monopoly guidelines which may guide both the competition agency and courts.[16] This brings up the question: what attitudes do the anti-monopoly guidelines hold towards the refusal to license IPRs?

In 2017, the Anti-monopoly Commission issued draft *Anti-monopoly Guidelines on the Abuse of Intellectual Property Rights* (hereafter 'draft IP Guidelines') for public comment. The draft IP Guidelines addressed the concept of 'essential facilities'. They stated that a refusal to license an IPR could constitute the abuse of

---

[13] The State Administration for Industry and Commerce of the PRC was one of three competition agencies in China before 2018. These three competition agencies became a uniform one (SAMR) in 2018.

[14] Article 7 of this document says that '[A] business operator with market dominance shall not, without a proper reason, refuse to license its intellectual property rights to other business operators under reasonable conditions if the said intellectual property constitutes essential facilities for manufacturing and business activities, so as to eliminate or restrict competition.'

[15] As discussed in previous chapters, laws enacted by the National People's Congress and judicial interpretations made by the SPC are legally binding for a Chinese court. The Chinese competition agency (SAMR), as an administrative regulator, can enact its own regulations. According to the Legislation Law of the PRC, these regulations are binding for SAMR itself and the sub-agencies of SAMR in different provinces, but are not legally binding for a court. However, Chinese courts would respect regulations of the competition agency in most circumstances.

[16] Article 12 of the AML.

dominance if the IPR that a dominant undertaking holds is regarded as an 'essential facility'.[17] The US strongly opposed this approach. For the record, the American Bar Association Sections of antitrust law, intellectual property law and international law commented that:

> Applying the essential facilities doctrine to IPRs would substantially impinge upon IPR holders' core right to exclude, create disincentives for competitors to develop their own competing IPR, and create long term disincentives to innovate in general.[18]

Obviously, the US government worried that if Chinese competition agencies adopt the 'essential facilities' doctrine, the Chinese government could easily force US companies to share their valuable intellectual property (e.g. a patent) with their Chinese counterparts, if their intellectual property could be identified as an 'essential facility'. Despite this, Chinese antitrust authorities or courts have never declared intellectual property as an essential facility in specific cases before.

The Anti-monopoly Commission of the State Council released the final *Anti-monopoly Guidelines for the Field of Intellectual Property Rights* ('IP Guidelines') in September of 2020. Article 16 of the IP Guidelines is concerned with the refusal to license IPRs. It clarifies that the refusal to license IPRs is a way that undertakings exercise their IPRs, and thus companies do not have a duty to license IPRs to their competitors in most circumstances. Nevertheless, it also states that a dominant firm can be found to be abusing market dominance if it refuses to license IPRs without justification. This article includes some elements that the competition agency and courts may consider in refusal to license cases.[19]

Surprisingly, compared with provisions in the draft IP Guidelines, the final IP Guidelines do not contain the concept of an 'essential facility' at all. As explained by Xianlin Wang, one of the counselors of the Anti-monopoly Commission and who was responsible for drafting the IP Guidelines, the removal of the 'essential facilities' doctrine was a response (or compromise) to addressing the concerns of the US

---

[17] Article 15 of the draft IP Guidelines.

[18] See Comments of the American bar association sections of antitrust law, intellectual property Law, and international law on the draft anti-monopoly guidelines on abuse of IP rights. *ABA*. https://www.americanbar.org/news/abanews/aba-news-archives/2017/04/aba_sections_comment/. Accessed 25 Mar 2025.

[19] Article 16 of the IP Guidelines says that 'The following factors may be considered in the specific analysis:

(I) the commitments made by the undertaking as to the licensing of such intellectual property rights;
(II) whether it is necessary for other undertakings to obtain the license of such intellectual property rights for entering the relevant market;
(III) the impact of refusal to license related intellectual property rights on market competition and innovation of undertakings and the extent thereof;
(IV) whether the refused party lacks willingness and capability to pay reasonable license fee;
(V) whether the undertaking has ever made a reasonable offer to the refused party; and.
(VI) whether refusal to license intellectual property rights will harm the interests of consumers or the public.'

regarding the so-called forced technology transfer[20] during the US-China trade negotiations.[21] Nevertheless, this does not mean that a dominant firm is immune from the antitrust duty to license if its refusal to license IPRs constitutes an abuse of dominance under the AML. The US government believed that the essential facilities doctrine was a way of forcing US companies to share IPRs with their Chinese rivals. Instead, Xianlin Wang argued that the AML has set out an antitrust duty of not violating the refusal to deal law. Previously, the draft IP Guidelines introduced the concept of essential facilities because there were intentions to establish a stricter criterion for the law concerning the refusal to license IPRs.[22] Even without mentioning the essential facilities doctrine, the Chinese competition authority and courts can still be able to find a company abusing market dominance through refusing licensing IPRs.

5.2.2.3 Refusal to Disclose Trade Secrets: A Case Study of Hytera V Motorola

As mentioned earlier, by the end of 2020, there was only one case regarding the refusal to license an IPR under the AML in China. The underlying intellectual property in the case of *Hytera v Motorola* was a trade secret (confidential information). Therefore, this book will analyse this case to illustrate how a Chinese court would deal with cases with respect to a refusal to disclose a trade secret, the topic of this book.

The Terrestrial Trunked Radio (TETRA) is a standard which is commonly used in private communication networks. Underground railways in China usually adopt TETRA equipment which is purchased by way of competitive bidding. Before 2019, Chengdu city[23] invited bids for its 14 lines of underground railways. The defendant, Motorola, won bids for all 14 of its lines, and was able to provide its own TETRA equipment in these 14 lines. The plaintiff, Hytera, intended to bid for the TETRA equipment of new lines for underground railways in Chengdu. However, the bidding documents required that the equipment for the new lines must be able to interoperate with the equipment on other lines, which was supplied by Motorola. Hytera believed that it was only when Motorola would disclose its Application Programming Interface (API) information, which was protected as secret information, to Hytera, that the TETRA equipment of Hytera could connect to Motorola's counterparts. Hytera argued that other competitors, including Hytera, de facto could not enter the relevant

---

[20] See Office of the United States Trade Representative. 2018. Update concerning China's acts, policies and practices related to technology transfer, intellectual property, and innovation. https://ustr.gov/sites/default/files/enforcement/301Investigations/301%20Report%20Update.pdf. Accessed 25 Mar 2025.

[21] Wang Xianlin gave a speech on the drafting of the IP Guidelines at Shanghai Jiao Tong University in the November of 2020. See KoGuan Jiao Wu Jun. Anti-monopoly issues in the field of intellectual property. https://mp.weixin.qq.com/s/l1ZkKyRowLswjrlnPsYdZQ. Accessed 25 March 2025.

[22] 王先林 [Wang Xianlin]. 2015. *关于制定我国滥用知识产权反垄断指南的若干思考*[Relevant thoughts on the enactment of the antimonopoly guidelines of the abuse of IPRs in China]. 价格理论与实践 [*Price Theory & Practice*] 10: 25–29, 29.

[23] Chengdu city is the capital of Sichuan Province in the southwest of China.

market and compete with Motorola as a result of Motorola's refusal to disclose API information. In this regard, Hytera accused Motorola of abuse of market dominance before the Beijing Intellectual Property Court.

The court discussed whether the refusal to deal under the AML is a form-based or effects-based illegal practice. The court held that the AML is aimed at protecting consumers' interests, instead of competitors' interests. Only if a refusal will harm the competition as such can it be found to be an illegal practice. Arguably, this is similar to the views of the SPC found in the Tencent case.

When it came to Motorola's alleged refusal to disclose API information, the court put forward three requirements to determine whether the refusal violated the AML. Firstly, there should be an actual refusal. The court held that Motorola did refuse Hytera's request to acquire Motorola's confidential API information.

Secondly, the court considered whether the refusal would cause anti-competitive effects. The court found in this case that even if Motorola disclosed its API information to other rivals, the TETRA equipment of other competitors would still be unable to interconnect to Motorola's equipment installed on previous underground lines in the way Motorola's own equipment could.[24] Since interconnection was a mandatory requirement imposed by the bidding documents, whether Motorola disclosed its API information or not would not have any impact on the competition in the relevant market.

Lastly, the courts analyzed several justifications Motorola proposed. During trials, Motorola claimed that even though the disclosure of API information could allow for other competitors' equipment to interconnect to Motorola's TETRA equipment, it was not an indispensable method of connecting the equipment. The court confirmed this justification by holding that there were another three methods that Hytera could use to achieve its goals.[25]

The second justification of Motorola was that the plaintiff who requested intellectual property, and the defendant who refused to license intellectual property, should be in two separate markets (upstream and downstream markets).[26] However, both Hytera and Motorola were competitors in the same market of providing TETRA equipment. The court disagreed with this argument. It held that whether there were

[24] Hytera argued that the API information had been used to interoperate TETRA equipment in Shenzhen underground lines. The court noted it was a false fact, as the API information was not applied in Shenzhen underground lines. The court held that Hytera failed to take the burden to prove the function of API information to interoperate TETRA equipment.

[25] For example, the court held, also as recognized by Hytera during the trial, that the ISI method was a successful way to interoperate TETRA equipment. For more details of the ISI, see *LTE technology. 2017.* The future of ISI for PMR TETRA network is now. https://www.criticalcommunicationsreview.com/lte/news/33962/the-future-of-isi-for-pmr-tetra-networks-is-now. Accessed 25 March 2025.

[26] In the EU competition law of refusals to supply, two separated markets are usually defined. The following sections will further explain this. In this case, Hytera did not provide more on this justification.

separate markets was irrelevant to the refusal to deal law. Although the two companies were both TETRA equipment providers, the underlying 'dealing' in this case was the disclosure of API information, rather than the sale of TETRA equipment.

Additionally, Motorola argued that its API information was protected by intellectual property law (more precisely, trade secret law), and thus it should not be forced to share this information with rivals. The court held that the intellectual property protection cannot act as a justification of the antitrust duty to deal.

Overall, as the first (and the only one) case involving the refusal to disclose secret information in China, the *Motorola* case sets out an approach to analyzing whether the refusal violates the AML. Although the court did not find that the defendant engaged in an illegal refusal as there was no effect on competition, it clarified that a refusal to disclose confidential information could constitute the abuse of dominance if all the outlined requirements were met.

5.2.2.4 Issues Identified in the Current Legal Practices in China

By reviewing current legal practices in China that are relevant to the refusal to disclose trade secrets, this book identifies several problems as follows.

Whether Chinese authorities will adopt the essential facilities doctrine as a rationale in cases of refusal to disclose trade secrets remains an open question. The Chinese competition agency (SAMR) introduced the concept of an 'essential facility' in its provisions regarding the prohibition of the abuse of dominance and abuse of IPRs. In theory, the competition agency needs to assess whether an intellectual property (such as a trade secret) at issue constitutes an 'essential facility' as a precondition of declaring a refusal to license as an abuse of dominance. In spite of that, it is unclear whether SAMR will adopt the essential facilities doctrine in specific cases because there have been no cases related to this issue.

In the civil litigation between Hytera and Motorola, the court did not bring up the concept of an essential facility in its judgement. Nevertheless, the court analyzed whether the underlying secret information was 'essential' or 'indispensable'. For example, the court noted that the API information could not help achieve the aim of interoperability with Motorola's equipment. In other words, the secret information was not 'essential' for the plaintiff to compete with Motorola. Furthermore, the court affirmed that there were three different ways the plaintiff may adopt to interconnect to Motorola's equipment. This also demonstrated that the API information was not 'essential'.

The Tencent case provided a general test about the refusal to deal in China, without specializing in the field of intellectual property. The analysis of refusal to license in the Motorola case is still general. Under the IP Guidelines, it is possible for a dominant firm to abuse market dominance through refusing to license intellectual property to others. However, the IP Guidelines and the Motorola case failed to provide a viable coherent test for interpreting the refusal to license law.

That said, current legal practices ignore the potential influence which an antitrust duty to disclose secret information may have on innovation. In the Motorola case, the court recognized the possibility that a refusal to disclose trade secrets could be a form of the abuse of market dominance. Although the court did not find Motorola's refusal illegal, an antitrust duty to disclose may be imposed on a dominant firm in the future. Such a duty, however, might have negative effects on the dominant firm's incentives to invest in innovation.[27] The Chinese court did not appear to pay much attention to this issue, as it did not assess whether the underlying API information was technical information in nature or not.

5.2.3 *Lessons of Refusal to Disclose Trade Secrets in the US and EU*

5.2.3.1 Lessons from the US

It is well recognized that the refusal to deal is an area that enforced by the US antitrust law of monopolization.[28] As a typical case-law country, the US developed its jurisprudence regarding the refusal to deal in several leading cases.

In the *Colgate*[29] case, the US Supreme Court claimed that a private company in principle can freely 'exercise his own independent discretion as to parties with whom he will deal'. This argument confirmed the right of a trader to refuse to deal with anyone the firm disliked. Nevertheless, one exception may occur, also argued by the Supreme Court, if there existed 'any purpose to create or maintain a monopoly.' The *Colgate* case did not reveal more about a refusal to deal.

The *Aspen Skiing*[30] case is one of the leading cases in which the US Supreme Court found an unlawful refusal to deal. The plaintiff (Aspen Highlands) and the defendant (Aspen Skiing) were two skiing competitors in Aspen, Colorado. Aspen Skiing was a larger firm which owned three mountains and the plaintiff had only one. Prior to the dispute, the two parties engaged in various joint ventures that could let skiers to exploit all four mountains by selling 'All-Aspen' tickets. The plaintiff and the defendant would calculate the actual use of each mountain and separated revenues according to the actual use. Despite their previous cooperation, Aspen Skiing wanted a larger proportion of the revenue and refused to participate in the joint ventures with the plaintiff and supplied its own ticket for three mountains.

The Court of Appeals for the Tenth Circuit held that the defendant's refusal had violated Section 2 of the Sherman Act, as the multi-mountain ticket ('All-Aspen') constituted an 'essential facility'. Yet, when the case was appealed to the Supreme

[27] Fox, Eleanor M. 2005. Monopolization, abuse of dominance, and refusal to license intellectual property to competitors–Do antitrust duties help or hurt competition and innovation? How do we know? *European Competition Law Annual* 59(1): 129–152, 133.

[28] Fox, Eleanor M., and Daniel A. Crane. 2017. *Global issues in antitrust and competition law*. St. Paul: West Academic Publishing, 80.

[29] United States v Colgate & Co., 250 U.S. 300 (1919).

[30] Aspen Skiing Co. v. Aspen Highlands Skiing Corp., 472 U.S. 585 (1985).

Court, the Court upheld the lower court's decision without referring to the essential facilities doctrine. Hovenkamp stated that three elements were taken into account by the Supreme Court to find an illegal refusal to deal. First, the two parties must have a previous cooperation relationship which the plaintiff relied on. Second, the defendant cannot provide 'any efficiency justification whatever for its pattern of conduct'. Lastly the refusal should be harmful to consumers and at least one competitor, as the refusal to continue the joint venture evidently impaired skiers' preference for a combine mountain ticket.[31]

Closely related to the refusal to deal in the US is the so-called 'essential facilities' doctrine, which the Court of Appeals for the Tenth Circuit also cited in the *Aspen* case. Put simply, the essential facilities doctrine means that the holder of an essential facility has a competition duty to share it with other competitors, and a refusal to do so may be considered as the abuse of market dominance.[32]

The *MCI* case is the most famous decision in respect of the essential facilities doctrine which influenced many subsequent cases.[33] The dominant US network company AT&T refused to provide local telephone networks for MCI which wanted to enhance its long-distance call service. The Seventh Circuit established four elements for the application of the essential facilities doctrine:

> (1) control of the essential facility by a monopolist; (2) a competitor's inability practically or reasonably to duplicate the essential facility; (3) the denial of the use of the facility to a competitor; and (4) the feasibility of providing the facility.[34]

While some courts have applied the doctrine to determine if a refusal to deal violated antitrust rules, some antitrust scholars are highly critical of it. For example, Hovenkamp argued that the essential facilities doctrine is 'the most troublesome, incoherent and unmanageable of bases' for antitrust liability, and 'the antitrust world would be well off without it.'[35] What these commentators worry about is that a dominant firm may often have an antitrust duty to share a crucial asset if it could be regarded as an 'essential facility'. In this regard, they in essence oppose not only the essential facilities doctrine but also the antitrust duty to deal.

---

[31] Hovenkamp, Herbert. 2020. *Federal antitrust policy:The law of competition and its practice(Sixth edition)*. St. Paul: West Academic Publishing, 382–383.

[32] Ibid 401. Some commentators believe that *Otter Tail Power* was the first one that seemed like a modern essential facilities case adjudicated by the Supreme Court. In this case, the Otter Tail Power, which was an electricity company, refused to market electricity to the public system, and refused to acquire power from other firms. The Supreme Court held such refusal was prohibited under Section 2 of the Sherman Act. See Massadeh, Ali. 2011. The essential facilities doctrine under scrutiny: EU and US perspective: 1–38, 12.

[33] MCI Communications Corp. v. AT&T Co., 708 F.2d 1081 (7th Cir. 1983).

[34] Worth noting is that not only a tangible asset but also an intangible asset can act as an 'essential facility'. For example, some courts held that a customer list may constitute an essential facility.

[35] Hovenkamp, Herbert. 2020. *Federal antitrust policy:The law of competition and its practice(Sixth edition)*. St. Paul: West Academic Publishing, 401. See some similar arguments in Areeda, Phillip. 1989. Essential facilities: An epithet in need of limiting principles. *Antitrust Law Journal* 58(3): 841–853, 841.

In 2004, the US Supreme Court decided the landmark *Trinko* case with respect to the refusal to deal.[36] This case was about the failure of an incumbent telecommunications exchange carrier, Verizon, to grant a competitive exchange carrier access to its network infrastructure.[37] The Supreme Court, with an opinion delivered by Justice Scalia, dismissed the claim that the refusal contravened Section 2 of Sherman Act.

Justice Scalia stated that the monopoly power and monopoly prices that arose from such power is 'an important element of the free-market system'. The opportunities of charging monopoly prices attract 'business acumen' and bring about incentives of innovation and economic growth. His Honour attached great importance to the infrastructure that a company may depend on to create monopoly power. Simultaneously, the opinion pointed out three drawbacks to compelling a firm to share crucial assets with others. The first defect is that forced sharing may chill innovation as such an antitrust duty may lessen the incentive for a monopolist to invest. Secondly, enforced sharing requires a court to determine specific terms and prices of the deal—a role for which an antitrust court is 'ill-suited'.[38] Lastly, the Supreme Court predicted that compelling competitors to negotiate could result in 'the supreme evil of antitrust: collusion'.

The Supreme Court discussed the essential facilities doctrine in this case. As Justice Scalia argued, lower courts created the doctrine and the Supreme Court never recognized it, so it had no reason 'either to recognize it or to repudiate it here'. Additionally, the Supreme Court would be very cautious in recognizing circumstances where a refusal to deal may violate Section 2. The Court invoked the precedent of *Aspen Skiing* where the dominant firm sacrificed short-term profits[39] through terminating a pre-existing cooperation relationship with rivals.

After *Trinko*, many lawyers believed that the law of refusal to deal and the essential facilities doctrine would not play a significant part in the US antitrust law.[40] The Supreme Court merely recognized a rather 'narrow' exception of the general principle of the right-not-to-deal.[41] In fact, by reviewing later cases of *Trinko*, it has been

---

[36] Verizon Communications v. Law Offices of Curtis V. Trinko, LLP, often shortened to Verizon v. Trinko, 540 U.S. 398 (2004).

[37] Roger van den Bergh, Camesasca, Peter. D. and Andrea Giannaccari. 2017. *Comparative competition law and economics*. Cheltenham: Edward Elgar Publishing, 308.

[38] Hovenkamp believes that forced sharing requires price administration instead of antitrust courts on the same ground. See Hovenkamp, Herbert. 2020. *Federal antitrust policy: The law of competition and its practice (sixth edition)*. St. Paul: West Academic Publishing, 405.

[39] Fox, Eleanor. 2005. Is there life in Aspen after Trinko? The silent revolution of Section 2 of the Sherman act. *Antitrust Law Journal* 73 (1): 153–169.

[40] Roger van den Bergh, Peter D Camesasca and Andrea Giannaccari, *Comparative competition law and economics, 309*. Cheltenham: Edward Elgar Publishing. See also Shelanski, Howard. 2009. Unilateral refusals to deal in intellectual and other property. *Antitrust Law Journal* 76 (2): 369–397.

[41] See Fox, Eleanor. 2005. Monopolization, abuse of dominance, and refusal to license intellectual property to competitors–Do antitrust duties help or hurt competition and innovation? How do we know? *The Antitrustt Bulletin* 59(1): 129–152; A Melamed, Douglas. 2005. Exclusionary conduct under the antitrust laws: balancing, sacrifice, and refusals to deal. *Berkeley Technology Law Journal* 20 (2): 1247–1266.

suggested that the US courts almost spare no room for the refusal to deal claims under the Sherman Act.[42]

There are no reported cases in the US in which a court or competition agency has imposed antitrust liability for a refusal to disclose trade secrets.[43] Nevertheless, as Fox argued, 'if there is no duty to deal without the involvement of intellectual property, there would be no duty to share intellectual property.'[44] As the *Trinko* case has demonstrated the US Supreme Court's unwillingness to apply an antitrust duty to deal, it can be inferred that it is unlikely for a US court to apply an antitrust duty for a dominant firm to disclose trade secrets.

5.2.3.2 Lessons from the EU

Refusal to Supply and the Bronner Test

Under the EU law, a general principle is that companies have the right to select those with whom they deal and freely decide how to use their property.[45] However, a refusal to supply could be an abuse of dominance in violation of Article 102 TFEU. In the context of EU competition law, the EU Commission and EU courts mainly target vertically integrated firms which are in a dominant position in the upstream market that refuse to supply rivals downstream.[46]

Several leading cases have defined the landscape. The *Commercial Solvents* case[47] was an archetypal example of an unlawful refusal to supply. Commercial Solvents was a chemical undertaking providing a raw material from which a derivative (ethambutol) can be manufactured in the downstream market. Commercial Solvents then refused to supply raw materials to traders of the derivative, when Commercial Solvents decided to be active on its own in the downstream market. The ECJ held in the case that:

---

[42] See Adediji, Damola. United State's law on refusal to deal after the Trinko decision of the Supreme Court (Seminar Paper, Intellectual Property and Competition Law Seminar under the direction and tutelage of Professor Dr. Josef Drexl, July 2016).

[43] There are also no reported cases in the domain of other intellectual property, such as patents and copyright. Hovenkamp believes that forced sharing requires price administration instead of antitrust courts on the same ground. See Hovenkamp, Herbert. 2010. *Federal antitrust policy: The law of competition and its practice (sixth edition).* St. Paul: West Academic Publishing, 434.

[44] See Fox, Eleanor. 2005. Monopolization, abuse of dominance, and refusal to license intellectual property to competitors–Do antitrust duties help or hurt competition and innovation? How do we know? *The Antitrustt Bulletin* 59(1): 129–152.

[45] See EU Guidance Paper para. 75.

[46] Jones, Alison, Sufrin, BE and Niamh Dunne. 2019. *EU competition law:Text, cases, and materials (7th ed).* Oxford: Oxford University Press, 484. The European Commission specifies that 'competition problems arise when the dominant undertaking competes on the "downstream" market with the buyer whom it refuses to supply.' This is the only scenario that the European Commission focuses on. See EU Guidance Paper para. 76.

[47] Joined cases 6 and 7–73, Istituto Chemioterapico Italiano S.p.A. and Commercial Solvents Corporation v Commission EU:C:1974:18.

> …an undertaking which has a dominant position in the market in raw materials and which, with the object of reversing such raw material for manufacturing its own derivates, refuses to supply a customer, which is itself a manufacturer of these derivates, and therefore risks eliminating all competition on the part of this customer, is abusing its dominant position…

In this case, Commercial Solvents was about to integrate vertically and compete with its former existing customers in the downstream market. However, unlike the US *Aspen* case requiring a preexisting cooperation relationship, the ECJ later clarified that a refusal to deal with new customers could constitute an abuse.[48]

The US *Trinko* case in essence denied the essential facilities doctrine, yet the concept flourishes on the other side of the Atlantic. The EU Commission first used the concept of 'essential facilities' in its decision of *Sealink/B&I Holyhead*[49] in 1992, in which the Commission defined an essential facility as 'a facility or infrastructure without access to which competitors cannot provide services to their customers.'[50] Under some circumstances, an 'essential facility' may be also called an 'indispensable' facility or input that is 'objectively necessary for operators to be able to compete effectively on the market'.[51]

The landmark EU case in terms of essential facilities and the refusal to supply is the *Oscar Bronner* case.[52] In this case, the ECJ set out several restrictions on the grant of access to the assets of a dominant undertaking, in setting out what is called the 'Bronner test'. The Bronner test has three requirements. Firstly, the alleged refusal to supply must be likely to eliminate all competition in the downstream market. Secondly, the conduct must be incapable of being objectively justified. Lastly, the asset/service in question should be indispensable to doing business, meaning that there is no actual or potential substitute for it in the market.[53] This three-step Bronner test sets out the legal framework of the application of the law of refusal to supply in the EU.

Refusal to Supply Intellectual Property Rights in the EU

As the EU Guidance Paper stated, the concept of refusal to supply in the EU is rather broad, including refusals to supply products, refusals to license intellectual property

[48] Case 311/84, Télémarketing EU:C:1985:394.

[49] 34174 Sealink/B&I—Holyhead: Interim Measures Decision 11 June 1992.

[50] Some commentators argue that Commercial Solvents was the first essential facilities case in the EU, although the ECJ did not adopt such concept clearly. See Muller, Ulf and Anselm Rodenhausen. 2008. The rise and fall of the essential facility doctrine. *European Competition Law Review* 29 (5):310–330, 316.

[51] See EU Guidance Paper para. 83. The ECJ also shows preference to 'indispensable' rather than 'essential' facilities.

[52] Case C-7/97, Oscar Bronner GmbH & Co. KG v Mediaprint EU:C:1998:569.

[53] Ibid. See also Jones, Alison, Sufrin, BE and Niamh Dunne. 2019. *EU competition law: Text, cases, and materials (7th ed)*. Oxford: Oxford University Press, 493.

rights and so on.[54] The leading cases of *Magill* and *IMS* reflect how EU courts would handle cases of refusal to license intellectual property rights.

The *Magill*[55] case concerns the refusal to license copyright material. Television listings were protected under the copyright law in the UK and Ireland.[56] At the time of this case, RTE possessed a statutory monopoly of TV broadcasting in Ireland while BBC and IBA were the merely two broadcasting companies in North Ireland. RTE and BBC had the copyright on their own television listings and ITP owned copyright in IBA's listings. Before the case, these three firms published their own TV listings respectively. Magill was a publishing company which began to publish a listing of programs of all three companies. The three television companies applied for an injunction against Magill under national intellectual property law. By contrast, Magill believed that the exercise of these intellectual property rights constituted an abuse of market dominance under the EU competition law.

The ECJ noted that there was a potential battle between the exercise of IPRs and the intervention of competition law. It opposed the view that the exercise of copyright 'can never be reviewed in relation to Article [102].' Instead, the ECJ ruled that a refusal to license may establish an abuse under 'exceptional circumstances'. In addition to the requirements in the Bronner test, the ECJ also provided a 'new product' rule as follows:

> [t]he appellants' refusal to provide basic information by relying on national copyright provisions thus prevented the appearance of a new product, a comprehensive weekly guide to television programmes, which the appellants did not offer and for which there was a potential consumer demand.

Some lawyers believe that when the requested property is intellectual property, the requirement of hinderance of a new product is added in a refusal to supply case.[57] Therefore, *Magill* demonstrated that there were four conditions that the ECJ would consider identifying such 'exception circumstances' as follows:

Firstly, the requested intellectual property (program information as a raw material) was indispensable to provide a by-product (derivatives) in the downstream market, which meant in *Magill* that there was no substitute to make a comprehensive television listing. Secondly, the refusal prevented the emergence of a new product (a comprehensive television guide). Thirdly, the defendant cannot justify its refusal. Lastly, the three television companies planned to exclude all competition in the secondary market and provided their own listings.

---

[54] See EU Guidance Paper para. 78.

[55] Joined cases C-241/91 P and C-242/91 P, Radio Telefis Eireann (RTE) and Independent Television Publications Ltd (ITP) v Commission EU:C:1995:98.

[56] Some leading intellectual property lawyers argue that TV listings did not deserve copyright protection in any sense. However, it is a question of intellectual property law. See Drexl, Josef. 2007. Abuse of dominance in licensing and refusal to license-a 'more economic approach' to competition by imitation and to competition by substitution'. In T*he interaction between competition law and IP law*, 647–664. Oxford: Hart publishing. 647, 654.

[57] Hou Liyang. 2012. The essential facilities doctrine—What was wrong in Microsoft? *IIC International Review of Intellectual Property and Competition Law* 43 (4): 251–271, 252.

IMS[58] was another leading case in relation to the refusal to license IPRs. IMS was a German pharmaceutical firm and had the copyright of its '1860 brick structure'.[59] The brick structure was popular among German pharmaceutical industry for many years and became a de facto industry standard. When IMS' competitors wanted to enter the market and supply pharmaceutical data services to customers, they found it impossible to do so without having access to the brick structure. As IMS obtained injunctions to preserve its '1860 brick structure', IMS' rivals complained that such refusal was an abusive practice.

In compliance with the Bronner and Magill criteria, the ECJ reiterated in *IMS* that there were several prerequisites for identifying an anti-competitive refusal to license and named them as 'cumulative conditions'.

> [i]n order for the refusal by an undertaking which owns a copyright to give access to a product or service indispensable for carrying on a particular business to be treated as abusive, it is sufficient that three cumulative conditions be satisfied, namely, that that refusal is preventing the emergence of a new product for which there is potential consumers demand, that it is unjustified and such as to exclude any competition on a secondary market.[60]

In addition, the ECJ further interpreted two major issues. On the one hand, as discussed, the EU law mainly focuses on vertically integrated companies and usually identify an upstream and a downstream market. The problem in *IMS* was that IMS had never marketed the '1860 brick structure' before, only reserving it to its own use.[61] The ECJ held that 'it is sufficient that a potential market or even hypothetical market can be identified',[62] and 'it is determinative that two stages of production may be identified and that they are interconnected, the upstream product is indispensable in as much as for supply of the downstream product.'[63] This indicates that the true issue is not to tell two markets apart clearly,[64] but to determine whether the intellectual property is indispensable for production of another downstream product.[65]

The ECJ discussed why a 'new product' rule was required. Having noted that there was a need to keep a reasonable balance between the protection of copyright

---

58 Case C-418/01, IMS Health GmbH & Co. OHG v NDC Health GmbH & Co. KG EU:C:2004:257.

59 IMS designed the '1860 Brick structure' which was used to collect and analyse pharmaceutical sales information.

60 Case C-418/01, IMS Health GmbH & Co. OHG v NDC Health GmbH & Co. KG EU:C:2004:257, para. 38.

61 This was different in *Magill*. In *Magill*, the three broadcasting firms used to license their television program listings to others.

62 Case C-418/01, IMS Health GmbH & Co. OHG v NDC Health GmbH & Co. KG EU:C:2004:257, para. 44.

63 Ibid, para. 45.

64 One lawyer claims that it would be sufficient 'even if the input is a competitive advantage of a kind which has never previously been marketed or licensed by any company, and which it would not be economically rational to license to a direct competitor.' See Lang, J. Temple. 2003. Anti-competitive non-pricing abuses under European and national antitrust law. *Fordham Corporate Law Institute*: 235–240, 307.

65 Mark Patterson. 2007. The peculiar 'New Product' requirement in European refusal to license cases: a US perspective. *European Competition Law Annual* 2007:705–722, 707.

and free competition, the ECJ referred to the opinion in Magill again that the intervention of competition law can prevail 'only where refusal to grant a license prevents the development of the secondary market to the detriment of consumers.' In other words, competitors cannot request to achieve intellectual property from the dominant firm merely because they are attempting to duplicate goods similar to those of the dominant firm. Competitors must be supplying new products for which there is a potential consumer need. This requirement indicates that even though the court orders a dominant firm to license IPRs to competitors, such a license is for the sake of consumers, rather than competitors.[66]

Case Study: Microsoft V EU Commission

The EU Microsoft case may be the most famous case worldwide in respect of the refusal to disclose trade secrets. This case is not only highly relied on, but also further developed the tests in *Magill* and *IMS*.

Sun Microsystems was a competitor of Microsoft. In 1998, Sun accused Microsoft of the abuse of dominance through refusal to disclose secret information. During the investigation, the European Commission, following jurisprudence in previous case-law, defined the upstream market (the client PC operating system market) and the downstream market (the workgroup server operating system market). As discussed in Chap. 4, the Commission identified the dominant position of Microsoft in the upstream market.[67] Windows was the most popular product around the 2000s and served as "a de facto standard operating product for client PCs'.[68] Microsoft possessed the interface information (interoperability information) which was kept as a trade secret, as Microsoft itself acknowledged.[69] Software providers could only operate with Windows if they could get access to such information. The Commission noted that Microsoft had provided workgroup server software providers with full interface information for free for many years before Microsoft entered the workgroup server operating system market itself. Microsoft then refused to disclose the secret interface information to its competitors, such as Sun. It became difficult for other rivals to survive in the downstream market without the information. The EU Commission ordered Microsoft to provide its interoperability information for requesting competitors. The General Court (GC) upheld Commission's decision.

---

66 Jones, Alison, Sufrin, BE and Niamh Dunne. 2019. *EU competition law: Text, cases, and materials (7th ed)*. Oxford: Oxford University Press, 509.

67 In fact, the Commission also found that Microsoft had market dominance in the downstream market.

68 Surblyte, Gintare. 2011. *The refusal to disclose trade secrets as an abuse of market dominance-Microsoft and beyond*. Bern: Stämpfli, 8.

69 Fox, Eleanor and Crane A. Daniel. 2017. *Global issues in antitrust and competition law*. St. Paul: West Academic Publishing, 89.

Josef Drexl has argued that the standard of analysis for the refusal to disclose trade secrets should not be different from that of the refusal to licence IPRs.[70] The EU Commission and the GC assessed the *Microsoft* case basically, but not totally, dependant on requirements in *Magill* and *IMS*.

The Commission adopted a two-stage approach in determining the indispensability of the secret information.[71] Firstly, the Commission considered what degree of interoperability non-Microsoft work group server operating systems need to allow competitors to remain viable in the market. Secondly, it assessed whether the interface information Microsoft refused to disclose can achieve such degree of interoperability. The Commission noted that users substantially valued interoperability. Through empirical research (customer surveys), the Commission found that even though other rivals' systems might perform better, users showed preference to Microsoft's because it could operate more effectively with Windows.[72] The Commission concluded that other competitors found it hard to compete with Microsoft in the downstream market without access to the interoperability information. The GC upheld the Commission's arguments and the conclusion that the interface information was indispensable.

The European Commission considered whether Microsoft's refusal to disclose eliminated competition in the derivate downstream market and concluded that it did. Although Microsoft argued that there was still some competition in the downstream market, the GC reaffirmed the decision and further held that Article 102 should apply even before all competition had been eliminated in the downstream market,[73] particularly considering that the market was 'characterized by significant network effects'[74] and 'the elimination of competition would therefore be difficult to reverse.' Noting that there were still some providers in the downstream market,[75] the GC held that 'a marginal presence (of competitors of the dominant firm) in certain niches in the market cannot suffice to substantiate the existence of such competition'. Therefore, the GC corrected the requirement of 'the elimination of all competition' used in previous cases and developed the concept of 'the elimination of effective competition' in the market. The GC concluded that Microsoft's refusal had eliminated effective competition in the derivate market.

---

[70] Drexl, Josef. 2011. Refusal to grant access to trade secrets as an abuse of market dominance. In *Intellectual property and competition law-new frontiers*. Oxford: Oxford University Press, 165, 183.

[71] Fox, Eleanor and Daniel A. Crane. 2017. *Global issues in antitrust and competition law.* St. Paul: West Academic Publishing, 84.

[72] Jones, Alison, Sufrin, BE and Niamh Dunne. 2019. *EU competition law:Text, cases, and materials (7th ed).* Oxford: Oxford University Press, 511.

[73] Fox, Eleanor and Daniel A. Crane. 2017. *Global issues in antitrust and competition law.* St. Paul: West Academic Publishing, 85.

[74] In this case, the popularity of Windows locked in many consumers and led to the network effects.

[75] For instance, the market share of Linux products continued to grow in the downstream market because Linux required less interoperability information. See Hou Liyang. 2012. The essential facilities doctrine—What was wrong in Microsoft? *IIC International Review of Intellectual Property and Competition Law* 43 (4): 251–271, 267.

It should be noted that the European Commission issued its decision against Microsoft shortly before the *IMS* judgement, without knowing that the ECJ would use the 'new product' rule as it did in *Magill*.[76] Therefore, the Commission did not analyse this requirement. It was no surprise that Microsoft later contested the decision before the GC. Microsoft claimed that because Microsoft had supplied work group server operating systems to customers in the downstream market, the systems provided by Microsoft's rivals were not 'new products'.

In response to this argument, the GC modified the 'new product' test set out in the previous case law.[77] The GC referred to Article 102 (b) which prevents a dominant company from limiting 'technical development to the prejudice of consumers', and held that the avoidance of a 'new product' cannot be 'the only parameter which determines whether a refusal to license an intellectual property right is capable of causing prejudice to consumers within the meaning of Article [102] (b).'[78] The GC also upheld Commission's decision that non-Microsoft work group server operating systems were better than Microsoft's products in many ways. If other competitors could acquire the interface information, they would not merely reproduce Microsoft's products, but had no choice but to differentiate their products in order to survive. Therefore, the GC concluded that the requirement of 'technical development' (the modification of the 'new product' rule) was met. In this regard, some commentators argue that this ruling demonstrates that the list of exceptional circumstances in the previous cases is not exhaustive.[79]

Microsoft put forward two arguments to justify its refusal. On the one hand, Microsoft claimed that the protection of intellectual property law (trade secret law) could be an objective justification for a refusal to deal. The GC, not surprisingly, dismissed this argument, and held that the possession of an IPR cannot be a justification, as pre-existing case law had demonstrated. Microsoft also proposed a justification that the remedy of compulsory disclosure may harm its incentives to innovate, similar to the views of the US Supreme Court in *Trinko*. The GC dismissed this argument on two grounds. Firstly, the GC stated that it should be Microsoft's burden to testify to what disincentives to innovation it would suffer. However, Microsoft had failed to prove this with its 'vague, general and theoretical' arguments. Secondly, the GC noted that the disclosure of the interface information to third parties was a

---

[76] Drexl, Josef. 2011. Refusal to grant access to trade secrets as an abuse of market dominance. In *Intellectual property and competition law-new frontiers*. 165–185, Oxford: Oxford University Press. 173.

[77] Ansari, Dina. 2009. The EC essential facilities doctrine, the Microsoft case and the treatment of trade secrets. Bern: Stämpfli, 41.

[78] It should be noted that some lawyers argue that the GC improperly changed the 'new product' criteria to 'technical development' standard. See Hou Liyang. 2012. The essential facilities doctrine—what was wrong in Microsoft? *IIC international review of intellectual property and competition law* 43 (4): 251–271, 251. This could misunderstand the court's ruling, as the GC only followed what the TFEU clearly stipulates.

[79] Roger van den Bergh, Camesasca, D Peter and Andrea Giannaccari. 2017. *Comparative Competition Law and Economics*. Cheltenham: Edward Elgar Publishing, 315–316.

common practice in the industry, and none previously claimed that this would reduce incentive to innovate before.

The GC finally upheld that Microsoft's refusal to disclose constituted the abuse of dominance under Article 102 and ordered Microsoft to share the underlying secret information with competitors as the remedy.

5.2.4 Suggestions for Improving Legal Practices of Refusal to Disclose Trade Secrets in China

5.2.4.1 Why Should China Mainly Learn from the EU Law?

The comparative analysis above indicates that there is great divergence between the US antitrust law and EU competition law with respect to the refusal to disclose trade secrets. Generally, the US attaches more importance to the right of refusal and is reluctant to find illegal refusals to deal after the landmark *Trinko* case. In contrast, the European Commission and courts are more likely than US law to require the supply of IPRs, including trade secrets. This brings up the question: which method is more appropriate for China? This book argues that the EU approach would be a more fitting option.

There are some problems with the US approach, particularly relating to the *Trinko* case. In *Trinko*, the US Supreme court argued that 'the opportunity to charge monopoly prices—at least for a short period—is what attracts business acumen in the first place'. However, since Verizon had charged monopoly prices for more than 20 years, it is questionable whether that was a 'short period'.[80]

The Supreme Court outlined three reasons to justify its non-intervention in the refusal to deal. The most important was that intervention would lessen the incentive to innovate. This argument has also influenced many subsequent cases in the US. Judge (now Supreme Court Justice) Neil Gorsuch also held in a recent US Microsoft case that '[T]he monopolist might be deterred from investing, innovating, or expanding (or even entering a market in the first place) with the knowledge anything it creates it could be forced to share.'[81] Josef Drexl criticized this argument, stating that the US Supreme Court endorsed a static and one-sided opinion about the relationship between market power and innovation, as it heavily relied on the Chicago School approach that the monopolist can innovate more.[82] However, he argued that even a monopolist would also lose its incentives to innovate in the long run if it does not

[80] Gallego, Beatriz Conde. 2008. Unilateral refusal to license indispensable intellectual property rights—US and EU approaches. In *Research Handbook on Intellectual Property and Competition Law,*215–238. Cheltenham: Edward Elgar, 220.

[81] Novell v. Microsoft, 731 F. 3d 1064 (10th Cir. 2013).

[82] Drexl, Josef. 2004. IMS health and trinko–antitrust placebo for consumers instead of sound economics in refusal-to-deal cases. *IIC* 35: 759–792.

have to worry about competitive pressure.[83] This explains the necessity of an antitrust duty to deal in restoring competition in the market.

The US Supreme Court also stated that forced negotiation may facilitate collusion. This argument is at odds with the facts in *Aspen Skiing*, in which the plaintiff and defendant had a preexisting dealing partnership. Despite that there being concerns of collusion in such a relationship, the court did not find collusion in *Aspen Skiing*.[84]

The last point the US Supreme Court made was that an antitrust court would be 'ill-suited' to determine the terms of the dealing, and thus it should not intervene in a refusal to deal. In view of this, the intellectual property law might provide a solution to this problem when it comes to a forced license of intellectual property. The compulsory license of an IPR ('forced sharing' in *Trinko*) is the remedy for an anti-competitive refusal to license. The TRIPS provides that the framework for compulsory licensing results not only from anti-competitive practices,[85] but also from other reasons of public interest, such as protection of public health.[86] Antitrust law is responsible for identifying whether an illegal refusal to license exists, whereas it is the task of intellectual property law, including trade secret law, to determine the specific terms of licensing. In this regard, the inability of an antitrust court to decide the license terms cannot give rise to the impossibility of finding an anti-competitive refusal to deal.[87] For instance, intellectual property judges may refer to the royalties of the underlying intellectual property in previous transactions to determine a royalty term.

It is also worth noting that the US Congress strongly disagreed with the Supreme Court's *Trinko* decision. As discussed in Chap. 2, in a recent US Congress report, the Congress argued that the Supreme Court's judicial decisions focused primarily on price and output ('a narrow construction of "consumer welfare"'), rather than the competitive process, and that such decisions contravene legislative history and intent. Particularly, the report referred to the Supreme Court's disfavour of the essential facilities doctrine and the refusal-to-deal law in *Trinko*. It claimed that the Congress should 'consider revitalizing the "essential facilities" doctrine and 'overriding judicial decisions'.[88]

---

83 Some scholars claim that the continual creation of monopoly and its correction by competitive entry result in a never-ending innovation process. See Bohannan, Christina and Herbert Hovenkamp. 2012. Chapter 1. In C*reation without restraint promoting liberty and rivalry in innovation*, 1–15. Oxford: Oxford University Press.

84 Hovenkamp, Herbert. 2020. *Federal antitrust policy:the law of competition and its Practice (Sixth edition)*. St. Paul: West Academic Publishing, 382–383.

85 Article 8.2 of the TRIPS.

86 Article 31 of the TRIPS.

87 Hovenkamp argues that forced sharing requires price administration. See Hovenkamp, Herbert. 2020. *Federal antitrust policy:the law of competition and its practice (sixth edition)*. St. Paul: West Academic Publishing, 405.

88 See Sub-committee on Antitrust Commercial and Administrative Law of the Committee on the Judiciary. 2020. Investigation of competition in digital markets. https://judiciary.house.gov/uploadedles/competition_in_digital_markets.pdf. Accessed 25 March 2025.

In contrast, the European approach is more fitting to the Chinese context, especially regarding intellectual property and trade secrets. The EU competition law recognizes that under 'exceptional circumstances' a refusal to license IPRs (or refusal to disclose trade secrets) may constitute an abuse of market dominance. It draws a clear boundary line between the general principle that each firm is entitled to refuse to supply, and the anti-competitive refusal, by introducing the 'exceptional circumstances' test.

Additionally, the 'exceptional circumstances' test is based on a legal theory which intends to balance the potential tension between IP law and competition law. Professor Drexl called it as 'the theory of complementarity' and it has been discussed earlier in Chap. 1 of this book.[89] According to this theory, fundamental conflicts between IPRs and competition do not exist. The rights holder of an IPR can prevent competitors from using the IPR in question but may not prevent competitors from developing competing or superior technology or services.[90] In other words, IP law authorises a rights holder to exclude competition by imitation, while the exercise of an IPR cannot hinder competition by substitution.[91] One commentator thus concluded that Article 102 can be applied only if competition by substitution is harmed.[92]

This explains why the GC required 'technical development' to be demonstrated in the *Microsoft* case. If competitors merely wanted to acquire the secret interface information and duplicate exactly the same products as Microsoft had already provided, competition law would not apply. The intervention of Article 102 was not targeted at Microsoft's competitors, but at the interests of customers with more choices.[93]

In conclusion, despite the fact that the US Supreme Court was unwilling to apply an antitrust duty to deal in the landmark *Trinko* case,[94] the ruling might be challenged for several reasons as discussed. It also appears that the US Congress is intending to override the *Trinko* case and revitalize the antitrust duty to deal and the essential facilities doctrine.

On the other side of the Atlantic, the EU competition law has developed a successive case-law on the refusal to license IPRs and disclose trade secrets. The EU approach is supported by 'the theory of complementarity',[95] which reasonably defines the relationship between the exercise of IPRs and the antitrust duty to license.

---

[89] Drexl, Josef. 2007. Abuse of dominance in licensing and refusal to license-a 'more economic approach' to competition by imitation and to competition by substitution. In *The interaction between competition law and IP law,* 647–648. Oxford: Hart publishing.

[90] Ibid 648.

[91] Ibid.

[92] Gallego, Beatriz Conde. 2008. Unilateral refusal to license indispensable intellectual property rights—US and EU approaches. In *Research Handbook on Intellectual Property and Competition Law,* 215–238. Cheltenham: Edward Elgar, 236.

[93] This is also in accordance with the European Ordoliberal thinking. See Behrens, Peter. 2018. The ordoliberal concept of abuse' of a dominant position and its impact on Article 102 TFEU. In *Abusive Practices in Competition Law*, 21–22. Cheltenham: Edward Elgar Publishing.

[94] As discussed above, the US courts spare little room for the refusal to deal claims after *Trinko.*

[95] For more details on the complementarity of theory between competition and intellectual property, see Chap. 1.

As stated earlier, China believes that a dominant company has the antitrust duty to disclose trade secrets if the refusal to disclose constitutes an abuse of dominance. Unfortunately, China lacks a detailed framework to analyse these cases. Considering the similar framework of abuse of dominance between China and the EU, this book argues that China can learn a lot from the EU case-law regarding the refusal to disclose trade secrets.

5.2.4.2 Suggestions for the Application of the Refusal to Disclose Trade Secrets Law in China

Section 5.2.2.4 outlines several issues in existing Chinese legal practices. The comparative experience, primarily the EU approach, can help address these problems.

There has never been a precise definition of the 'essential facilities' doctrine. As discussed, the GC and ECJ did not refer to the concept of 'essential facilities' in *Magill*, *IMS* and *Microsoft*. However, Drexl argued that the court applied a 'restrictive' essential facility theory[96] in assessing whether the property/information at issue was indispensable or not. This demonstrates that whether it is called 'essential facilities' doctrine does not matter. Despite that China's IP Guidelines not referring to the concept of 'essential facilities' because pressure from the US, it is suggested that Chinese competition agencies and courts should consider the indispensability of the secret information, when dealing with cases of the refusal to disclose trade secrets. More importantly, China should adopt a definite framework for assessing such cases. In this regard, the EU Microsoft test can be considered a good model. China's IP Guidelines failed to provide a detailed framework, yet there are some similarities between the EU *Microsoft* case and China's *Motorola* case. For example, both courts examined whether the secret information was indispensable for competition and whether the refusal would eliminate competition. They also held that the defendants cannot justify their practices by arguing that the underlying information was protected by trade secret law.

This book argues that Chinese competition agencies and courts should seek to differentiate upstream products from downstream products in a refusal to disclose trade secrets case. The Chinese court in *Motorola* dismissed the argument that two separate markets should be identified, yet the court in effect differentiated the upstream product (API information) and the downstream product (TETRA equipment) in this case. The *IMS* case reminds us that "it is determinative that two stages of production may be identified and that they are interconnected, the upstream product is indispensable in as much as for supply of the downstream product.' This book proposes that Chinese courts may accept the experience of *IMS* and the later EU case-law to differentiate upstream from downstream products in the assessments of the refusal to disclose trade secrets cases.

---

[96] Drexl, Josef. 2007. Abuse of dominance in licensing and refusal to license-a 'more economic approach' to competition by imitation and to competition by substitution. In *The Interaction between competition law and IP law*, 647–664. Oxford: Hart publishing, 661.

This book proposes the following test for cases of refusal to disclose trade secrets in China.[97] Firstly, the court or competition authority should examine the indispensability of the secret information. The indispensability could arise, as Josef Drexl stated, particularly when the secrecy of the information leads to de facto standards and network effects.[98] The competition agency and court should also examine whether the underlying trade secret can be easily reverse-engineered. If competitors can easily reverse engineer the secret holder's information, it usually means the trade secret is not indispensable for other competitors. Secondly, the competition authorities and courts should examine whether the refusal eliminated effective competition in the downstream market. The competition agency and courts may rely on the degree of indispensability of the secret and empirical research (such as customer questionnaires) to determine this. Thirdly, the competition authorities and courts need to examine whether the refusal prevents 'technical developments'. China's IP Guidelines also regard the hindrance of technical innovation and development as an element of anti-competitive effects.[99] In compliance with the complementarity theory, the requesting competitors cannot request the disclosure of a trade secret merely for the duplication of a product but for purposes of technical developments. Lastly, the dominant firm should be entitled to justify its refusal. For example, if the secret is technical and with great innovation, the dominant undertaking can argue a duty to disclose may harm its incentives to invest and to innovate with convincing evidence.

Moreover, it would be more likely to find a refusal to disclose secret information unlawful when a previous disclosure exists. Despite the fact that the US *Trinko* case was reluctant to determine an anti-competitive refusal to deal, it recognized the jurisprudence in *Aspen Skiing*. In the *Aspen Skiing* case, the plaintiff and defendant had a preexisting cooperation relationship before the defendant's refusal to deal. In *Microsoft*, the European Commission also noted that Microsoft had disclosed its interface information free of charge for many years. As a result, if a dominant corporation discloses its secret information for a long period, and it later declines to disclose the same because its attempt to enter a downstream market, the competition agency and courts are more likely to find an abuse of market dominance.

5.2.5 Conclusion

China's AML prohibits the abuse of market dominance through the refusal to deal. The SPC clarified in the Tencent case that it would examine the anti-competitive effects of a refusal to deal, instead of taking a form-based approach. During the

[97] It should be noted that the company under review should be in the dominant position in the relevant market. As Chap. 4 discusses the dominance issue, this chapter provides tests regarding the analysis of abusive practices.

[98] This is also called 'external market failures'. The problems of de facto standards and network effects resulting from trade secrets are discussed in Chap. 4 regarding market dominance.

[99] Article 5 of China's IP Guidelines.

enactment of China's IP Guidelines, the US government pressured China to abandon the concept of 'essential facilities'. Notwithstanding this, the final IP Guidelines still recognize that the refusal to license IPRs (including the refusal to disclose trade secrets as a sub-group) may constitute an abuse of market dominance.

From the perspective of comparative law, the US and the EU take divergent approaches to the refusal to deal. The US, despite being the first to use the essential facilities doctrine, is unlikely to find illegal refusals to deal after the Supreme Court's *Trinko* decision. By contrast, the EU developed an 'exceptional circumstances' test to apply Article 102 to the field of refusal to license, through a series of leading cases. In *Microsoft*, the European Commission and the GC successfully handled the issue of refusal to disclose trade secrets, and proposed a thorough criteria for applying Article 102.

The EU case-law regarding the refusal to disclose trade secrets may be more fitting in the Chinese context. The EU law holds as a general principle that even a dominant firm has the right to refuse to disclose trade secrets. Under 'exceptional circumstances', the EU competition law may regard the refusal to disclose trade secrets as an abuse. The *Microsoft* criteria are not only concerned with the potential anti-competitive effects of a refusal to disclose trade secrets, but also deals effectively with the relationship between competition and innovation.

Therefore, this book suggests that Chinese legal practices in relation to the refusal to deal should be shaped mainly by the EU competition law. When dealing with cases of refusal to disclose trade secrets, Chinese competition agencies and courts should separate upstream products from downstream products. They can also apply the balance test which was provided in the EU *Microsoft* case.

This section (see Sect. 5.2) analyzes the refusal to disclose trade secrets by a dominant company as an abuse of market dominance. The next sections will further assess other abusive practices of a dominant undertaking regarding trade secrets which might constitute the abuse of dominance.

5.3 Bad Faith Litigation of Trade Secrets

5.3.1 Introduction

In addition to the refusal to disclose trade secrets, some antitrust scholars also identify that bad faith litigation of trade secrets initiated by a dominant firm as conduct which might constitute the abuse of market dominance.[100]

---

[100] For example, Professor Harry First considers refusal to supply and sham litigation as two primary abusive practices in relation to trade secrets that may violate the US monopolisation law. See First, Harry. 2011. Trade secrets and antitrust law. In *The law and theory of trade secrecy: A handbook of contemporary research*, eds. Rochelle C Dreyfuss. 358–365. Cheltenham: Edward Elgar Publishing.

See also Oliver, D Michael. 1989. Antitrust liability for bad faith assertion of trade secrets. *University of Baltimore Law Review* 18(3): 544–569.

Access to justice is universally recognized as a part of human rights[101] and a basic principle of the rule of law.[102] Any individuals and companies, including a dominant undertaking, may gain remedies from the court if they are harmed by others. Nevertheless, a dominant firm may conduct bad faith litigation not for legal remedies but in order to hamper its competitors, giving rise to detriment to the competitive process. Such anti-competitive bad faith litigation may arise as a type of antitrust counterclaim, particularly in the context of intellectual property infringement lawsuits.[103] Therefore, it is necessary to keep a reasonable balance between the right of access to the court and antitrust intervention, finding a workable standard for the antitrust intervention in anti-competitive bad faith litigation, especially with respect to trade secrets in China.

This section is divided into three parts. Since the US and EU have long-standing case law with regard to anti-competitive bad faith litigation, the first part analyses comparative lessons from both sides of the Atlantic. Subsequently, this section provides several suggestions for Chinese competition agencies and courts. It first examines *Huawei v InterDigital*, the only case in China where bad faith litigation was held to be an abuse of market dominance. It then gives specific suggestions on the identification of bad faith litigation of trade secrets in China. The last part presents the conclusion.

5.3.2 Lessons from the US and the EU

5.3.2.1 Lessons from the US

Bad Faith Litigation Under the US Antitrust Law

In the US, the *Noerr-Pennington* doctrine usually protects litigation from being reviewed by antitrust laws. However, if the litigation is initiated in bad faith by a dominant firm, the litigation may constitute monopolization in violation of Section 2 of the Sherman Act. The following provides specific analysis of the bad faith litigation in the US.

---

[101] Francioni, Francesco. 2007. *Access to justice as a human right.* Oxford: Oxford University Press.

[102] United Nations. Access to Justice. https://www.un.org/ruleoflaw/thematic-areas/access-to-justice-and-rule-of-law-institutions/access-to-justice/. Accessed 25 March 2025.

[103] For instance, competition law scholars argued that in the context of intellectual property litigation, it is necessary for antitrust law to intervene if some litigants abuse the litigation process. See Lianos, Ioannis and Pierre Regibeau. 2017. 'Sham' litigation: When can it arise and how can it be reduced? *Antitrust Bulletin* 62 (4): 643–689, 647. See also First, Harry. 2011. Trade secrets and antitrust law. In *The law and theory of trade secrecy: A handbook of contemporary research,* ed. Rochelle C. Dreyfuss, 332–380. Cheltenham: Edward Elgar Publishing, 363 ('A familiar problem in antitrust law is the alleged bad faith assertion of an intellectual property right as part of an effort to exclude competitors.') Leading intellectual property lawyers, such as Mark Lemley, also noted that antitrust claims are a crucial part of IP lawsuits. See Lemley, Mark. 1994. Antitrust counterclaims in patent and copyright infringement cases. *Texas Intellectual Property Law Journal* 3 (1): 1–8.

The US Supreme Court forbids antitrust intervention in the right to petition the government through two cases,[104] which formed the so-called *Noerr-Pennington* doctrine. It should be noted that the term 'government' in the context of the US refers to all three branches, namely the legislative, executive and judicial branches. As a result, although the two cases (*Noerr* and *Pennington*) were about petitioning activity of the executive administration, the *Noerr-Pennington* doctrine may apply to the judicial branch—lawsuits.[105]

In *Noerr*, railroads and truckers were competitors in the market for long-haul freight business. Both industries organized campaigns aiming at encouraging shippers to use their own method in order to gain more competitive advantages. The railroads, by making deceptive and untruthful claims, successfully petitioned Pennsylvania's governor for legislation that imposed disadvantages on truckers.[106] Having noted that the petition by the railroads had severe anti-competitive effects, the Supreme Court, however, held that an undertaking which petitions the government to harm rivals will have antitrust immunity, even though those claims are misleading or even unethical.[107]

The US Supreme Court in *Noerr* recognized that under some circumstances a petition 'is mere sham to cover what is actually nothing more than an attempt to interfere directly with the business relationships of a competitor'.[108] For example, the Supreme Court acknowledged 'the use (of) the governmental process as opposed to the outcome of that process as an anti-competitive weapon' in *City of Columbia v Omni Outdoor Advertising*.[109] The sham exception in *Noerr* may be bad faith litigation since petitioning activity includes filing a lawsuit.

Consequently, bad faith litigation is likely to violate the US antitrust laws. In view of the OECD, bad faith litigation might be the most egregious form of non-price predation.[110] The following question becomes what constitutes bad faith litigation.

---

[104] See Eastern R. Conference v. Noerr Motors, 365 U.S. 127 (1961); United Mine Workers v. Pennington, 381 U.S. 657 (1965).

[105] The Noerr-Pennington doctrine applies in the decision-making of all three branches of the government—which might be legislative, executive or judicial. See Bona, Jarod. 2021. What is Noerr-Pennington Immunity and Is this Doctrine a Defense to an Antitrust Case? *Bona Law PC*. https://www.theantitrustattorney.com/what-is-noerr-pennington-immunity-and-is-this-doctrine-a-defense-to-an-antitrust-case/. Accessed 25 March 2025.

[106] The railroads petitioned the Governor's veto for legislation that would have more flexible standards for truckers.

[107] As the First Amendment to the US Constitution protects freedom of speech, the press, assembly, and the right to petition the Government for a redress of grievances, the railroads' lobbying fell into the scope of the First Amendment and thus was granted immunity from antitrust liability. *Pennington* was a similar case. A mine workers' union and some large mining companies tried to induce the Labour State to set minimum wages for employees that would be more difficult for smaller companies to compete in the market. The Supreme Court reiterated again that such lobbying was immune from competition law liability.

[108] See Eastern R. Conference v. Noerr Motors, 365 U.S. 127 (1961).

[109] See City of Columbia v. Omni Outdoor Advertising, 499 U.S. 365 (1991).

[110] OECD. Competition policy and intellectual property rights. https://www.oecd.org/regreform/sectors/2376247.pdf. Accessed 25 March 2025.

As Mark Lemley noted, previously the US lower courts had mainly concentrated on whether 'sham' referred to as claims that were objectively or subjectively baseless.[111]

The US Supreme Court clarified the requirements of bad faith litigation in *Professional Real Estate Investors v Columbia Pictures Industries* (PREI).[112] In this case, the Supreme Court for the first time identified the 'sham' in a case relevant to the enforcement of copyright claims. Columbia filed a copyright infringement suit against PREI while PREI counterclaimed that the lawsuit itself was bad faith litigation and constituted monopolization. The Supreme Court set out a two-fold test to examine the issue of bad faith litigation. Firstly, a bad faith lawsuit 'must be objectively baseless in the sense that no reasonable litigant could realistically expect success on the merits.'[113] Secondly, if the objective requirement was met, the court would further examine the antitrust defendant's subjective motivation to analyse if the 'lawsuit conceals an attempt to interfere directly with the business relationships of a competitor'.[114] The PREI two-fold test is cumulative with both objective and subjective requirements. The PREI test from the US Supreme Court's decision remains a good law today.[115]

The US Supreme Court identified a type of bad faith litigation particularly in the context of patent infringement lawsuits.[116] This was indicated in *Walker Process*.[117] Food Machinery (the patentee) filed a patent infringement lawsuit against Walker Process. Walker Process, however, counterclaimed that (1) Food Machinery's patent was invalid because it committed a fraud on the US Patent and Trademark Office in order to achieve the patent[118]; and (2) Food Machinery's effort to enforce the invalid patent violated Section 2 of the Sherman Act.[119]

The Supreme Court held that there was a violation of article 2, US monopolization law. Justice Harlan clarified the elements of the *Walker Process* claim, saying that:

> the relevant patent is shown to have been procured by knowing and willful fraud practiced by the defendant on the Patent Office or, if the defendant was not the original patent applicant, he had been enforcing the patent with knowledge of the fraudulent manner in which it was

---

[111] Lemley, Mark. 1994. Antitrust counterclaims in patent and copyright infringement cases. *Texas Intellectual Property Law Journal* 3 (1): 1–8, 2.

[112] Professional Real Estate Investors, Inc. v. Columbia Pictures Industries, Inc., 508 U.S. 49 (1993).

[113] Ibid.

[114] Ibid.

[115] For instance, the Supreme Court reiterated in *ICON* that the sham litigation needs 'baseless claims in an attempt to thwart competition'. See Octane Fitness, LLC v. ICON Health & Fitness, Inc., 572 U.S. 545 (2014).

[116] Juckniess, Frederick and Suzanne Larimore Wahl. 2012. Antitrust and intellectual property rights—the ultimate counter weapon? *Michigan Bar Journal* 12: 22–26, 23.

[117] Walker Process Eqpt., Inc. v. Food Machinery Corp., 382 U.S. 172 (1965).

[118] In detail, when Food Machinery applied the underlying patent, it stated to the patent office that it did not know the invention had been in use in the US before the application. Nevertheless, Food Machinery withheld information that itself had been involved in the prior use of the invention before patent application. See Hovenkamp, Herbert. 2020. *Federal antitrust policy: the law of competition and its practice (Sixth edition)*. St. Paul: West Academic Publishing, 425.

[119] Ibid 424.

obtained; and (2) all the elements otherwise necessary to establish a § 2 monopolization charge are proved.

The above case-law reveals the attitudes of antitrust law on bad faith litigation in the US. One may also observe that bad faith litigation may also be scrutinized by the intellectual property law at the same time. This kind of bad faith litigation may occur in the context of the 'patent troll' litigation in the US.

A patent troll is someone who does not use the patent but wants to earn a large amount of money from the patent.[120] As patents can be bought and sold, a patent troll can purchase patents from inventors who are not willing to use patents on their own. Patents trolls can file patent infringement litigation against other companies and gain remedies from a court or force other firms to accept settlements. A research study showed that roughly 63% of patent infringement lawsuits in 2013 were brought by NPEs (non-practising entities) in the US.[121] Hence, the bad faith litigation initiated by a patent troll is a considerable concern in the US.

As many US lawyers suggest, the patent troll problem stems primarily from the weakness of the US patent system, instead of the litigation.[122] An interesting phenomenon is that patent troll problems are less frequent in European and Asian countries.[123] One reason might be because it is possible to gain substantial remedies in patent infringement cases in the US. Compared with the US approach where punitive damages are easily available,[124] civil law traditions believe that the goal of remedies is to 'put the injured party in the position in which it would have been had the act that gave rise to the damage not occurred.'[125] As a patent troll does not produce patented products at all, it would be difficult for a troll to prove actual losses

[120] Paul Gugliuzza. Patent Trolls and Patent Litigation Reform. *Oxford Handbooks Online* https://www.oxfordhandbooks.com/view/10.1093/oxfordhb/9780199935352.001.0001/oxfordhb-9780199935352-e-15. Accessed 25 March 2025. However, some scholars, such Professor Josef Drexl, consider it inaccurate to call such companies 'patent trolls'. Instead, non-practicing entities (NPEs) or patent assertion entities (PAEs) would be better names. See Concurrences. 2015. Standard Setting Organizations and Processes: Challenges and opportunities for competition and innovation. https://www.concurrences.com/en/review/issues/no-3-2015/conferences/standard-setting-organizations-and-processes-challenges-and-opportunities-for. Accessed 25 March 2025.

[121] Fiona M. Scott Morton and Carl Shapiro. 2014. Strategic Patent acquisitions. *Antitrust law journal* 79 (2): 463–499, 467.

[122] See generally Burk, Dan and Lemley Mark. 2009. Fence posts or sign posts? rethinking patent claim construction. *University of Pennsylvania Law Review* 157 (6): 1743–1799.

[123] Sokol, Daniel. 2017. Introduction in *Patent Assertion Entities and Competition Policy*, 1–8. Cambridge: Cambridge University Press, 6. Professor Josef Drexl also argues that patent trolling is a phenomenon more of an immediate concern in the US than the EU. See Concurrences. 2015. Standard setting organizations and processes: Challenges and opportunities for competition and innovation. https://www.concurrences.com/en/review/issues/no-3-2015/conferences/standard-setting-organizations-and-processes-challenges-and-opportunities-for. Accessed 25 Mar 2025.

[124] See generally Zhu Li. 2017. Punitive damages under patent law: Where should we go after halo? *China Patents & Trademarks* 1: 25–35.

[125] 2018. *Guide to damages in international arbitration*, ed. John A. Trenor. Law Business Research Ltd.

before a court in a civil law jurisdiction, let alone to achieve substantial profits from the litigation.

Arguably the patent trolling problem itself has little to do with the abuse of market dominance.[126] From the perspective of competition law, it is rather difficult or even impossible for a patent troll which does not actually use patents to become a competitor of a manufacturer of patented goods.

Despite these facts, a patent troll may file bad faith litigation in order to gain profits. It is meaningful to examine bad faith litigation under the intellectual property law as opposed to such litigation under the antitrust law. Conventionally, the standard of distinguishing bad faith and good faith in the US patent enforcement is focused on the subjective side.[127] The plaintiff is in good faith if she 'sincerely believe[d] in the truth of his statement.'[128] Nevertheless, a very interesting trend is that the US Courts tend to apply the antitrust standard of 'sham exception' in cases of patent enforcement.[129] For instance, the Federal Circuit in *Globetrotter Software v Elan Computer Group*[130] held that the plaintiff must indicate 'that the claims asserted were objectively baseless' in order to determine bad faith litigation. Some lawyers observe that the US courts have applied the two-part test of PREI in not only antitrust cases but also intellectual property infringement cases.[131]

In summary, the US Supreme Court bars the application of antitrust law in the field of petitions to the government through the *Noerr-Pennington* doctrine, even though such petitions may be anti-competitive. The Supreme Court also acknowledges that bad faith litigation is an exception to the *Noerr-Pennington* doctrine and might violate Section 2 of the Sharman Act. In PREI, the Supreme Court clarified that both objective and subjective requirements are necessary to establish a violation of antitrust law. The PREI test has become a key standard to decode bad faith litigation in both antitrust cases and intellectual property infringement cases in the US.

---

126 As patent trolling issues are mainly coming from problems of the US patent system, it is understandable that it was the White House and the Congress, rather than courts, which made their efforts to address these issues. See Hu, Christopher. 2014. Some observations on the patent troll litigation Problem. *Intellectual Property & Technology Law Journal* 26(8): 10.

127 See e.g. Emack v. Kane, 34 F. 46 (1888).

128 Louis Altman and Malla Pollack, *Callmann on Unfair Competition, Trademarks, and Monopolies* (Thomson Reuters, 2008) § 11, 10.

129 Gugliuzza, Paul. 2015. Patent trolls and preemption. *Virginia Law Review* 101(06):1579–1647, 1625 ('The Federal Circuit brought the bad faith rule even closer to the sham litigation test under *Noerr* and its progeny.').

130 Globetrotter Software v. Elan Computer Group, 63 F. Supp. 2d 1127 (N.D. Cal. 1999).

131 Gugliuzza, Paul. 2015. Patent trolls and preemption. *Virginia Law Review* 101(06):1579–1647, 1625.

Case Study: CVD V Raytheon

CVD v Raytheon[132] is a US case on anti-competitive bad faith litigation of trade secrets. It is not a Supreme Court decision, yet antitrust lawyers[133] and competition agencies[134] recognize it as a leading case. This section analyses the *CVD* case for the purpose of examining how US courts would identify bad faith litigation related to trade secrets.

Robert Donadio and Joseph Connolly were former employees of Raytheon (defendant). Raytheon was a company that produced zinc selenide (ZnSe) and zinc sulfide (ZnS) through a process called chemical vapor deposition. During their employment, Donadio and Connolly signed agreements in which they promised to protect Raytheon's secret information, because both of them had access to the manufacture process of ZnSe and ZnS. Donadio and Connolly then left Raytheon and founded a company named CVD. The main business of CVD was also to manufacture ZnSe and ZnS through chemical vapor deposition.

Raytheon believed that CVD could not produce ZnS and ZnSe without using trade secrets of Raytheon. Raytheon threatened to sue if CVD started to produce without a license from Raytheon. However, Donadio and Connolly argued that there were not trade secrets. This was because the product that Raytheon manufactured was primarily made for agreements with the US federal government, and the technology used to produce materials had been published in government reports. In spite of these disputes, CVD and Raytheon signed a license contract in which CVD agreed to pay Raytheon a 15% royalty on earnings for ZnSe and 8% for ZnS. After the signing of the contract, CVD did not pay and sued Raytheon, alleging that the license was invalid as a result of the violation of US antitrust laws. Raytheon counterclaimed that CVD misappropriated its trade secrets.

The Court considered that *Walker Process* was an analogous case that could be used to deal with *CVD*. Bad faith litigation of trade secrets, as bad faith litigation of patents, is likely to constitute a monopolisation under the Sherman Act. In order to identify whether there was a violation of Section 2, the Court examined whether Raytheon had substantial market power in the relevant markets. In this case, the Court defined two markets, which were markets of ZnSe and ZnS.[135] Prior to the establishment of CVD, Raytheon was the exclusive global undertaking manufacturing ZnSe and ZnS for commercial use. Accordingly, the Court held that Raytheon had substantial market power as to both ZnSe and ZnS.

---

132 CVD, Inc. v. Raytheon. Co., 769 F.2d 842, 850 (1st Cir. 1985).

133 See e.g. First, Harry. 2011. Trade Secrets and Antitrust Law in C ed Dreyfuss Rochelle. *The law and theory of trade secrecy:a handbook of contemporary research*, Cheltenham: Edward Elgar Publishing. 363. Juckniess, Frederick and Suzanne Larimore Wahl. 2012. Antitrust and Intellectual Property Rights—the Ultimate Counterweapon? *Michigan Bar Journal* 12: 22–26, 26.

134 For example, the US Antitrust Guidelines for the Licensing of Intellectual Property (2017) issued by DOJ and FTC points out that sham litigation to enforce IPRs may lead to a violation of Sherman Act. It particularly refers to as the *CVD* case regarding trade secrets. See Antitrust Guidelines for the Licensing of Intellectual Property (2017) p. 36.

135 Chapter 4 (4.2.2.1) has discussed the method of market definition in *CVD* case.

Different from *Walker Process*, Raytheon did not actually initiate an infringement lawsuit against CVD but threatened to sue it in order to form a license agreement from CVD. The Court considered that such threat might violate antitrust laws provided that all other requirements were met. It was notable that CVD successfully proved before the court that Raytheon's alleged secret information were already published in government reports. The process information of producing ZnSe and ZnS had entered public domain. Raytheon thus had no trade secrets. The Court considered that through threatening to sue, Raytheon in fact provided three options for the plaintiffs[136]:

> (1) defend a trade secrets infringement suit against Raytheon; (2) refrain from competing with Raytheon in the manufacture of ZnS/cvd and ZnSe/cvd; or (3) take a license from Raytheon for the use of alleged trade secrets.[137]

As the plaintiffs testified, even if they knew that there were no trade secrets in the manufacture process, Raytheon's threat of infringement suits would prevent them from achieving financing for the newly-established CVD company. This may prevent them from entering the market. The Court affirmed this argument and held that the first two choices would be more than detrimental to the existence of CVD. CVD had no choice but to accept the license agreement offered by Raytheon.

The Court held that the dominant firm Raytheon knew it did not possess legally-defined trade secrets, yet it threatened to file lawsuits in bad faith, so as to compel CVD to accept a license contract of the secret information. The Court concluded that Raytheon's threat of litigation was intended to restrict competition and monopolise markets of ZnSe and ZnS.

In conclusion, the US *Noerr-Pennington* doctrine in principle forbids the application of antitrust laws in the field of the petitioning activity, including litigation. However, bad faith litigation is not immune from the Noerr-Pennington and may be scrutinized by antitrust law. The US Supreme Court set out a two-fold test to determine the litigation in bad faith, focusing on both subjective and objective aspects. The CVD case demonstrated that bad faith litigation of trade secrets initiated by a dominant firm may constitute the monopolization under the US Sherman Act.

5.3.2.2 Lessons from the EU

EU competition law also forbids bad faith litigation that may restrain competition. As Professor Lianos noted, European literature often calls it 'vexatious litigation'.[138] While there are noticeable differences between the EU competition law and the US

---

[136] Robert Donadio, Joseph Connolly and the CVD company were plaintiffs in this case.

[137] CVD, Inc. v. Raytheon. Co., 769 F.2d 842, 850 (1st Cir. 1985).

[138] Lianos, Ioannis and Regibeau, Pierre. 2017. 'Sham' litigation. *Antitrust Bulletin* 62(4): 643–689, 643.

antitrust law, both EU and US share 'singularly close' doctrine in terms of bad faith litigation.[139]

ITT Promedia[140] is the sole case in the EU with regard to anti-competitive vexatious litigation. This case demonstrated that it might be an abuse if a dominant company files a lawsuit against its competitors. In this case, Belgacom was a dominant company which supplied voice telephony in Belgium. Promedia was a company which had cooperated with Belgacom for several years. Promedia had been able to have access to the database of Belgacom in order to publish telephone directories. However, the two companies broke up later. Belgacom sued Promedia for misappropriation of its database in the national court. Promedia complained to the European Commission, arguing that Belgacom abused market dominance through filing national lawsuits against it.

The European Commission rejected Promedia's complaints. At the same time, the Commission recognized the issue of likelihood of vexatious litigation being the abuse of market dominance under the EU competition law. The Commission also provided a two-part test to assess whether a dominant company abuses its dominance through vexatious litigation: (1) the conduct cannot reasonably be considered as an attempt to establish the rights of the undertaking concerned and can therefore only serve to harass the opposite party; and (2) the conduct is conceived in the framework of a plan whose goal is to eliminate competition.

Promedia did not challenge the application of the two-part test. It argued that the test set out by the Commission was not properly applied and contested the decision before the General Court (the former Court of First Instance). The General Court affirmed the correctness of the two-part test,[141] holding that '[A]s access to the Court is a fundamental right and a general principle ensuring the rule of law, it is wholly exceptional circumstances that the fact that legal proceedings are brought is capable of constituting an abuse of a dominant position.'[142]

When analyzing the first part of the test, the General Court held that it was not the Court's task to examine whether there existed legal rights when the dominant firm filed a lawsuit, but to determine whether the company reasonably believed that they have legal basis.[143] The General Court found that even though Belgacom brought litigation against Promedia, Belgacom subjectively considered these actions had legal foundations and were not vexatious. The first part of the criteria was not met here. The two-part test is cumulative, so the General Court upheld the Commission's decision,

---

139 A report of WIPO considers sham litigation as a potential type of anti-competitive enforcement of intellectual property rights. After researching on issues of sham litigation in different member states, this report believes that the EU and US share the similar doctrine. See WIPO, 'Study on the Anti-competitive Enforcement of Intellectual Property Rights' CDIP/9/INF/6, 14.

140 Case T-111/96, ITT Promedia NV v Commission of the European Communities EU: T:1998:183.

141 Jones, Alison, Sufrin, BE and Niamh Dunne. 2019. *EU competition law:Text, cases, and materials (7th ed).* Oxford: Oxford University Press, 534.

142 Case T-111/96, ITT Promedia NV v Commission of the European Communities EU: T:1998:183.

143 Jones, Alison, Sufrin, BE and Niamh Dunne. 2019. *EU competition law:Text, cases, and materials (7th ed).* Oxford: Oxford University Press, 535.

considering that it was unnecessary to move to the assessment of the second part of the test.

The two-prong test in *ITT Promedia* contains objective and subjective requirements. From the wording of the test, the first part examines whether a dominant firm believes it possesses legal rights when it wants to assert the right before a court. If the dominant undertaking does not have a right, its assertion would be a harassment to the other party (probably its competitor). The second test identifies the aim of the dominant company to bring a lawsuit. If a firm files a baseless suit only because of its negligence, this lawsuit should be out of the scope of the competition law.

US antitrust law, particularly the *Noerr-Pennington* doctrine (including the 'sham exception' in *PREI*) and *Walker Process*, apparently influenced the formation of the two-part test in the EU *ITT Promedia*.[144] On the one hand, the EU and US both attach great importance to the right of a company to have access to the court. Competition agencies on both sides of the Atlantic take a quite cautious approach to the antitrust intervention of litigation.

On the other hand, under certain circumstances competition authorities need to focus on bad faith litigation conducted by a dominant company. In order to gain a reasonable balance between the right of access to the court and the antitrust intervention, the US and EU courts developed a similar test to examine bad faith litigation.

5.3.2.3 Conclusion

The US Supreme Court developed the *Noerr-Pennington* doctrine, which in principle proscribes petitioning activities (including litigation) from being scrutinized by antitrust laws. However, the Supreme Court provides a 'sham exception' to the *Noerr-Pennington* doctrine, indicating that bad faith litigation might not gain immunity from antitrust laws. The two-fold test in *PREI* examines the circumstances in which a lawsuit may establish anti-competitive bad faith litigation.

When it came to bad faith litigation of trade secrets, the US court in *CVD* ruled that a threat of filing an infringement lawsuit of trade secrets may constitute a violation of Section 2 of Sherman Act. By quoting *Walker Process*, the Court there made it clear that if a dominant company knew there were not legally-defined trade secrets and sued (or threatened to sue) the potential rival for the misappropriation of secret information, the dominant firm may be liable for the abuse of dominance.

The EU case-law closely follows the US approach on bad faith ('vexatious') litigation. The European Commission proposes a two-part test in *ITT Promedia*, which is similar to the US PREI test. The General Court affirms these criteria, meanwhile requiring that the test should be applied 'strictly'.[145]

---

[144] See e.g. Maggiolino, Mariateresa. 2012. *Intellectual property and antitrust—A comparative economic analysis of US and EU law*. Cheltenham: Edward Elgar Publishing, 198.

[145] Case T-111/96, ITT Promedia NV v Commission of the European Communities EU: T:1998:183.

5.3.3 *Suggestions for Improving Anti-monopoly Enforcement of Bad Faith Litigation of Trade Secrets in China*

Comparative lessons have demonstrated that bad faith litigation of trade secrets might be the abuse of market dominance. As discussed in Chap. 3, article 17 of China's AML lists several practices that may be regarded as the abuse of market dominance. Bad faith litigation is not specifically included in this list, yet the catch-all provision of article 17 authorizes the competition agency or courts to identify new kinds of abusive practices other than the list. There have been no competition cases about bad faith litigation of trade secrets in China to date.

Despite this, the Chinese court held that bad faith litigation of intellectual property rights may establish an abuse of dominance in a landmark competition case relevant to patents in *Huawei v InterDigital*.[146] This part will firstly analyse how the Chinese court examined sham litigation in *Huawei*. Subsequently, through learning from the US and EU experience, this book provides several suggestions on the assessment of bad faith litigation under China's AML, particularly when it is relevant to trade secrets.

5.3.3.1 Huawei V InterDigital[147]

China is not a case law jurisdiction, yet cases play an important role in China's anti-monopoly analysis. Since the AML has been effective for only 13 years in China, there are not many competition cases compared with the other large antitrust jurisdictions (the US and EU). Existing cases in China, especially those adjudicated or recognized by the SPC (or the central competition agency SAMR), may reflect China's current approach to dealing with certain anti-monopoly issues.

It is undisputed that *Huawei v InterDigital* was a landmark anti-monopoly case in China. This is 'the first antimonopoly civil case in China that was decided entirely in favour of the plaintiff, and also the first monopoly case arising out of SEP licensing.'[148] The SPC recognized the Huawei case as 'one of the top ten cases in Chinese courts in 2013',[149] and one of the two most important anti-monopoly cases (with *Qihoo v Tencent*) adjudicated by Chinese courts during the first 10 years

[146] Commentators argue that Huawei v InterDigital was a leading case in China that stood at the crossroads of antitrust and intellectual property. See Han, Michael and Li Kexin. 2013. Huawei v InterDigital: China at the crossroads of antitrust and intellectual property, competition and innovation. Competition Policy International Asia Column.

[147] 华为公司与交互数字公司滥用市场支配地位案 [Huawei v InterDigital—Abuse of Market Dominance case], 广东省高级人民法院 [Guangdong High People's Court], (2013) 粤高法民三终字第306号 [Economic Appeal No. 306], 21 October 2013.

[148] Wang Xianlin. 2017. Recent developments in China's antimonopoly regulations on Abuse of intellectual property rights. *Antitrust Bulletin* 62 (4): 806–814, 808.

[149] Ibid.

of the implementation of the AML.[150] Also noteworthy is the fact that Huawei was the first and the only case in China where bad faith litigation of intellectual property was found to constitute the abuse of market dominance. Accordingly, this section provides a case study of *Huawei.*

Huawei is a Chinese producer of wireless telecom equipment. InterDigital is a US company which holds a number of standard essential patents (SEPs)[151] of 3G in the domain of wireless telecom technology. SEPs are indispensable for manufacturers to manufacture similar technology, so companies like Huawei have no alternative but to make use of these SEPs. The Court identified InterDigital as a dominant firm in the market for licensing each SEP it holds.

Huawei had negotiated with InterDigital on the license for SEPs from 2008. Huawei argued that the royalty fees offered by InterDigital were much higher than those InterDigital had offered to other undertakings, such as Apple and Samsung. Since InterDigital had promised to license its SEPs on a FRAND term, Huawei sued InterDigital before a Chinese court. Huawei argued that InterDigital abused its market dominance to impose unreasonable license terms.

It is worth noting that during the negotiations between these two companies, InterDigital sued Huawei for patent infringement before a court in Delaware, and requested an injunction to prohibit Huawei from manufacturing, using, selling and importing products that encompassed InterDigital's patents. In front of the Chinese court, Huawei claimed that the lawsuit initiated by InterDigital constituted the abuse of market dominance. In this case, InterDigital had SEPs for the 3G technology. As SEPs were indispensable for manufactures to produce the relevant technology, InterDigital had 100% market share in the relevant market. The Chinese court thus considered that InterDigital was a dominant company.

The Court held that InterDigital's litigation against Huawei in the US was not intended to protect its patents, but merely a sham. As these two companies were still in the process of negotiation on license terms, the Court held that InterDigital's assertion of patent rights in the US was aimed at forcing Huawei to accept its unreasonable license terms. Huawei had been negotiating with InterDigital on license terms in good faith before the conflict. As InterDigital had committed to offering FRAND terms to willing licensees, it could not stop Huawei negotiating in good faith to use its SEPs through filing bad faith infringement litigation.

Noteworthy is the fact that *Huawei* was a special case relevant to SEPs. SEP holders, such as InterDigital, have promised to license their patents to all willing licensees on FRAND terms in order for the incorporation of the patents into industry

[150] Supreme People's Court. A forum was held in memory of the enforcement of the anti-monopoly law for 10 years by the Supreme People's Court. https://www.court.gov.cn/fabu-xiangqing-130481.html. Accessed 25 March 2025.

[151] As WIPO states, patents which are essential parts of technical standards are SEPs. SEPs are ubiquitous in technical standards, ranging from mobile phones to memory devices. Standard setting organisation often requires SEP holders to commit to licensing their SEPs on fair, reasonable and non-discriminatory (FRAND) terms. See Hines, Doris Johnson and Yang Ming-Tao. 2019. Worldwide activities on licensing issues relating to standard essential patents. *WIPO*. https://www.wipo.int/wipo_magazine/en/2019/01/article_0003.html. Accessed 25 March 2025.

standards. If a SEP holder is allowed to file infringement lawsuits against potential licensees which are expected to achieve the license in good faith, these lawsuits may compel potential licensees to accept unreasonable terms. As the FRAND commitments requires InterDigital to license SEPs on fair and reasonable conditions, it is arguable that InterDigital's practice may not be compatible with the FRAND commitments.[152] As stated by the European Commission,[153] there may be two aspects of anti-competitive effects arising from bad faith SEP litigation: (1) it may exclude potential competing companies from the market; and (2) it may induce potential licensees to accept disadvantageous licensing terms, compared to those which potential licensees may have accepted under FRAND conditions.[154]

In summary, the landmark *Huawei* case identified that bad faith litigation of intellectual property rights by a dominant undertaking may constitute the abuse of market dominance in China. However, the court merely dealt with the case under SEP-related circumstances. The court neither dealt with the relationship between the right of access to justice and the antitrust intervention on bad faith litigation, nor developed a test to analyse what may constitute an anti-competitive bad faith litigation.

5.3.3.2 Suggestions for Identifying Bad Litigation of Trade Secrets in China

China has witnessed a rapid increase in the number of infringement cases of trade secrets over the past few years.[155] While so far no cases have been reported in China where a dominant firm abuses dominance and makes use of infringement litigation of trade secrets to harm competitors, this is likely to occur in the future. At the same time, Chinese lawmakers have realized that bad faith litigation of intellectual property rights is illegal. For example, the latest Chinese Trademark Law (2019) provides a new article that prohibits bad faith litigation of trademark.[156] This article is rather general and fails to examine what may constitute bad faith litigation.

---

[152] Ibid.

[153] In 2011, Samsung applied for injunctions before some courts of member states in the EU against competing mobile device makers (e.g. Apple), arguing that they infringed Samsung's patents which were incorporated into technology standards. The EU Commission opened an investigation on Samsung for the abuse of market dominance under Article 102 TFEU. See Antitrust: commission opens proceedings against aamsung. *European Commission.* https://ec.europa.eu/commission/presscorner/detail/en/IP_12_89. Accessed 25 March 2025.

[154] EU Commission, Case At. 39939, para. 62. See https://ec.europa.eu/competition/antitrust/cases/dec_docs/39939/39939_1501_5.pdf. Accessed 25 March 2025.

[155] A latest report shows that there were 499 infringement cases of trade secrets adjudicated by Chinese courts in 2015. However, the number of cases surged to 1348 in 2019. See Data analysis of trade secret Cases in China (2015–2019). *Hefei IP lawyer.*https://hfiplaw.cn/details/20610.html. Accessed 25 March 2025.

[156] Article 68 of the Chinese Trademark Law (2019 amendment) says that '[W]hoever maliciously applies for trademark registration shall be subject to subject to a warning, a fine or any other administrative punishments, as the case may be; and whoever maliciously lodges a trademark lawsuit shall be penalized by the People's Court according to law.'

Comparative experience from the US and EU indicates that competition agencies and courts need to keep a reasonable balance between the right of access to justice and antitrust interference. Chinese lawyers also regard the right of access to the court as a fundamental right of individuals.[157] In terms of the relationship between competition law and trade secrets, China is now under great pressure to ensure that the AML enforcement is fair and transparent with respect to intellectual property.[158] Undue antitrust intervention in lawsuits may chill the incentives of trade secret holders to protect their secret information, and this may harm innovation. As a consequence, it is critical for China to develop a clear test to analyse what kind of litigation of trade secrets may constitute abuse of market dominance under the AML. The following parts propose some specific suggestions:

1. Generally, in accordance with the comparative lessons from both sides of the Atlantic, this book proposes a two-fold test for Chinese competition authorities and courts. In cases where a dominant company brings an infringement suit about trade secrets against its competitors, the competition agency or court should consider that it is bad faith litigation only if the lawsuit is objectively baseless. That is, a reasonable secret holder would not expect to prevail in such an infringement case, such that the litigation can only act as a harassment to other rivals.

   As the ECJ ruled in *ITT Promedia*, sometimes it is more important to determine whether the dominant firm reasonably considers that the lawsuit is baseless, rather than to determine whether a legal right exists.[159] This is critical when it comes to trade secrets. For example, as examined in Chap. 2, it is essential for one to take reasonable precautions to keep information secret. Otherwise the information in question cannot be protected by trade secret law.[160] Nevertheless, it is often difficult for a court to determine what is a 'reasonable' step to protect the information. This requirement of 'reasonable precautions' hence becomes 'the most challenging of all requirements'.[161] Supposing a dominant company (X) requires its employees to keep the firm's information secret merely through

[157] 张卫平 [Zhang Weiping]. 2016. 民事诉讼法 [Civil Procedure Law]. 北京: 法律出版社 [Beijing: Law Press], 45.

[158] See 2021 Special 301 Report. *Office of the US Trade Representative* https://ustr.gov/sites/default/files/files/reports/2021/2021%20Special%20301%20Report%20(final).pdf48. Accessed 25 March 2025. The Special 301 Report is enacted by the US government annually to reflect whether other jurisdictions provide sufficient intellectual property protection.

[159] Case T-111/96, ITT Promedia NV v Commission of the European Communities EU: T:1998:183, para 73. ('Furthermore, when applying that criterion, it is not a question of determining whether the rights which the undertaking concerned was asserting when it brought its action actually existed or whether that action was well founded, but rather of determining whether such an action was intended to assert what that undertaking could, at that moment, reasonably consider to be its rights.').

[160] For the assessment of the requirement of reasonable secrecy measures, see Bone, Robert. 2010. Trade secrecy, innovation, and the requirement of reasonable secrecy precautions. In *The law and theory of trade secrecy: a handbook of contemporary research,* eds. Rochelle Dreyfuss and Katherine Strandburg T, 1–35. Cheltenham: Edward Elgar Press.

[161] Nuno Sousa e Silva. 2014. What exactly is a trade secret under the proposed directive? *Journal of Intellectual Property Law & Practice* 9 (11): 923–932, 931.

word-of-mouth, the company may consider this as a 'reasonable' step. In cases where X's employees are hired by its competitor (Y), X might sue Y for misappropriation of secret information. However, the court may consider that X has not taken reasonable measures to protect information. Therefore, no trade secrets exist. Because X believes that there is a legal basis at the moment of filing the lawsuit, the infringement suit brought by X should not be regarded as bad faith litigation under the competition law.

2. In addition to the objective requirement, the competition agency and court need to examine whether the dominant undertaking has an intention to restrict competition through bad faith litigation. Anti-competitive intention may be inferred from the conduct of the dominant company. For instance, notwithstanding the *PREI* case has shown that a single lawsuit could be in bad faith and therefore constitute monopolisation, commentators argue that repetitive bad faith lawsuits brought by a dominant firm may reflect that the company has a 'plan' and intention to eliminate competition.[162]
3. In particular, there are two scenarios of bad faith litigation as to trade secrets that deserve assessment. The *CVD* case defines the first landscape where there does not exist a legally-defined trade secret. As discussed earlier,[163] a trade secret is construed as information with secrecy, commercial value, and the information holder should take reasonable measures to protect it. In *CVD*, as Raytheon's alleged that secret information in fact entered the public domain, the US court ruled that Raytheon did not possess information that deserved protection. There was no probable cause in Raytheon's threat of infringement lawsuits against CVD.

The above example in relation to trade secrets tells a different story from *Walker Process* which concerned patents. A patent is a registered right. This means that a company needs to submit its patent application to a national (or regional) patent office for the grant.[164] Food Machinery in *Walker Process* committed a fraud before the Patent Office to obtain a patent. Therefore, the following patent litigation it initiated was found to be baseless and a sham since the 'patent' should not have been granted at first.

A trade secret is not a form of registered intellectual property in China. The Walker Process scenario, where the patent office was deceived into granting a patent, is unlikely to happen in cases of trade secrets. Nonetheless, the *CVD* case indicates that bad faith litigation may occur when the plaintiff knows that there is not a legal trade secret due to lack of the requirements of a trade secret, and files an infringement suit against competitors. Similarly, the Chinese authorities may take the *CVD* scenario into account where the plaintiff does not have legally-defined trade secrets but alleges misappropriation. For example, Chinese law allows an individual to reverse engineer

---

162 Vezzoso, Simonetta. 2012. Towards an EU doctrine of anticompetitive IP-related litigation. *Journal of European Competition Law & Practice* 3 (6): 521–530.

163 See Chap. 2 of this book.

164 See Frequently asked questions: patents. *WIPO*. https://www.wipo.int/patents/en/faq_patents.html. Accessed 25 March 2025.

a product to acquire another's secret information.[165] If a dominant firm sues its rival for misappropriation of secret information, realizing that the defendant obtains the information via reverse-engineering, such a lawsuit might be baseless and in bad faith.

Another scenario may occur when a trade secret is related to a de facto standard. *Huawei v InterDigital* provides an overview of bad faith litigation with respect to SEPs. The ECJ describes the characteristics of SEP-related cases from two aspects: (1) the patent in question is so indispensable to a standard that all manufacturers must use it for products that should comply with the standard and (2) since SEP holders have made a FRAND commitment, implementers have legitimate expectations to gain the license of SEPs through FRAND terms.[166] As a result of these characteristics, SEP holders' conduct which is incompatible with the FRAND commitment, such as filing bad faith litigation to obtain unreasonable terms, might constitute an abuse under the competition law.

Usually a trade secret cannot be included in a formal standard published by a standardization organization,[167] yet it can act as a de facto standard which can confer market power.[168] Accordingly, there might be a circumstance regarding trade secrets which are similar to *Huawei v InterDigital*. For instance, in the EU *Microsoft* case, as Microsoft's refusal to disclose secret interface information constituted the abuse of market dominance, the European Commission ordered Microsoft to supply the secret information to 'any undertaking that has an interest in developing products that constitute a competitive constraint to Microsoft in the work group server operating system market.'[169] Like FRAND terms promised by SEP holders, the Commission required Microsoft to deal with other competitors on 'reasonable and non-discriminatory'[170] conditions.[171]

It can be inferred that in these circumstances, if Microsoft had filed a lawsuit against its rivals so as to extract unreasonable royalties for the disclosure of secret information, this may constitute bad faith litigation because it violates the Commission's decision on 'reasonable and non-discriminatory' conditions of license. It is hence likely that Chinese competition agencies and courts would identify anti-competitive bad faith litigation if (1) the dominant firm has an antitrust duty to disclose trade secrets; (2) the dominant firm has a FRAND duty imposed by the

165 See Chap. 2 of this book.

166 See Case C-170/13, Huawei Technologies Co. Ltd v ZTE Corp. and ZTE Deutschland GmbH., EU:C:2015:477, paras 49 and 53.

167 See Chap. 4.3.2. A formal standard should be public. Thanks to the secrecy requirement of a trade secret, it cannot be incorporated into a formal standard.

168 Section 2 of this chapter examines how secret information can lead to a de facto standard in the EU *Microsoft* case.

169 Commission Decision of 24 May 2004 relating to a proceeding pursuant to Article 82 of the EC Treaty and Article 54 of the EEA Agreement against Microsoft Corporation (Case COMP/C-3/37.792—Microsoft), para 30.

170 Ibid para 31.

171 Ibid. Under the Commission's requirement, the remuneration that Microsoft would take should not 'reflect the strategic value stemming from Microsoft's market power' in the relevant market.

Chinese competition authority; and (3) the dominant firm initiates legal proceedings for unreasonable trading terms.

5.3.4 Conclusion

As the two largest antitrust jurisdictions, the US and the EU both demonstrate that bad faith litigation of intellectual property, including trade secrets, may constitute the abuse of market dominance. As discussed earlier, China's AML enforcement, to a large extent, has been influenced by these two jurisdictions. This book thus analyses experience from the US and the EU as comparative lessons for China's anti-monopoly enforcement.

The US Supreme Court developed the *Noerr-Pennington* doctrine which in principle prevents the application of antitrust law in the field of petitioning activities, including legal proceedings. There is an exception to the *Noerr-Pennington* doctrine where bad faith litigation might constitute monopolization under the US antitrust law. The *PREI* and *Walker Process* cases further define the landscape of bad faith litigation. Bad faith in this context requires the court to examine whether the lawsuit brought by the dominant firm is objectively without probable cause and whether the dominant company subjectively intends to harm competition. *CVD* is a landmark case in the US where the court identified bad faith litigation of trade secrets as a type of abuse.

The EU competition agency and court also hold that vexatious litigation may constitute the abuse of market dominance under Article 102 TFEU. The two-prong test developed in *ITT Promedia* is similar to the US approach, which requires both objective and subjective conditions.

Chinese competition authorities and courts have less experience in assessing anti-competitive bad faith litigation. In *Huawei v InterDigital*, the Chinese court for the first time ruled that bad faith litigation relevant to SEPs may violate the AML. Nevertheless, the court failed to deal with the relationship between the right of access to the court and antitrust intervention, and did not provide a specific test.

In this respect, this book provides Chinese competition agencies and courts with several suggestions on the assessment of bad faith litigation with regard to trade secrets. As a premise of analyzing the abuse of market dominance, the company at issue should possess substantial market power in the relevant market. The book proposes that China should learn from comparative experience to examine bad faith litigation from both objective and subjective aspects. In China, bad faith litigation of trade secrets may occur mainly in two circumstances. In one case like *CVD*, a dominant firm may file lawsuits against competitors for misappropriation of trade secrets, although there was not a legally-defined trade secret. In another, when the trade secret becomes a de facto standard, a dominant undertaking may initiate bad faith lawsuits just as InterDigital did in the *Huawei* case regarding SEPs.

Bad faith litigation is the second abusive practice that a dominant firm may conduct examined in this Chapter. The next section is going to look at a third abusive practice in relation to trade secrets, which is the non-challenge clause of trade secrets.

5.4 Non-challenge Clauses of Trade Secrets

5.4.1 Introduction

As previously stated, the exploitation of intellectual property rights may lead to concerns about the competitive impact. It is generally acknowledged that these concerns may occur particularly in the context of licensing practices for intellectual property rights. For example, the TRIPS[172] is intended to provide a universal standard for the protection of intellectual property. The TRIPS recognizes that licensing practices related to intellectual property rights may have anti-competitive effects and thus have negative influences on trade and the transfer of technology.[173] Article 40.2 of the TRIPS lists the non-challenge clause in a license as an example of conduct that may have anti-competitive effect arising from intellectual property rights.

Non-challenge clauses are contractual clauses imposed by the licensor that require the licensee not to challenge the validity of the licensed intellectual property. Such clauses usually occur in patent licenses.[174] However there might be non-challenge clauses in the licensing terms of other kinds of intellectual property, such as trade secrets. As the abuse of market dominance pertaining to trade secrets is the main topic of this book, this section will use existing patent cases to analyse cases in the field of trade secrets.

Abundant comparative experience from the US and the EU has demonstrated that competition law should apply under certain circumstances to the licensing practices involving non-challenge clauses. In contrast, China has less mature regulations and competition cases about non-challenge clauses of intellectual property rights. This section thus firstly analyses comparative experience from the US and the EU (see Sect. 5.4.2). It then examines the current anti-monopoly practices in China, focusing on several regulations or guidelines of the Chinese competition agency and on the famous Qualcomm case (see Sect. 5.4.3). Through identifying some problems with the anti-monopoly practices in China and learning from comparative experience, Sect. 5.4.4 provides some suggestions on improvements for anti-monopoly

---

172 The TRIPS agreement is under the WTO framework. It is believed to introduce intellectual property rules into the multilateral trading system for the first time. See Intellectual property: Protection and enforcement. *WTO*. https://www.wto.org/english/thewto_e/whatis_e/tif_e/agrm7_e.htm. Accessed 25 March 2025. As most countries all over the world are members of the WTO, the TRIPS agreement has substantial implications on many jurisdictions worldwide.

173 See Article 40.1 of the TRIPS agreement.

174 The following parts will analyse some patent cases that include non-challenge clauses.

enforcement in China, particularly related to trade secrets. The last part presents the conclusion.

5.4.2 *Comparative Lessons from the Assessment of Non-challenge Clauses*

As discussed earlier, US antitrust law and the EU competition law encompass quite a few differences on specific issues. Notwithstanding this, commentators have argued that the two dominant antitrust jurisdictions share more similarities than divergences when it comes to the regulation of non-challenge clauses.[175] This part will introduce how the US and EU prohibit anti-competitive non-challenge clauses in order to provide some experience for Chinese competition enforcement.

5.4.2.1 The US Approach

The US courts, for a long time, used the doctrine of estoppel when ruling on the issue of non-challenge clauses. This doctrine was largely based on *Kinsman v Parkhurst*,[176] a US Supreme Court case. The doctrine stated that wherever a license of intellectual property exists, the licensee should be regarded as having recognized the validity of the underlying intellectual property (e.g. a patent). Therefore, the licensee was prohibited from challenging the validity of intellectual property thanks to the doctrine of estoppel.

The estoppel doctrine prevailed in the US until *Lear v Adkins*,[177] a leading case of the US Supreme Court.[178] There, the Supreme Court there examined two conflicting policies: the equitable consideration of estoppel and the public policy of eliminating invalid intellectual property (in Lear, patents). The Supreme Court finally decided that the latter should prevail by holding that:

> Surely the equities of the licensor do not weigh very heavily when they are balanced against the important interest in permitting full and free competition in the use ideas which are in

[175] See Lawrance, Sophie. 2014. The competition law treatment of no-challenge clauses in licence agreements: An unfortunate revolution. *Journal of intellectual property law & practice* 9 (10): 802–811, 804. Lawrance opined that there is relevance between the US *Lear* case and the EU *Windsurfing* case. These cases are discussed in the following parts.

[176] Kinsman v. Parkhurst, 59 U.S. 289 (1855).

[177] Lear, Inc. v. Adkins, 395 U.S. 653 (1969). Typically, the *Lear* case was not an antitrust case. However, antitrust academia often referred to this case because the US Supreme Court ruled on the legality of non-challenge clauses which can also be learned in the sense of antitrust.

[178] It should be noted that there was not an absolute non-challenge clause in *Lear*. Nevertheless, as some commentators argued, there existed some contractual clauses that were equivalent to non-challenge clauses, which 'required the licensee to continue paying royalties during the pendency of the patent challenge.' See Miller, Alan and Michal Gal. 2015. Licensee patent challenges. *Yale journal on regulation* 32 (1): 121–160, 131.

> reality a part of the public domain. Licensees may often be the only individuals with enough economic incentive to challenge the patentability of an inventor's discovery.[179]

The Supreme Court held that the need to clear invalid patents overrides other equitable considerations in contract law. While *Lear* was not a technical antitrust case, the Supreme Court was concerned that muzzling licensees may lead to the public continually being 'required to pay tribute to a would-be monopolist without need or justification'.[180] The public interest in eliminating invalid patents and promoting competition won out in the *Lear* case.

The US Supreme Court stated that one important reason that non-challenge clauses are improper is that '[L[icensees may often be the only individuals with enough economic incentive to challenge the patentability of an inventor's discovery.' This argument makes sense. A patent holder is usually entitled to sue anyone who infringes the patent. A patent license enables the licensee to use the patent in issue without taking the risk of infringing the licensor's right. Meanwhile, the licensee has to exploit the technology in compliance with the contractual terms and pay royalties for the use of the patent. If the patent is proven to be invalid, the licensee may take advantage of relevant technology freely without any royalties.[181] This explains why a licensee is in a good position to challenge the validity of the intellectual property. In order to avoid the economic motivation of a licensee to challenge the validity of a patent, the patentee often includes non-challenge clauses in the license. In that case, the licensees may be accountable for liquidated damages if they launch patent challenges against the licensor.

Several US cases follow the *Lear* doctrine regarding non-challenge clauses.[182] For instance, in *Bendix Corp v Balax Inc*,[183] the license contract prevented the licensee from challenging the validity of the patent in question even after the termination of the license. The Seventh Circuit held that this clause created 'a danger of unwarranted monopolization,'[184] particularly because the clause extended the non-challenge obligation beyond the duration of the license.[185]

Lear and its progeny, although concerning non-challenge clauses, are not antitrust cases.[186] However, the US Supreme Court referred to as *Lear* in *Actavis*,[187] which was an antitrust reverse payment (also known as 'pay-for-delay') case.

---

[179] Lear, Inc. v. Adkins, 395 U.S. 653 (1969).

[180] Ibid.

[181] Alison, Jones, BE, Sufrin and Dunne Niamh. 2019. *EU competition law:Text, cases, and Materials*(7th ed). Oxford: Oxford University Press, 820.

[182] See Chadd Taylor, Christian. 1993. No-challenge termination clauses: incorporating innovation policy and risk allocation into patent licensing law. *Indiana law journal* 69(01): 215–253, 241.

[183] Bendix Corporation v. Balax, Inc., 471 F.2d 809 (7th Cir. 1970).

[184] Ibid.

[185] Cheng Thomas. 2016. Antitrust treatment of the no challenge clause. *Journal of intellectual property and entertainment law* 5 (2):437–512, 453.

[186] In other words, the plaintiffs in these cases filed lawsuits because they believe that non-challenge clauses should be illegal, without alleging that the defendants violated antitrust laws.

[187] FTC v. Actavis, Inc., 570 U.S. 136 (2013).

Commentators believe that there are similarities between reverse payments and non-challenge clause cases.[188] *Actavis* concerned disputes between Solvay which manufactured brand-name drugs, and Actavis which manufactured generic drugs. Under the US Hatch–Waxman Act, if generic drug manufacturers intend to enter the market prior to the expiration date of the patent of brand-name drugs, they can challenge the validity of the patent (the so-called 'Paragraph IV Challenges'[189]). Actavis launched Paragraph IV Challenges against Solvay, while Solvay in turn counterclaimed that Actavis infringed its patent. These two companies finally achieved a settlement in which Solvay agreed to pay a large sum of money in exchange for Actavis's not entering the market. Such an agreement is called a reverse payment deal or a pay-for-delay agreement in that 'it is the patent holder—who brought the infringement suit—that pays a substantial sum to settle it.'[190]

Antitrust scholars have noted the potential anti-competitive effects of a reverse payment deal.[191] This is roughly because a reverse payment agreement, especially that proposed by a dominant drug manufacturer, may deter new entry to the market and thus harm competition and consumer welfare.[192]

In *Actavis*, the Eleventh Circuit held that a reverse payment settlement was 'immune from antitrust attack so long as its anticompetitive effects fall within the scope of the exclusionary potential of the patent.'[193] Nonetheless, the majority of the Supreme Court found that the reverse payment agreement needed antitrust scrutiny. As far as the Supreme Court stated, the reverse payment settlement would violate antitrust laws by substantially hampering competition through lowering the risk of patent invalidation.[194]

Although there was no clear non-challenge clause in *Actavis*, as some lawyers suggest, the majority indicated that any motivation to restrain challenges of the patent validity were anti-competitive.[195] Similarly, a non-challenge clause of intellectual property may prevent the licensee from challenging the validity of the intellectual property. Therefore, reverse payment cases and non-challenge clause cases share

---

[188] Gal, Michal and Alan Miller. 2017. Patent challenge clauses: a new antitrust offense? *Iowa law review* 102 (4): 1477–1532 ('[T]his new antitrust offense is a natural extension of the logic of the Supreme Court's landmark case of Federal Trade Commission v Actavis, Inc.').

[189] See generally Paragraph IV challenges: exploring 2017 trends, developments and updates. *MINTZ*. https://www.mintz.com/insights-center/events/2017/paragraph-iv-challenges-exploring-2017-trends-developments-and-updates. Accessed 25 March 2025.

[190] Gal, Michal, and Alan Miller. 2017. Patent challenge clauses: a new antitrust offense? *Iowa law review* 102 (4):1477–1532, 1492.

[191] See e.g. Hovenkamp, Hebert, Janis, Mark, and Mark Lemley. 2003. Anticompetitive settlement of intellectual property disputes. *Minnesota law review* 87 (6):1719–1775.

[192] Fialkoff, Michael. 2014. Pay-for-delay settlements in the wake of actavis. *Michigan telecomm. & technology law review* 20: 523–546, 524.

[193] FTC v. Watson Pharmaceuticals, Inc., et al., No. 10-12729 (11th Cir. 2012). Watson changed its name to Actavis when the case was dealt with by the Supreme Court.

[194] Gal, Michal, and Alan Miller, 'Patent Challenge Clauses: A New Antitrust Offense?' (2017) 102 (4) *Iowa Law Review* 1477–1532, 1493.

[195] Crane, Daniel. 2014. Actavis, the reverse payment fallacy, and the continuing need for regulatory solution. *Minnesota Journal of Law, Science & Technology* 15 (1): 51–59, 53.

similarities in the same antitrust doctrine. This is why the US Supreme Court cited *Lear* in *Actavis*.

In summary, the US Supreme Court held that the non-challenge clause might contravene the public interest of clearing an invalid patent in *Lear*. The Supreme Court also recognized the potential anti-competitive effects of a reverse payment deal, which shows the motivation to restrict challenges of patent validity in *Actavis*. These cases reflected US antitrust concerns of the non-challenge clause of intellectual property.

5.4.2.2 The EU Approach

The ECJ encountered the competition issue of non-challenge clauses in a landmark case *Windsurfing*.[196] The patentee in the case imposed a non-challenge obligation on its licensees. The European Commission claimed before the Court that:

> [E]ven where a licensee is only able to challenge a patent because of the information which has become available to him as a result of his privileged relationship with the licensor, the public interest in ensuring an essentially free system of competition and therefore in the removal of a monopoly perhaps wrongly granted to licensor must prevail over any other consideration.[197]

The ECJ affirmed the Commission's arguments. The ECJ, as well as the European Commission apparently placed more value more on the needs of clearing invalid patents for the sake of free competition. It has been suggested that the policy was influenced by US case law, especially the *Lear* case.[198]

The ECJ developed its analysis of non-challenge clauses of intellectual property in another case *Bayer*.[199] The Court there proposed two scenarios where non-challenge clauses might be deemed legal: (1) 'when the licence granted is a free licence inasmuch as, in those circumstances, the licensee does not suffer from the competitive disadvantage involved in the payment of royalties'[200]; and (2) 'when the licence relates to a technically outdated process which the licensee undertaking did not use.'[201]

Aside from these two cases, it is worth noting that non-challenge clauses often occur in SEP-related cases in the EU. As discussed in previous sections, patents can

---

[196] Windsurfing International Inc. v Commission of the European Communities, Case 193/83, EU:C:1986:75.

[197] Ibid.

[198] See e.g. Lawrance, Sophie. 2014. The competition law treatment of no-challenge clauses in licence agreements: An unfortunate revolution? *Journal of intellectual property law & practice* 9 (10): 802–811, 804. Gal, Michal and Miller, Alan. 2017. Patent challenge clause: a new antitrust offense. *Iowa law review.*102 (4):1477–1532, 1488–1489.

[199] Bayer AG and Maschinenfabrik Hennecke GmbH v Heinz Süllhöfer, Case 65/86, EU:C:1988:448.

[200] Ibid.

[201] Ibid.

be incorporated into standards if the patents are essential for implementers to conduct the technology. In *Huawei v ZTE*,[202] the ECJ considered whether the licensee had the right to challenge the validity of SEPs even though there was a non-challenge clause in the license. As the Court pointed out, standard-setting organizations (SSOs) usually do not review whether the SEPs are valid or not.[203] The ECJ held:

> [A]n alleged infringer cannot be criticized either for challenging, in parallel to the negotiations relating to the grant of licences, the validity of those patents and/or the essential nature of those patents to the standard in which they are included and/or their actual use, or for reserving the right to do so in the future.[204]

It has been suggested that non-challenge clauses of SEPs may result in more serious competitive problems than those of non-SEPs.[205] If a patent is incorporated into the technology standard, it means that all manufacturers must make use of the patent at issue to produce goods complying with the standard. In other words, all consumers of the technology need to pay for the value of the SEP. In cases where the SEPs are invalid, consumers should not pay for invalid SEPs.[206] The European Commission noted this problem in a recent SEP-related case, explaining that:

> Implementer of standards and ultimately consumers should not have to pay for invalid or non-infringed patents. Implementers should therefore be able to ascertain the validity of patents and contest alleged infringements.[207]

The practice of non-challenge clauses might constitute violations of both Article 101 (which prohibits anti-competitive agreements) and Article 102 (which prevents the abuse of market dominance) violations under the EU competition law. Article 102 (a) of the TFEU prohibits a dominant firm from directly or indirectly imposing unfair trading conditions on other companies. Non-challenge clauses thus are likely to constitute a part of unfair trading terms imposed by a dominant firm.

The ECJ ruled in *Ahmed Saeed*[208] that an agreement which seems to be the mutual will of both parties might be actually established by the dominant company. The underlying agreement may simply constitute 'the formal measure setting the

---

[202] Huawei Technologies Co. Ltd v ZTE Corp. and ZTE Deutschland GmbH, Case C-170/13, EU:C:2015:477.

[203] In practice, it is not the duty for SSOs to examine the validity of SEPs. National patent offices are responsible for the validity of patents.

[204] Ibid.

[205] Cheng Thomas. 2016. Antitrust treatment of the no challenge clause. *Journal of intellectual property and entertainment Law* 5 (2): 437–512, 462.

[206] Some lawyers claimed that SEP enforcement, the patent of which might be invalid, can threaten the successful operation of implementers, affecting price, innovation and choice in the downstream market. See Jones, Alison. 2014. Standard-essential patents: FRAND commitments, injunctions and the smartphone wars. *European competition journal* 10 (1):1–36, 5.

[207] Antitrust: commission finds that Motorola mobility infringed EU competition rules by misusing standard essential patents. *European commission.* https://ec.europa.eu/commission/presscorner/detail/en/IP_14_489. Accessed 25 March 2025.

[208] Case 66/86, Ahmed Saeed Flugreisen and Silver Line Reisebüro GmbH v Zentrale zur Bekämpfung unlauteren Wettbewerbs e.V., EU:C:1989:140.

seal on an economic reality characterized by the fact that an undertaking in a dominant position has succeeded in having the tariffs in question applied by other undertakings.'[209]

Antitrust analysis relevant to non-challenge clauses under Article 101 TFEU may help understand antitrust assessment under Article 102.[210] The European Commission Regulation on the application of Article 101 (3) to categories of technology transfer agreements (TTBER)[211] concerns non-challenge clauses. Under the TTBER, the competition agency usually does not consider technology transfer agreements as a category of anti-competitive agreements under Article 101 (1) TFEU. However, this does not include technology transfer agreements containing non-challenge clauses.[212]

While the TTBER does not provide any explanations, the Guidelines on the application of Article 101 of the Treaty on the Functioning of the European Union to technology transfer agreements (TTBER Guidelines) set out the potential anti-competitive effects of non-challenge clauses in technology transfer agreements. These Guidelines, not surprisingly, reiterate the US *Lear* doctrine that 'licensees are normally in the best position to determine whether or not an intellectual property right is invalid.'[213] The TTBER Guidelines explain that invalid intellectual property should be eliminated because it not only restricts undistorted competition but undermines the principles of the protection of intellectual property.[214] These anti-competitive effects may occur especially when the licensed technology 'is valuable and therefore creates a competitive disadvantage for undertakings that are prevented from using it or are only able to use it against payment of royalties.'[215]

It is also notable that the TTBER Guidelines concern technical trade secrets (know-how) in particular. In view of the TTBER Guidelines, as it would be rather

---

[209] Ibid. Some scholars take the so-called 'most favoured nation' (MFN) clauses as an example. While some national competition agencies analyzed the MFN clauses under Article 101, the EU Commission examined such clauses as an Article 102 violation in the Amazon case. See Jones, Alison, Sufrin, BE and Niamh Dunne. 2019. *EU competition law:Text, cases, and materials*(7th ed). Oxford: Oxford University Press, 567–568.

[210] This book focuses on the abuse of market dominance, which is prohibited by Article 102 TFEU under the EU competition law. For the reason that both Article 101 (restrictive agreements) and Article 102 TFEU are both applicable in the assessment of non-challenge clauses, this section will also learn from non-challenge clauses from the perspective of Article 101. However, it should be kept in mind that Article 102 violations need the establishment of market dominance while Article 101 violations do not.

[211] Commission Regulation (EU) No. 316/2014 of 21 March 2014 on the application of Article 101(3) of the Treaty on the Functioning of the European Union to categories of technology transfer agreements.

[212] Article 101 (1) prohibits any agreements that can have an object or effect to restrict competition within the internal market. Any agreements that complied with Article 101 (3) may fall outside the scope of Article 101 (1). Under Article 2 of the TTBER, technology transfer agreements are in principle fall within the scope of Article 101 (3).

[213] Para 134 of the TTBER Guidelines.

[214] Ibid.

[215] Ibid.

difficult or even impossible to recover the licensed know-how once it is disclosed, the European Commission tends to give a more favourable opinion on non-challenge clauses which concern know-how. If a stronger licensee obtains a trade secret from a weaker licensor and challenges the existence of the secret, it is likely that the licensee discloses the know-how. In that case, the weaker licensor may suffer substantial losses in that the trade secret disappears. Consequently, the non-challenge obligation may allow 'weaker licensors to license stronger licensees without fear of a challenge once the know-how has been absorbed by the licensee.'[216]

In conclusion, the US and the EU have both developed respective and similar case law regarding non-challenge clauses of intellectual property. These two jurisdictions share similarities through recognizing the importance of the ability of licensees to challenge the validity of intellectual property. Both find that the policy of clearing invalid intellectual property should override other policies in order to obtain a free market. After comparative analysis from both sides of the Atlantic, the next part examines how China views non-challenge clauses.

5.4.3 China's Existing Approach to Prohibiting Non-challenge Clauses

The last section analyses how the US and EU antitrust authorities treat non-challenge clauses in intellectual property. China has made substantial efforts in the competition enforcement of the abuse of intellectual property rights during recent years.[217] While there is not as much competition experience in China as in the US and the EU, Chinese competition agencies and courts have concentrated recently on non-challenge clauses.

The following analysis based on current Chinese competition enforcement is divided into two parts. Firstly, the book analyses several provisions regarding non-challenge clauses in *Regulation on Prohibition of Abuse of Intellectual Property Rights to Exclude and Restrict Competition* (IP Regulation), which was enacted by the Chinese central competition authority SAMR.[218] Apart from the IP Regulation, the Anti-monopoly Commission of the State Council published IP Guidelines in 2019, in which non-challenge clauses are also mentioned. Secondly, the then (one

[216] Para 140 of the TTBER Guidelines.

[217] To some extent, China made these efforts owing to some pressures of the US. The US government keeps urging that 'China's AML enforcement [in the field of intellectual property] be fair, transparent, and non-discriminatory, afford due process to parties, focus only on the legitimate goals of competition law.' See 2021 Special 301 Report. *Office of the US Trade Representative*. https://ustr.gov/sites/default/files/files/reports/2021/2021%20Special%20301%20Report%20(final).pdf. Accessed 25 March 2025.

[218] As the State Administration for Industry and Commerce (SAIC) was one of the three competition agencies in China, the IP Regulations were enacted by SAIC in 2015. In 2019, the three competition agencies combined and formed a new Chinese competition authority SAMR. In 2020, SAMR recognized that the IP Regulations are still effective.

of three) competition authorities, NDRC,[219] penalized Qualcomm for its abuse of market dominance in 2015. The NDRC Qualcomm case was the first and the only case in China where non-challenge clauses were found illegal. Therefore, this book assesses this landmark case in some detail.

5.4.3.1 The SAMR Regulations and the IP Guidelines

Very similarly to the EU competition law, Article 22 (5) of China's AML prohibits a dominant company from imposing unreasonable trading terms on other undertakings. As a consequence, the IP Regulation[220] also prevents a dominant firm from imposing unfair trading terms in the course of the implementation of intellectual property rights.[221] Article 10 of the IP Regulation lists some potential abusive practices that might constitute unfair trading terms, including 'prohibitions of transaction counterparties from challenging the validity of intellectual property rights.'[222] While there are no interpretations of this provision, it indicates that the Chinese competition agency regards non-challenge clauses as a category of abuse of market dominance in the domain of licensing practices of intellectual property.[223]

The IP Guidelines examine non-challenge clauses when discussing both its restrictive agreements[224] and its abuse of market dominance.[225] This approach is similar to the EU but different from the approach in the IP Regulation which assesses non-challenge clauses merely under the framework of the abuse of dominance. The influential Professor Xianlin Wang has argued that, in terms of anti-competitive license agreements of intellectual property, if the licensor is in a dominant position, the

[219] NDRC refers to National Development and Reform Commission of the PRC. It is a ministerial department of the central government of China (namely the State Council). It undertakes many duties related to the economic development of China. One of its duties was to conduct price-related anti-monopoly enforcement before 2018. After 2018 when the new unified competition agency (SAMR) was established, the NDRC no longer undertakes duties of anti-monopoly enforcement.

[220] The AML is the fundamental anti-monopoly rule in China, which was enacted by the Standing Committee of the National People's Congress. The IP Regulation is a type of secondary law which was published by the competition agency. The IP Regulation should follow the basic rules of the AML and can be applied in the public enforcement of the AML led by the competition agency. The IP Guidelines are a type of soft law in China which can guide competition enforcement of competition agencies and courts. More details about China's anti-monopoly enforcement can be found in Chap. 6.

[221] See Article 10 of the IP Regulation.

[222] See Article 10 (2) of the IP Regulation.

[223] Moreover, Chinese antitrust academia believes that non-challenge clauses may have anti-competitive effects. See e.g. 王晓晔 [Wang Xiaoye]. 2017. 滥用知识产权限制竞争的法律问题 [Legal issues surrounding the misuse of intellectual property rights to restrict competition]. *中国社会科学 [Social Sciences in China]* 4: 130–144 + 207, 139.

[224] See Article 10 of the IP Guidelines, which is in the Chap. 2 (Intellectual Property Agreements that may Eliminate or Restrict Competition).

[225] See Article 18 of the IP Guidelines, which is in the Chap. 3 (Abuse of Market Dominance involving Intellectual Property Rights).

licensing practices may be assessed under the framework of restrictive agreements and the abuse of dominance at the same time.[226]

There are two main differences between the assessment of restrictive agreements and the abuse of dominance. The first difference is, restrictive agreements are bilateral practices, which means both the licensor and the licensee agree to non-challenge clauses. By contrast, the abuse of dominance is a unilateral practice. The dominant licensor may compel the weaker licensee to accept non-challenge clauses it offers. The second difference is, only a conduct of a dominant firm may constitute the abuse of market dominance. Parties between a restrictive agreement do not need to be dominant undertakings.

However, these differences are not black-and-white. If a dominant licensor forces the licensee to accept the non-challenge clause, this practice might be considered under the framework of restrictive agreements and abuse of dominance concurrently. Under such circumstance, it has been suggested that 'there is no reason why different analytical factors are considered when no challenge clauses are treated as a restrictive agreement as opposed to an abuse of dominance.'[227]

Article 10 of the IP Guidelines looks at the non-challenge clause as an intellectual property agreement that may restrict competition. This Article lists some considerations that the competition agency may take into on the assessment of anti-competitive effects of such clauses.[228] Article 18 of the IP Guidelines, which is similar to Article 10 of the IP Regulation, prohibits a dominant firm from imposing unreasonable terms as a category of the abuse of market dominance. Article 18 provides a list involving some potential abusive practices, one of which is the non-challenge clause.[229]

---

[226] See 王先林 [Wang Xianlin]. 2020. *知识产权与反垄断法 [Intellectual property and anti-monopoly law]*. 北京: 法律出版社 [Beijing: Law Press China], 243.

[227] Cheng Thomas. 2016. Antitrust treatment of the no challenge clause. *Journal of intellectual property and entertainment law* 5 (2): 437–512, 467. It means that the practice of non-challenge clauses should be treated the same under restrictive agreement cases and abuse of dominance cases. However, abuse of dominance cases are different from restrictive agreement cases in other aspects. For example, only a firm is in a dominant position can it conduct the abuse of dominance.

[228] These considerations are:

(1) whether the licensor requires all licensees not to challenge the validity of its intellectual property rights;
(2) whether the licensing of intellectual property rights involved in the non-challenge clause is paid;
(3) whether the intellectual property rights involved in the non-challenge clause may constitute a barrier to enter downstream market;
(4) whether the intellectual property rights involved in the non-challenge clause obstruct the implementation of other competitive intellectual property rights;
(5) whether the licensing of intellectual property rights involved in the non-challenge clause is exclusive; and
(6) whether the licensee may suffer material losses if it challenges the validity of the licensor's intellectual property rights.' See Article 10 of the IP Guidelines.

[229] See Article 18 (2) of the IP Guidelines.

5.4.3.2 The NDRC Qualcomm Decision

The NDRC began its anti-monopoly investigation of Qualcomm in 2013 and concluded the case in 2015.[230] Qualcomm was found to have abused market dominance with respect to SEPs. The NDRC finally fined Qualcomm 6.088 billion yuan (approximately one billion US dollars), which was one of the highest fines imposed by Chinese competition agencies. As this case was related to competition issues of intellectual property, some scholars believed that it was a milestone because it indicated that 'China is not only stressing IPR protection, but also resolute in fighting against any abuses of IPRs that eliminate or restrict competition.'[231]

Qualcomm is a worldwide giant company making baseband processors in the smartphone sector. The NDRC determined that Qualcomm was a dominant firm in the SEP licensing market (including CDMA, WCDMA and LTE wireless communication SEP licensing market) and the baseband chip market globally.[232] After the establishment of market dominance, Qualcomm was accused of having conducted a series of abusive practices resulting from its licensing practices.[233] Of them, the non-challenge clause, is the focus of this section.

The NDRC decided that Qualcomm had imposed unreasonable trading terms when selling its baseband chips. In particular, Qualcomm required its trading partners to accept the non-challenge clause if they intended to acquire Qualcomm's chips protected as SEPs. If potential licensees refused to accept the non-challenge clause, Qualcomm refused to sell chips to them. In addition, if a licensee challenged the validity of Qualcomm's patents after accepting the non-challenge clauses, Qualcomm would no longer provide the chips.

The NDRC argued that the licensee had the legal right to challenge the validity of patents in question. In this regard, Qualcomm abused its market dominance by imposing non-challenge clauses, depriving the licensee of its right to challenge Qualcomm's patents. Furthermore, the non-challenge clauses practically excluded those potential or actual licensees who refused to take such terms from the market. This conduct restricted the competition. Accordingly, the NDRC decided that Qualcomm had imposed unreasonable trading terms by compelling licensees to accept non-challenge clauses.

The NDRC *Qualcomm* case is the only anti-monopoly case in China so far which includes a non-challenge clause in intellectual property. This section provides details of this case to show the attitude of the Chinese competition agency. The NDRC

---

[230] The overview of the Qualcomm case and the brief of the NDRC decision can be found in a book edited by Eleanor Fox and Daniel Crane. See Fox, Eleanor and Crane, Daniel. *Global issues in antitrust and competition law,* 129–132. St. Paul: West Academic Publishing.

[231] Wang Xianlin. 2017. Recent developments in China's antimonopoly regulations on abuse of intellectual property rights. *Antitrust bulletin* 62 (4): 806–814, 810.

[232] Ibid 809. When discussing the non-challenge clauses in the Qualcomm case, it is relevant that Qualcomm had market dominance in the baseband chip market.

[233] For example, the NDRC found that Qualcomm had charged unfairly high royalties, tied the licensing of non-SEPs with SEPs and imposed unreasonable conditions to the sales of baseband chips. See Ibid 809.

Qualcomm case, as well as relevant provisions in the IP Regulation and IP Guidelines defined the landscape of how Chinese authorities view non-challenge clauses. The following section examines problems in the current anti-monopoly practices and puts forward several suggestions for improvements.

5.4.4 Suggestions on Improving China's Future Anti-monopoly Enforcement

The above analysis reveals that non-challenge clauses have been under antitrust scrutiny in all three jurisdictions (the US, EU and China). Notwithstanding this, there are some divergences in the assessment of non-challenge clauses among these jurisdictions. The following section concentrates on a problem existing in China's current approach, and provides some suggestions particularly with respect to trade secrets.

Compared to comparative experience from the US and the EU, one problem is that Chinese anti-monopoly doctrine fails to explain why non-challenge clauses should be proscribed. For example, the IP Regulation merely says that non-challenge clauses required by a dominant firm may constitute the abuse of market dominance. The IP Guidelines provide some assistance by listing some considerations when examining the extent of anti-competitive effects. Yet the IP Guidelines do not explain why non-challenge clauses might give rise to competition concerns. Additionally, few Chinese antitrust lawyers have discussed this issue. In other words, the prohibition of the non-challenge clause in China lacks legal explanation. It may make the competition enforcement against the non-challenge clause in China less clear.

The NDRC Qualcomm case, as the only case in China concerning non-challenge clauses, provides some reasons why non-challenge clauses ought to be prevented. A non-challenge clause deprives a licensee's legal right to challenge the validity of the licensor's patents. One may understand this argument in the context of the Chinese Patent Law. Article 45 of the Chinese Patent Law (2020) authorizes anyone who regards a granted patent invalid to challenge the validity of the underlying patent.[234] As a result, anyone including the licensee has the legal right to challenge the validity of a patent according to the Patent Law. In this regard, a dominant firm forcing a licensee to accept non-challenge clauses may violate Chinese intellectual property law.

Secondly, the NDRC in *Qualcomm* stated that any potential or actual licensees who was unwilling to take the non-challenge clause might be excluded from the market. Arguably this is an argument that is related to antitrust analysis.

---

[234] Article 45 of the Patent Law of the PRC (2020) says that '[W]ith effect from the date of announcement by the patent administrative department under the State Council on grant of patent rights, any organisation or individual that holds the view that the grant of such patent rights does not comply with the relevant provisions of this Law may request the patent administrative department under the State Council to declare that such patent rights are invalid.'

As discussed in Chap. 3, Chinese authorities use an effects-based approach in cases of the abuse of dominance, especially after the landmark *Qihoo v Tencent* case.[235] The NDRC also considered whether the practice might restrict competition in the Qualcomm case. Some antitrust lawyers argued that the NDRC's arguments, especially the latter one, are questionable. They suggest that even though many licensees were unwilling to take on Qualcomm's non-challenge clauses, it could not be demonstrated that competition was restricted. In other words, even a dominant company does not have an obligation to provide licensing terms that are all acceptable to its licensees.[236] As a result, the NDRC's opinion on non-challenge clauses may not be correct.

The key question is whether a non-challenge clause of intellectual property may harm competition. The following analysis takes patents as an example. The patent law entitles a patentee to charge supra-competitive prices from licensees and consumers[237] as long as the patent at issue is valid.[238] While this practice may harm consumers, it is a necessary step to maintaining incentives for innovation. In other words, the patent law allows for a sacrifice of 'short-run consumer welfare for long-run dynamic efficiency gains.'[239] Competition rules should not intervene in such cases.

Notwithstanding this, it is obvious that the patent law does not protect invalid patents. From the perspective of patent law, patentees of invalid patents have no right to charge supra-competitive prices to licensees, resulting in damages to consumer welfare.[240] The anti-competitive effects of a non-challenge clause arise from its protection of possible invalid intellectual property.

Not every patentee is capable of charging supra-competitive prices that harm consumers. As discussed in Chap. 4, the exclusivity of intellectual property does not necessarily lead to market power in the sense of competition law analysis. In a competitive environment where many substitutes of the underlying technology exist, a patentee is unable to price above the competitive level. Therefore, the prerequisite

---

[235] See 3.4.2 and 3.4.3 in Chap. 3. However, Chap. 3 also notices that the meaning of 'effects' in the context of Chinese law is different from the US and EU (Commission) approaches. Chinese authorities consider both economic and other potential effects.

[236] See Cheng Thomas. 2017. The PRC NDRC case against Qualcomm: a misguided venture or justified enforcement of competition law. *Journal of Antitrust Enforcement* 5(1): 76–99, 96.

[237] A licensee pays royalties to a licensor directly, yet the licensee will earn its profits from end-user consumers.

[238] Hovenkamp, Herbert, Janis, Mark, Lemley, Mark, and Christopher Leslie. In *IP and antitrust: An analysis of antitrust principles applied to intellectual property law*, 11–19. Austin: Aspen Publishers.

[239] Cheng Thomas. 2016. Antitrust treatment of the no challenge clause. *Journal of intellectual property and entertainment law* 5 (2):437–512, 477.

[240] It is obvious that patentees of invalid patents have no right to charge at all, not because of antitrust reasons. However, this section discusses antitrust concerns arising from the non-challenge clause imposed by a dominant licensor, instead of invalid patents as such.

of identifying an anti-competitive non-challenge clause is that the holder of the intellectual property has substantial market power.[241]

This part will now discuss non-challenge clauses with regard to trade secrets in China. As noted earlier, the most significant argument comparative experience has made is that a licensee is in a good position to challenge the validity of the underlying intellectual property. This argument relies on the need to eliminate invalid patents. Consumers are protected from paying for needless intellectual property which is in essence invalid. Because invalid intellectual property may harm consumers, competition law should apply in cases where non-challenge clauses exist.

The above argument is also applicable (or even more applicable) when the licensed intellectual property is a trade secret. In patent cases, the licensee is able to detect whether the patent at issue is invalid because the licensee herself is utilizing the technology, knowing the very subject matter of the underlying patent.[242] However, the patentee imposes a non-challenge clause, yet these clauses are only binding for the licensees instead of unrelated third parties.[243] Consequently, even though the licensee of a patent is in a good (perhaps the best) position with sufficient economic incentive to challenge the validity of a patent, it is still possible for other third parties to challenge it.

In terms of trade secrets, unlike a patent where patent claims are made public, the core element of a trade secret is its secrecy. As a result, theoretically there are only two parties who can get access to the licensed secret: the secret holder and the licensee(s). Unrelated third parties are unable to know the content of the trade secret. In this scenario, the licensee might be in not only a good but also the exclusive position to challenge the existence of the trade secret. For this reason, the *Lear* doctrine that protects the position of challenging the validity of intellectual property should apply in the domain of trade secrets. Accordingly, Chinese competition agencies and courts should in principle prohibit non-challenge clauses imposed by a dominant firm in the license of trade secrets.

It is arguable that most analysis above about non-challenge clauses of patents can be applied in the scenario of trade secrets. Additionally, there are some other suggestions on the assessment of non-challenge clauses of trade secrets in China:

Firstly, some non-challenge clauses of trade secrets might be more anti-competitive than others. Usually there is a specific duration of a license. The period of the existing of a non-challenge clause[244] is at most equivalent to the duration of a license in most circumstances. For example, supposing a secret holder licenses

---

[241] Elhaugec, Einer and Alex Krueger. 2012. Solving the patent settlement puzzle. *Texas law review* 91(2):283–330, 323.

[242] Jones, Alison, BE, Sufrin and Niamh Dunne. 2019. *EU competition law:Text, cases, and materials*(7th ed). Oxford: Oxford University Press, 820.

[243] Ørstavik, Inger Berg. 2005. Technology transfer agreements: grant-backs and no-challenge clauses in the New EC technology transfer regulation. *IIC: International review of intellectual property and competition law* 36 (1): 83–112, 87.

[244] Some commentators call the period 'licensing exclusion period'. See Cheng Thomas. 2016. Antitrust treatment of the no challenge clause. *Journal of intellectual property and entertainment law* 5 (2): 437–512, 479.

its secret information to a licensee for 10 years, the license terms may require the licensee not to challenge the existence of the secret for 10 years (or less).

However, in some circumstances a dominant licensor might extend the duration of non-challenge obligation even after the license has been terminated.[245] In patent cases, as the protection period of a patent is limited, all patents will enter the public domain when the patent is expired. Even though a patentee can extend the period of non-challenge clauses, the duration is unlikely to be extended after the expiration of the patent. A secret holder, however, may possess the trade secret forever without the requirement to disclose it to the public. Therefore, it is possible for a secret holder to require its licensee not to challenge the existence of a trade secret permanently. In a case where the licensed information may not constitute a trade secret, consumers will suffer from the long-standing non-challenge clause, as no one can challenge the existence of the underlying 'secret information'. As a consequence, it is arguable that Chinese competition agencies should pay attention to the duration of the non-challenge clauses when deciding the anti-competitive effects.

Secondly, the *Bayer* exception might in part apply to cases of trade secrets. It has been discussed that there existed two exceptions where a non-challenge clause might be legal provided in the EU *Bayer* case.[246] The first circumstance is that the license is granted for free. Arguably, as Cheng claimed, the first exception may be a misunderstanding of antitrust harm of non-challenge clauses.[247] In cases where the license is granted free of charge, the licensee may not have to pay royalties for the licensed intellectual property. However, the licensor may still hold market power arising from the licensed intellectual property, which might be invalid in essence. Consumers still need to pay for invalid intellectual property.[248] In light of the policy of clearing invalid intellectual property, the first exception does not make sense.

The second exception appears when the license relates to a technically outdated process which the licensee does not use. A technical trade secret (or know-how) may form a part of a technology. If the licensee does not use the technology protected as a trade secret, all clauses in the license, including a non-challenge clause, do not have impacts on consumers. As a result, it is suggested that Chinese competition agencies may consider the second exception from *Bayer*.

Thirdly, the dominant licensor may have some defenses for the non-challenge clauses of trade secrets. On the one hand, the anti-competitive harm of non-challenge clauses results from the invalidity of the underlying intellectual property. In cases

---

[245] Such situations have occurred in patent license cases. See e.g. Bendix Corporation v. Balax, Inc., 471 F.2d 809 (7th Cir. 1970).

[246] The EU Commission also affirmed the *Bayer* exception in its TTBER Guidelines. See para. 134 of the TTBER Guidelines ('However, if the licensed technology is related to a technically outdated process which the licensee does not use, or if the licence is granted for free, no restriction of competition arises.').

[247] See Cheng Thomas. 2016. Antitrust treatment of the no challenge clause. *Journal of intellectual property and entertainment law* 5 (2): 437–512, 461.

[248] The licensees may obtain the intellectual property for free, yet it is impossible for them to sell products to consumers for free.

where a trade secret in involved, if the licensor can prove that the licensed information is a legally-defined trade secret, competition law should not apply here.[249]

On the other hand, the EU TTBER Guidelines remind us that compared with other intellectual property, there is no trade secret once the secret information is disclosed to the public. A dominant firm may justify its non-challenge clauses through proving that these clauses are imperative to protect the secrecy of the information. It is the dominant licensor who needs to take the burden of proof.

Lastly, the EU experience demonstrates that a non-challenge clause may result in severe antitrust harm when the underlying intellectual property becomes a standard (e.g. SEPs). The Chinese competition law also notes the anti-competitive effects of a non-challenge clause in the SEP-related Qualcomm case. A trade secret may act as a de facto standard.[250] It is thus suggested that Chinese competition authorities and courts may pay more attention to the non-challenge clause of a trade secret which establishes a de facto standard.[251]

5.4.5 Conclusion

Licensing practices of intellectual property rights may raise concerns about competitive impact. A dominant licensor may take advantage of its market power and force a weaker licensee to agree not to challenge the validity of the licensed intellectual property. 'Non-challenge' clauses may be detrimental to competition and consumer interests.

Comparative analysis from the US and the EU provides some experience with regard to non-challenge clauses. The US Supreme Court's *Lear* decision reveals that licensees usually have sufficient economic incentive to challenge the validity of the licensed intellectual property. The public policy of eliminating invalid intellectual property should be the priority compared over other policies. While *Lear* was not a typical antitrust case, the US Supreme Court cited *Lear* to discuss antitrust doctrine in *Actavis*. The reverse payment issue in *Actavis* reflected a similar doctrine to that in *Lear*. The majority in *Actavis* held that any motivation to protect invalid intellectual property from being challenged might harm competition.[252]

---

[249] The same defense is applicable in fields of other intellectual property. Sometimes the licensor imposes a non-challenge clause merely because of the prevention of needless ligation expenses. See Cheng Thomas. Antitrust treatment of the no challenge clause. *Journal of intellectual property and entertainment law* 5 (2): 437–512, 508.

[250] See Sect. 5.2 of this book particularly related to the EU *Microsoft* case.

[251] As the interface information of Microsoft acts as a de facto standard, supposing Microsoft imposes a non-challenge clause to its licensees, this conduct may need antitrust scrutiny.

[252] Some scholars recently have argued that antitrust issues of reverse payment may happen in China as well. See e.g. Wang Yuting. 2020. The anti-monopoly regulation of reverse payment patent settlement agreements in the pharmaceutical industry in China. *Asia pacific law review* 28 (1): 202–224.

The EU competition law shares an analogous approach to the US path. The ECJ in *Windsurfing* opined that the public interest in the removal of monopoly resulting from invalid intellectual property should be ensured. Non-challenge clauses are usually relevant to SEP-related cases. As consumers have no choice but to use SEPs, the ECJ and the European Commission both criticized non-challenge clauses as a potential violation of the EU competition law. The EU TTBER and its Guidelines also consider non-challenge clauses. They recall the US *Lear* case and argue that licensees are in the best position to challenge the licensed intellectual property.

China's anti-monopoly law has looked at non-challenge clauses. The IP Regulation and the IP Guidelines make it clear that non-challenge clauses may give rise to anti-monopoly concerns by Chinese competition authorities. The NDRC Qualcomm case was the first and only competition case in China where non-challenge clauses were considered. The NDRC held that the non-challenge clause imposed by Qualcomm was an unreasonable trading term and constituted the abuse of market dominance.

In spite of these facts, the IP Regulation and IP Guidelines fail to explain why non-challenge clauses deserve the intervention of competition law. Neither the intellectual property law nor the competition law entitles an information holder to charge supra-competitive prices if the underlying information cannot constitute a trade secret. This may be the reason that a licensee should have the right to challenge the existence of a trade secret. It is suggested that Chinese competition agencies and courts need to challenge non-challenge clauses of trade secrets in principle. At the same time, there are some other specific recommendations on the determination of anti-competitive effect of non-challenge clauses. For instance, Chinese competition agencies may consider the duration of the non-challenge clause so as to determine the extent of anti-competitive effects. If a license is related to technically outdated process which the licensee does not use, the non-challenge clause in such license may not hamper competition. The dominant licensor might justify its practices by proving that the licensed information is a true trade secret, or the non-challenge clause is an indispensable method of protecting the secret in question. Every time the underlying secret information might create a de facto standard, the Chinese competition authority needs to consider the serious anti-competitive effects that a non-challenge clause may bring about.

5.5 Conclusion

In order to find an abuse of market dominance, the company in a dominant position must have conducted specific abusive practices. Chapter 5 of this book analyses three kinds of abusive practices that a dominant firm may engage in particularly in relation to trade secrets.

The first selected abusive practice is the refusal to deal in relation to trade secrets. The US antitrust case-law and the EU competition law have witnessed obvious differences in the analysis of the refusal to deal. The US courts may not find illegal refusal to deal after the landmark *Trinko* case. The EU competition authorities have developed a thorough criteria for applying Article 102 in cases of the refusal to license intellectual property, including in the *Microsoft* case as to the refusal to disclose trade secrets. This book suggests that China should primarily learn from the EU approach to the assessment of the refusal to disclose trade secrets.

The second abusive practice outlined is bad faith litigation of trade secrets. All three jurisdictions discussed in this Chapter (namely, the US, EU and China) recognize that bad faith litigation of intellectual property initiated by a dominant firm may constitute the abuse of market dominance. Compared to the other two jurisdictions, China does not have mature experience when dealing with cases of bad faith litigation of trade secrets. This book proposes that Chinese competition authorities should analyse these cases with both subjective and objective requirements. In particular, the competition authorities should consider two circumstances where no legally-defined trade secrets exist, and the secret information becomes a de facto standard.

The last possible abusive practice is the imposition of a non-challenge clause of trade secrets by a dominant licensor. Comparative lessons from the US and the EU have demonstrated that the non-challenge clause may raise antitrust concerns in that it prevents the licensee, who is in the best position to challenge the intellectual property, from challenging the validity of intellectual property. This book suggests that Chinese competition authorities may learn from comparative experience and consider some factors when dealing with specific cases of non-challenge clause of trade secrets, such as considering the duration of the license and the Bayer exception.

Chapters 4 and 5 assess market dominance and abusive practices in relation to trade secrets, which are two essential elements of constituting the abuse of market dominance in trade secrets. After the establishment of analytical and theoretical framework of the abuse of dominance as to trade secrets, Chapter 6 will provide detailed suggestions on the improvement of anti-monopoly enforcement in the context of Chinese laws.

Chapter 6
Proposed Recommendations for China's Anti-monopoly Legal Practices

6.1 Introduction

This book examines the research question of when the use of trade secrets will constitute the abuse of market dominance in China. To this end, previous chapters (Chapters 2–5) critically analyse the abuse of market dominance regarding trade secrets from a normative perspective. Chapter 6 now provides some specific recommendations for China's anti-monopoly legal practice in relation to this question.

This chapter is divided into five parts. Different jurisdictions have unique legal systems and traditions.[1] Anti-monopoly law in China should follow China's legal system in a broader sense. In this regard, Sect. 6.2 of this chapter provides an overview of current China's anti-monopoly enforcement based on China's legal traditions. It examines China's existing anti-monopoly rules centred on the AML (6.2.1). At the same time, this section briefly analyses the public and private anti-monopoly enforcement, and the roles that competition agencies and courts play in China (6.2.2).

The next parts provide specific suggestions relevant to the abuse of market dominance in trade secrets to improve anti-monopoly enforcement in China. Referencing from Chapter 4 (market dominance in trade secrets) and Chapter 5 (abusive practices in trade secrets), Sects. 6.3 and 6.4 provide suggestions on China's anti-monopoly enforcement regarding the identification of market dominance and the assessment of abusive practices related to trade secrets. Specifically, Sect. 6.3 proposes amendments to China's anti-monopoly enforcement in relation to market definition involving

[1] Chinese government describe China's legal system as 'the socialist system of laws with Chinese characteristics'. See Supreme People's Court of China. 2015. The socialist system of laws with Chinese characteristics. https://english.court.gov.cn/2015-07/17/c_761596_8.htm. Accessed 23 March 2025. Despite this, observers often describe that China has mainly civil law system because statutes are important reference for Chinese regulators and judges. See China Justice Observer. 2020. Does China have common law? https://www.chinajusticeobserver.com/a/does-china-have-common-law. Accessed 23 March 2025.

P. Wu, *Trade Secrets and Market Dominance*, Contemporary Chinese Civil and Commercial Law, https://doi.org/10.1007/978-981-95-1152-5_6

trade secrets (6.3.1), and suggests that China should amend the rules for determining market dominance in trade secrets (6.3.2). Section 6.4 provides recommendations on analysis of abusive practices during the exploitation of trade secrets. As the three types of abusive practices (the refusal to disclose trade secrets, bad faith litigation of trade secrets and non-challenge clauses of trade secrets) are discussed in Chapter 5, this section provides recommendations about these practices to improve China's anti-monopoly rules. The last Sect. 6.5 presents a brief conclusion.

6.2 An Overview of China's Anti-monopoly Rules and Enforcement

Before providing specific suggestions for Chinese anti-monopoly enforcement of the abuse of market dominance concerning trade secrets, it is necessary to introduce an overview of the existing anti-monopoly rules and enforcement in China. This section is divided into two parts. The first part presents some types of codified anti-monopoly rules in China. The second part focuses on public enforcement (led by Chinese competition agencies) and the private enforcement (led by Chinese courts) in China.

6.2.1 China's Anti-monopoly Rules Associated with This Book

The Introductory chapter (Chapter 1) has introduced the anti-monopoly rules and their status and hierarchy in China. This is presented in the following diagram (Fig. 6.1).

The AML is relevant to this book, providing general provisions on the abuse of market dominance in China. In addition to the AML, closely related to this book are the IP Guidelines. The IP Guidelines (a type of anti-monopoly guidelines in China)

Fig. 6.1 Chinese anti-monopoly rules

provide guidance for Chinese competition agencies and courts particularly in the field of intellectual property (including trade secrets).[2] This chapter thus provides recommendations primarily for the AML and the IP Guidelines.

6.2.2 *China's Public and Private Anti-monopoly Enforcement*

China's anti-monopoly enforcement can be divided into public and private enforcement. The Chinese competition agency leads the public enforcement. In other words, the Chinese competition agency (SAMR) has the authority to make antitrust investigations against companies. Also noteworthy is that the SAMR is a component of the central administrative government (State Council). As a result, the public enforcement of the AML, in a broader sense, is a part of administrative enforcement in China.

If the Chinese anti-monopoly authority finds that the undertaking under investigation has violated the AML, the authority may issue an administrative decision to punish the company. However, the decision is not effective immediately. According to the *Administrative Procedure Law of China*,[3] if the undertaking under investigation disagrees with the decision, it can apply for a judicial review before a court. For instance, a local branch of the NDRC in Hainan Province investigated and fined a firm named Yutai for its monopoly agreements in 2015.[4] Yutai disagreed with the administrative decision and sued the local branch of the NDRC before a court. After rounds of trials, this case was appealed to the SPC in 2018. The SPC finally upheld the decision of the local branch of the NDRC. Despite this case, a research report reveals that appeals against Chinese competition agencies have been extraordinarily

[2] The IP Guidelines were primarily drafted by Professor Xianlin Wang who acts as an expert of the Anti-monopoly Commission of the State Council. Professor Wang gave a speech on the draft of the IP Guidelines at KoGuan Law School of Shanghai Jiao Tong University in November 2020. As he said, he had taken over a decade to draft the IP Guidelines. The US expressed its concerns about the draft of the IP Guidelines because the US worried that the Chinese government may use the antitrust law to force US firms to transfer their technology to Chinese counterparts. As a result, the existing IP Guidelines published in 2019 are general guidelines. The IP Guidelines may be amended in the future with the easing of US-China tensions and the further research relevant to the specific categories of intellectual property (e.g. patents/copyright/trade secrets). See KoGuan Jiao Wu Jun. 2020. Anti-monopoly issues in the field of intellectual property. https://mp.weixin.qq.com/s/l1ZkKyRowLswjrlnPsYdZQ. Accessed 23 March 2025.

[3] The SPC used to select some leading cases where the judicial review applied in administrative decisions. See Supreme People' s Court Issues 10 Major Cases of Administrative Inaction (2017) 49 (2) Chinese Law & Government 101–119.

[4] 裕泰公司与海南省物价局垄断纠纷案 [Yutai v Hainan Price Administration—Monopoly Dispute Case], 最高人民法院 [Supreme People's Court], (2018)最高法行申4675号 [Administrative No. 4675], 18 December 2018. The Yutai case was a landmark case regarding vertical monopoly agreements in China.

rare.[5] There have been no reported cases in China where an undertaking has applied for a judicial review of antitrust decisions imposed by the central competition agency (SAMR).

Article 60 of the AML says that '[U]ndertakings which implement monopolistic activities and causing others to suffer losses therefrom shall bear civil liability pursuant to the law.' This provision is the legal basis of the private enforcement of the AML.[6] Any individuals or firms who suffer from anti-competitive practices are entitled to file a civil lawsuit against the monopolist before a court.[7] For example, Qihoo sued Tencent for the abuse of market dominance in *Qihoo v Tencent* (as discussed in Chapter 3).[8]

6.3 Recommendations on Identifying Market Dominance Related to Trade Secrets

Chapter 4 of this book analyses the market power a firm may possess concerning trade secrets. According to analysis in Chapter 4, competition agencies or courts need to define the relevant market and examine the market power a company has in that relevant market.

The AML is the fundamental antitrust rule in China. It applies generally and is not limited to trade secrets. Additionally, among all anti-monopoly rules in China, the IP Guidelines are the ones that targets at the exercise of intellectual property rights. Therefore, the following sections provide some suggestions for the AML and IP Guidelines.

---

[5] Ma, Jingyuan. 2020. *Competition law in China: A law and economics perspective,* 219. Cham: Springer.

[6] 王先林 [Wang Xianlin]. 2018. *竞争法学 [Competition Law].* 北京: 中国人民大学出版社 [Beijing: Renmin University of China Press], 314.

[7] Some may argue that individuals may use commercial arbitrations as a method of dealing with civil antitrust cases, which might be another type of private enforcement of the AML. See 吴佩乘 [Wu Peicheng]. 2020. 论作为私人实施方式的反垄断民事纠纷仲裁 [On the civil anti-monopoly dispute arbitration as the private enforcement]. *北京仲裁 [Beijing Arbitration Quarterly]* 4: 27–46. However, the SPC held that civil antitrust disputes cannot be arbitrated in China. See汇力公司诉壳牌公司横向垄断协议纠纷案 [Huili v Shell—Horizonal Monopoly Agreement Case], 最高人民法院 [Supreme People's Court] (2019) 最高法知民辖终47号 [Economic No. 47], 21 August 2019.

[8] Some scholars argue that China's SPC sometimes acts as a 'market regulator', which interprets laws on economic regulation. See Pan Su. 2021. The court as a market regulator: proactive rule-making of the Supreme People's Court of China on economic regulation. *China Information* 35: 219–238.

6.3.1 *Market Definition*

The current IP Guidelines have some provisions on market definition.[9] For example, the IP Guidelines recognize that both the intellectual property products and the intellectual property may be marketed. Therefore, in addition to the product market, sometimes it may be necessary to define a technology market relating to intellectual property. However, the IP Guidelines provisions are general without specific provisions on trade secrets. Arguably, the existing provisions are difficult to apply in a specific case involving trade secrets. Some recommendations are given as follows in accordance with assessments in Chapter 4:

6.3.1.1 The IP Guidelines Should Specify the Quantitative and Qualitative Tests for Market Definition

China's Anti-monopoly Commission enacted the *Guidelines on the Definition of a Relevant Market* (Market Definition Guidelines) in 2009, which govern some general rules of market definition in anti-monopoly cases. Article 10 of the Market Definition Guidelines stipulates that the quantitative SSNIP test is a useful analytical framework for market definition.[10] As analyzed in Chapter 4, it is likely for the competition authority to adopt the SSNIP test to define the relevant market in cases relevant to all types of intellectual property, including trade secrets. The IP Guidelines should reiterate the quantitative SSNIP test as a method of market definition in the domain of intellectual property.

Concurrently, the IP Guidelines should specify some limitations on the SSNIP test in cases of intellectual property (including trade secrets). The IP Guidelines should explain the possible 'cellophane fallacy' arising from the SSNIP test in the abuse of dominance cases.[11] The IP Guidelines should clarify that the SSNIP test can only be

[9] Article 4 of the IP Guidelines says that '[I]ntellectual property rights may either be the direct subject matter for transactions or be used to provide products or services (hereinafter collectively referred to as 'products'). Under normal conditions, it is required to define the relevant market in accordance with the Guidelines on the Definition of Relevant Market. If it is difficult to fully assess the competition impact of the conduct by only defining the relevant commodity market, it may be necessary to define the relevant technology market. The impact of the conduct on innovation, research and development and other factors may also be taken into account, as the case may be…In defining the relevant market, it is required to define the relevant geographic market and take into account the regional features of the intellectual property rights. Where the relevant transaction involves multiple countries or regions, it is also necessary to consider the impact of transaction conditions on the definition of the relevant geographic market.'

[10] Article 10 of the Market Definition Guidelines says that '[T]he Hypothetical Monopolist Test is an analytical theory for defining a relevant market, which can help solve any uncertainty that is likely to occur in defining a relevant market. At present, this test is generally adopted by all the counties and regions in the formulation of anti-monopoly guidelines.'

[11] See 4.2.2.1 in Chapter 4 of this book.

applied when the price is the primary variety of consumer choice.[12] If factors other than prices substantially influence the choice of consumers, it is difficult to use the SSNIP test to define a market.

The IP Guidelines should also include a qualitative test. That is, Chinese anti-monopoly authorities should consider the characteristics, prices and the intended use of the products consisting of intellectual property (e.g. *CVD v Raytheon*[13] concerning trade secrets). In order to define the relevant market precisely, the IP Guidelines should require the anti-monopoly authorities to consider both quantitative and qualitative tests in the part of General Provisions to deal with the abuse of dominance cases relevant to intellectual property (including trade secrets).

6.3.1.2 The IP Guidelines Should Provide More Guidance About the Technology Market Related to Trade Secrets

Chapter 4 explains that it is necessary to define a technology market when a trade secret as such is licensed. In accordance with analysis in Chapter 4, the IP Guidelines should consider some special factors when defining a technology market. In some cases, when applying the SSNIP test, Chinese authorities should consider whether it is difficult to calculate the baseline price (namely the license royalties of the license of a trade secret) of a specific trade secret license. For instance, it may be possible to determine the royalties in the license of a customer list protected as a trade secret. However, it may be challenging to identify the royalties when a technical secret only covers a small fraction of a product or cross-licenses exist.[14] In another case, as provided in Chapter 4, the IP Guidelines should clarify that network effects may have noticeable influences on market definition of a trade secret.[15]

6.3.1.3 The IP Guidelines Should Specify Some Factors for Defining the Geographic Market as to Trade Secrets

China's IP Guidelines have stipulated that 'it is required to define the relevant geographic market and consider the territoriality of intellectual property rights'[16] in a general sense. This may be the case when it comes to registered intellectual property, such as patents. In other words, a holder can achieve a patent only if a national

[12] Chapter 4 provides an example regarding Coca-Cola, the formula of which is a trade secret. The SSNIP test may help define a product market including Coca-Cola, Pepsi and Sprite. See ibid.

[13] See ibid.

[14] See ibid.

[15] See ibid.

[16] See Article 4 of the IP Guidelines. According to the principle of territoriality, intellectual property rights are limited to the territory of the jurisdictions where they have been granted. See Emmanuel Kolawole Oke. 2018. Territoriality in intellectual property law: examining the tension between securing societal goals and treating intellectual property as an investment asset. *SCRIPTed* 15: 313–348, 315.

authority grants the patent. Nevertheless, in accordance with the requirements of constituting a trade secret as discussed in Chapter 2, a secret holder can acquire a trade secret without the grant from a national authority. Consequently, the geographic market as to the trade secret might be worldwide. At the same time, the IP Guidelines should consider the potential implications of restrictions on technology licenses on the definition of a geographic market regarding trade secrets.[17] For instance, after the US-China trade war in 2018, the US government has imposed many restrictions on technology transfer from US-based companies to Chinese companies.[18] These restrictions may influence the definition of a geographic market in know-how.

To conclude, this book proposes some specific recommendations on the market definition in intellectual property (including trade secrets) or trade secrets in particular for China's IP Guidelines. The IP Guideline should consider both quantitative and qualitative tests when defining the relevant market as to intellectual property. The IP Guideline should provide more provisions about the technology market. It is also suggested that the IP Guidelines should consider some special factors for defining a geographic market related to trade secrets.

6.3.2 Market Dominance

As Chapter 3 suggests, the premise of finding that a company abuses market dominance is that the undertaking is in a dominant position in the relevant market. In a general sense, the IP Guidelines concern the determination of a dominant position with regard to intellectual property. Article 14 of the IP Guidelines provides that:

> If an undertaking owns intellectual property rights, it does not necessarily mean that it has dominant market position. In order to identify whether an undertaking which owns intellectual property rights has dominant market position in the relevant market, analysis shall be made according to the factors and circumstances of the dominant market position of the undertaking as prescribed in Articles 18 and 19 of the Anti-monopoly Law, in light of the characteristics of the intellectual property rights; in addition, the following factors may be specifically considered:
>
> (I) the possibility of the transaction counterparties switching to substitutable technologies or commodities and the switching costs;
>
> (II) the dependency of the downstream market on the products provided by applying intellectual property rights; and
>
> (III) the capability of restricting and balancing the undertaking by the transaction counterparty.

---

[17] See 4.2.4 in Chapter 4 of this book.

[18] See e.g. Mondaq. 2023. US imposes technology transfer and export restrictions on dozens of Chinese companies, including Top Chipmaker and Drone Manufacture. https://www.mondaq.com/unitedstates/export-controls-trade-investment-sanctions/1019498/us-imposes-technology-transfer-and-export-restrictions-on-dozens-of-chinese-companies-including-top-chipmaker-and-drone-manufacturer. Accessed 23 March 2025.

While Article 14 does not provide sufficient information about the establishment of market dominance, it has set out three key points: (1) Chinese lawmakers do not equate the possession of intellectual property to that of market dominance of a firm; (2) the general provisions regarding the identification of market dominance in the AML (including the market-share hypothesis in Article 24 of the AML) should apply to cases of the abuse of dominance in relation to intellectual property; (3) Chinese competition authorities and courts may consider some other factors when dealing with cases involving intellectual property.

However, it is arguable that article 14 of the IP Guidelines is too general and does not target certain intellectual property categories, such as the trade secret. The following recommendations are provided to strengthen the IP Guidelines in terms of trade secrets.

6.3.2.1 The IP Guidelines Should Clearly Clarify the Relationship Between the Exclusivity of a Trade Secret and the Market Dominance

Article 14 of the IP Guidelines states that the ownership of intellectual property, including trade secrets, does not necessarily lead to a dominant position in the market. However, it does not solve the problem of the circumstances in which the exclusivity of a trade secret may confer market power on the secret holder.

It is suggested that the IP Guidelines should discuss this issue. In detail, on the one hand, the exclusivity of a trade secret cannot confer substantial market power when consumers can switch to other close substitutes. On the other hand, a trade secret may bring about market power to the secret owner if the secret information becomes essential and a de facto standard.[19]

6.3.2.2 The IP Guidelines Should Consider Diverse Factors to Assess Market Power of the Trade Secret Holder

As discussed in Chapter 3, article 24 of the AML provides a rebuttable market-share presumption of market dominance. A firm with more than 50% market share in the relevant market should be regarded as a dominant undertaking. This article also clarifies that the market-share presumption may be rebutted by saying that '[W]here an undertaking which is deemed to hold dominant market position is able to prove that it does not hold dominant market position, it shall not be defined to be holding dominant market position.'[20] As discussed in Chapter 3, this presumption may unreasonably increase the burden of proof for the company under investigation because article 19

[19] See 4.3.2 in Chapter 4 of this book. Moreover, the IP Guidelines may consider adding an example to explain how a trade secret may become a de facto standard. It is suggested that the EU *Microsoft* case (which is discussed in 4.3.4 of Chapter 4) is a suitable example.

[20] See article 24 of the AML.

requires the company presumed to be in the dominant position to prove that it is not in such a position.

As the IP Guidelines provide, the market-share presumption in the AML should be applied in the field of intellectual property. Arguably, there are some problems with this presumption with respect to trade secrets. The first problem is that the market-share hypothesis concerns only the percentage but ignores the time-frame of that percentage. If a secret product can be quickly reverse engineered, the percentage of market share the secret owner holds (perhaps above 50%) may be decreased very soon.[21] The second problem is that market share might not reflect market power in markets where dynamic competition plays an important role.[22] In this regard, the percentage of market share may not indicate market dominance precisely.

This book proposes some suggestions to address these problems. Firstly, it is suggested that the IP Guidelines should consider diverse factors to determine the market dominance of intellectual property owners, including trade secret holders. Market share is a significant but not decisive factor when determining market dominance.[23] Secondly, when examining the market share of the owner of intellectual property, the IP Guidelines should require the percentage of market share, and require that the particular percentage should exist for a period of time. Thirdly, the IP Guidelines should provide some specific provisions related to trade secrets. For instance, if a trade secret can be promptly reverse engineered by other competitors, the secret holder may temporarily possess a high proportion of market share, but is unlikely to have that market share for an extended period. That is, the secret holder does not have market dominance.

6.3.2.3 The IP Guidelines Should Consider Barriers to Entry as a Crucial Factor When Identifying the Market Dominance Concerning Trade Secrets

Article 14 of the IP Guidelines do not explicitly consider barriers to entry. Yet Chapter 4 revealed that it is necessary to take barriers to entry into account when determining the market dominance in trade secrets. Specifically, the IP Guidelines should recognize trade secret protection as a significant part of a barrier to entry.

As discussed, if a trade secret becomes a de facto standard, the secret information may bring about substantial market power to the secret holder. Nevertheless, under circumstances where the law does not provide sufficient protection for trade secrets,

---

[21] See 4.3.3 in Chapter 4 of this book.

[22] See ibid.

[23] The AML provides the market-share presumption, yet Chinese competition agencies and courts rarely rely on market share only to determine the market dominance of an undertaking. In most circumstances, Chinese authorities examine both market share and other factors concurrently. The latest abuse of dominance case against Alibaba is an example. See 阿里巴巴滥用市场支配地位案 [Alibaba-The Abuse of Market Dominance Case]. 国家市场监管总局 [SAMR]. 国市监处 [2021] 28号 [Administrative Decision of the SAMR No. 28], 10 April 2008. This is another important reason that this book proposes the abandonment of the market-share presumption provision.

competitors can easily misappropriate the information even if a secret becomes a de facto standard. This may decrease the market power of a secret holder. By contrast, the high-level protection of trade secrets may maintain the de facto standard and the barrier to entry of the market.

China has noticeably promoted trade secret protection, particularly after the US-China trade conflicts, such as providing punitive damages for the secret holder.[24] In the future, a secret holder in China may use its secret information (e.g. licenses) without being concerned about misappropriation of the secret. The increased protection of trade secrets may influence the barrier to entry and market power analysis in China.

Furthermore, the IP Guidelines should consider the lack of access to key secret information as a barrier to entry. In accordance with assessments in Chapter 4, it is difficult for potential rivals to enter the market if they cannot acquire key secret information.[25] The EU *Microsoft* case demonstrated that interface secret information might constitute an essential facility, no matter whether it was technically advanced or not. Other companies were unable to connect to the Windows system unless they could get access to the interface information of Microsoft.[26] It is suggested that the IP Guidelines should consider the lack of access to key trade secrets.

When determining whether a trade secret is key secret information, the IP Guidelines should consider the difficulty of reverse-engineering and self-invention of the secret information. As Chapter 2 provides, individuals are entitled to obtain one's secret information through reverse-engineering and self-invention. Therefore, a secret that can be easily reverse engineered or self-invented is unlikely to act as a barrier to entry and confer market power.[27]

The IP Guidelines should also consider the superior technology of an incumbent as a barrier for potential entrants.[28] Professor Josef Drexl states that a trade secret may bring about market power because of its innovation and technological advancement.[29] The IP Guidelines should regard superior technology consisting of trade secrets as a factor when assessing barriers to entry.

In conclusion, even though the IP Guidelines provide some provisions on the establishment of market dominance, these provisions are general. They do not target trade secrets in particular. This book recommends that the IP Guidelines should explain the relationship between the exclusivity of a trade secret and market power in detail. It is suggested that the IP Guidelines should consider diverse factors to

---

[24] Wu Peicheng and Charlie Xiao-chuan Weng. 2020. Implications of the China–US trade agreement on the civil protection of trade secrets in China: Is it a game changer? *Asia Pacific Law Review* 28(2): 316–336.

[25] See 4.3.4 in Chapter 4 of this book.

[26] Ibid.

[27] Ibid.

[28] Ibid.

[29] Drexl, Josef. 2011. Refusal to grant access to trade secrets as an abuse of market dominance. In *Intellectual property and competition law-new frontiers,* 165, 182. Oxford: Oxford University Press, 2011.

establish market dominance. The IP Guidelines should consider specifying barriers to entry involving trade secrets that may cause market power.

6.4 Recommendations on Dealing with Abusive Practices Related to Trade Secrets

Article 22 of the AML lists six types of abusive practices of a dominant undertaking which might constitute the abuse of market dominance.[30] The list is not exhaustive because article 22 has a catch-all provision. Chinese competition agencies and courts have the discretion to determine new categories of abusive practices on a case-specific basis.

The last chapter examined three types of abusive practices related to the exploitation of trade secrets. Theoretically, the list in article 22 of the AML and its catch-all provision have already included all kinds of abusive practices. This book argues that it is unnecessary to amend the AML in relation to abusive practices.

The IP Guidelines are designed to guide Chinese competition agencies and courts in anti-monopoly cases relevant to intellectual property. One objective of the IP Guidelines is to further interpret the AML in the domain of intellectual property.[31] Therefore this section mainly provides some recommendations for the IP Guidelines on the abuse of dominance concerning trade secrets. The following recommendations are organized according to the three abusive practices analyzed in Chapter 5.

---

[30] Article 22 of the AML says that 'Undertakings which hold dominant market position shall not abuse their dominant market position to engage in the following activities:

(1) sell commodities at unfairly high prices or purchase commodities at unfairly low prices;
(2) sell commodities at below-cost prices without a valid reason;
(3) refuse to transact with trading counterparts without a valid reason;
(4) restrict trading counterparts to transact only with the undertaking or only with designated undertakings without a valid reason;
(5) bundle sale of commodities without a valid reason or imposition of any other unreasonable terms of transaction during a transaction; or.
(6) implement differential treatment for terms of transaction such as transaction price for similar trading counterparts without a valid reason; or.
(7) perform any other activities of abuse of dominant market position as defined by the anti-monopoly enforcement agency of the State Council.'

[31] 王先林 [Wang Xianlin]. 2015. 关于制定我国滥用知识产权反垄断指南的若干思考 [Relevant thoughts on the enactment of the anti-monopoly guidelines of the abuse of IPRs in China]. *价格理论与实践 [Price Theory & Practice]* 10: 25-29, 25.

6.4.1 *The Refusal to Disclose Trade Secrets*

The refusal to disclose trade secrets is a crucial abusive practice discussed in Chapter 5. The owner of a trade secret is in principle entitled to decide whether to disclose the secret information to others. However, the refusal to disclose trade secrets may constitute the abuse of market dominance in some circumstances. There is a potential tension between the right to exercise of trade secrets and the antitrust intervention.

This tension also exists in China. Chapter 5 has noted that the US imposed tremendous pressures for urging China not to adopt the essential facilities doctrine, which was closely related to the refusal to license intellectual property rights.[32] Aside from the issue of the essential facilities doctrine, the US government has shown noticeable concerns about the competition law intervention of intellectual property right in China. For example, an official report issued by the Office of the United States Trade Representative says that:

> Based on a limited number of investigations conducted to date, there is an ongoing concern among U.S. companies that Chinese competition authorities may target for investigation those foreign firms that hold IPR that may be essential to the implementation of certain technological standards. Reports of intimidating and non-transparent investigation conduct contribute to these concerns.[33]

To address these concerns, it is suggested that China should promote the coordinated development of anti-monopoly and intellectual property protection.[34] China must deal with the above tension between the right to exercise of trade secrets and the antitrust intervention.

Chapter 5 has discussed existing provisions on the refusal to license intellectual property in the IP Guidelines.[35] These provisions are too general to provide a clear standard for Chinese competition agencies and courts to deal with cases. Chinese competition authorities and courts may have too broad discretion to interpret these provisions in specific cases. The broad discretion may result in concerns—such as 'non-transparent investigation' as stated in the US report. As a result, this book recommends that China should establish a more definite test to assess the refusal to disclose trade secrets.

Chapter 5 provides two different approaches, namely the US and EU approaches, to the refusal to disclose trade secrets. It has been suggested that the US courts hesitate to determine an illegal refusal to deal after the landmark *Trinko* case.[36] In comparison, the EU authorities have developed a test of 'exceptional circumstances'

---

[32] See 5.2.2.2 in Chapter 4 of this book.

[33] Office of the United States Trade Representative. 2016. 2016 Special 301 Report. https://ustr.gov/sites/default/files/USTR-2016-Special-301-Report.pdf. Accessed 23 March 2025.

[34] Wang Xianlin. 2017. Some key issues concerning further development of China's anti-monopoly law. In *Competition policy for the new era: Insights from the BRICS countries,* eds. Tembinkosi Bonakele, Eleanor Fox and Liberty Mncube, 224. Oxford: Oxford University Press.

[35] See 5.2.2.2 in Chapter 5 of this book.

[36] See 5.2.3.1 in Chapter 4 of this book.

to deal with cases of the refusal to license intellectual property, including the refusal to disclose trade secrets (*Microsoft* case).

Chapter 5 explains why China should primarily adopt the EU experience (instead of the US counterpart) when it comes to analyzing the refusal to disclose trade secrets.[37] In addition to the advantages of the EU case-law which are examined in Chapter 5, China should not introduce the *Trinko* doctrine because it contradicts the anti-monopoly reality in China.

In *Trinko*, Justice Scalia was not confident of the antitrust intervention in the refusal to deal. His Honour was concerned that antitrust intervention may be detrimental to the free market system.[38] Under relevant anti-monopoly rules in China, the refusal to deal (including the refusal to license intellectual property and disclose trade secrets) may constitute the abuse of market dominance.[39] Consequently, Chinese competition agencies and courts should follow Chinese anti-monopoly rules, and cannot refuse to apply the refusal to deal doctrine as the US courts do.

In accordance with the EU case-law, this book provides recommendations for establishing a straightforward test of the refusal to disclose trade secrets. These suggestions are as follows:

6.4.1.1 The IP Guidelines Should Mainly Target Cases of the Refusal to Disclose Trade Secrets Where the Upstream and Downstream Markets Are Differentiated

As examined in Chapter 5, the Chinese court and EU court have in fact identified the upstream market and derivative market in their respective cases (China's *Motorola* and the EU *Microsoft* cases).[40] This book recommends that the IP Guidelines distinguish the upstream and derivative markets when assessing the refusal to disclose trade secrets cases.

6.4.1.2 The IP Guidelines Should Include a Four-Prong Test to Determine an Anti-Competitive Refusal to Disclose Trade Secrets[41]

(A) Chinese competition authorities and courts should assess whether the underlying secret information is indispensable (essential). A trade secret may encompass indispensability particularly when it becomes a de facto standard with network effects (EU *Microsoft* case).

[37] See 5.2.4.1 in Chapter 5 of this book.

[38] See 5.2.3.1 in Chapter 5 of this book.

[39] These rules involve the AML and relevant regulations of SAMR, as well as the IP Guidelines. See 5.2.2 in Chapter 5 of this book.

[40] See 5.2.4.2 in Chapter 5 of this book.

[41] Ibid.

(B) Chinese competition authorities and courts should examine whether the refusal to disclose trade secrets may eliminate effective competition in the downstream market. The Chinese authority may learn from comparative experience to conduct empirical research (e.g. customer questionnaires) to determine it.
(C) Chinese competition authorities and courts should analyse whether the refusal to disclose trade secrets may prevent technical developments. This requirement follows the IP Guidelines where the detriment to technical innovation may be considered as a type of anti-competitive effects in particular cases.[42]
(D) Chinese competition authorities and courts should allow the dominant firm to justify its refusal to disclose trade secrets. For example, the dominant firm may argue the disclosure might decrease the firm's incentive to innovate in the future. The dominant firm should have the burden of proof for these justifications.

6.4.1.3 The IP Guidelines Should Consider the Existence of a Previous Disclosure as a Vital Factor Constituting the Abuse of Market Dominance[43]

The four-prong test is a common rule for Chinese competition authorities and courts to determine an illegal refusal to disclose trade secrets. It will be more likely for the authority to identify the abuse of dominance if a previous disclosure exists (the US *Aspen Skiing* and EU *Microsoft*). A dominant company may disclose the secret to its competitors for some periods and refuse to disclose it for the convenience of entering the derivate market. In that case, it should be an indication of an illegal refusal to disclose trade secrets.

6.4.1.4 Chinese Law Should Include Provisions on the Remedy for a Refusal to Disclose Trade Secrets

The Chinese competition agency or court may determine a refusal to disclose trade secrets as a type of the abuse of market dominance under the AML. In that case, the reasonable remedy for the refusal is the imposition of a duty to disclose by the dominant firm. Arguably, the competition law is responsible for identifying the anti-competitive refusal to license intellectual property. The intellectual property law is responsible for determining a compulsory license of intellectual property, such as providing provisions on determining the royalty fees of the license. Nonetheless, existing Chinese law does not provide any provisions on a compulsory disclosure of a trade secret.

The Chinese Patent law can be an example to explain this issue. Article 53 of the Chinese Patent Law (Revised in 2020) provides that:

[42] See article 5 of the IP Guidelines.
[43] Ibid.

> 'Under any of the following circumstances, the patent administrative department under the State Council may, pursuant to an application by an organization or individual qualified for implementation, grant a mandatory licensing for implementation of the patent for an invention or a utility model:
>
> … (2) where the acts of exercising patent rights by a patentee have been determined as monopolistic acts pursuant to the law, and the mandatory licensing is granted to eliminate or reduce the adverse impact of such acts on competition.'

According to article 53 of the Chinese Patent Law, if a refusal to license a patent constitutes the abuse of market dominance under the AML, Chinese authorities can order the dominant patentee to license the patent to competitors. Nevertheless, this antitrust duty to license merely exists in Chinese Patent Law and cannot be applied to cases of trade secrets. As a result, this book recommends that the Chinese Law governing the protection of trade secrets (the Anti-unfair Competition Law) should learn from the Patent Law. The Anti-unfair Competition Law should contain a provision that allows the Chinese authority to impose an antitrust duty to disclose trade secrets if the refusal constitutes the abuse of market dominance under the AML.

6.4.2 Bad Faith Litigation of Trade Secrets

Chapter 5 identifies bad faith litigation of trade secrets initiated by a dominant undertaking as a category of the abuse of market dominance. Even though the *Huawei v InterDigital* case indicated that the Chinese court recognized bad faith litigation as an abuse,[44] the IP Guidelines do not include any provisions on bad faith litigation.

The IP Guidelines should include bad faith litigation of trade secrets initiated by a dominant firm as an abuse of dominance. This book argues that China should enable antitrust counterclaims in misappropriation lawsuits of trade secrets. The following also gives some specific suggestions on assessing bad faith litigation of trade secrets in the IP Guidelines.

6.4.2.1 China Should Consider Enabling Antitrust Counterclaims in a Misappropriation Lawsuit of Trade Secrets

If a dominant company (X) files an infringement lawsuit alleging that the defendant (Y) misappropriated the plaintiff's trade secret, this lawsuit might constitute the abuse of dominance provided that the dominant firm litigates in bad faith. There are three possible methods of dealing with this type of bad faith litigation of trade secrets in China:

(A) The Chinese competition agency may take an antitrust investigation against the dominant firm (X) for its bad faith litigation of trade secrets.

[44] See 5.3.3 in Chapter 5 of this book.

(B) Y (the defendant in the bad faith lawsuit) may file an independent civil anti-monopoly lawsuit against X through a separate legal proceeding. (e.g. *Huawei v InterDigital*)[45]
(C) During the misappropriation lawsuit of trade secrets, Y may directly counterclaim that the misappropriation litigation is initiated in bad faith and constitutes the abuse of market dominance. ('antitrust counterclaim')

The AML provides the legal foundations for the first two scenarios. For example, article 38 of the AML says that '[T]he anti-monopoly enforcement agency shall investigate alleged monopolistic activities pursuant to the law.' Meanwhile, article 50 of the AML authorizes individuals who suffer from monopolistic activities to file anti-monopoly civil lawsuits before a court.[46]

It may cost Y time and money to report the alleged bad faith litigation to the competition agency or file an independent antitrust civil lawsuit against X. This is why comparative experience reveals that bad faith litigation often occurs as a counterclaim in intellectual property infringement lawsuits as discussed in Chapter 5.[47] It may be much easier for Y to directly counterclaim that X abuses its market dominance by litigating in bad faith in the misappropriation lawsuit of trade secrets. If the judge upholds Y's argument by finding bad faith litigation, the court will dismiss the misappropriation case immediately.

However, Chinese law has not established antitrust counterclaims in a misappropriation lawsuit of trade secrets yet. Although there are over 1000 civil lawsuits of misappropriation of trade secrets each year in China,[48] there have been none reported cases where the judge held that bad faith litigation of trade secrets constitutes an anti-monopoly counterclaim.

This book recommends that China should allow antitrust counterclaims in misappropriation lawsuits of trade secrets. The SPC should amend its relevant judicial interpretations (which are binding for all Chinese courts) to allow this. For example, the SPC issued the *Provisions on Several Issues concerning the Application of Law in the Trial of Civil Cases involving Trade Secret Infringement* in September 2020. This is a judicial interpretation designed to deal with the application of laws in misappropriation litigation of trade secrets in China. It is suggested that this judicial interpretation should stipulate that the defendant is entitled to counterclaim that the litigation initiated by the plaintiff might constitute the abuse of market dominance. If the bad faith litigation of trade secrets constitutes the abuse of dominance, the court should dismiss the plaintiff's claims.

---

[45] See 5.3.3.1 in Chapter 5 of this book.

[46] Article 60 of the AML provides that '[U]ndertakings which implement monopolistic activities and causing others to suffer losses shall bear civil liability pursuant to the law.'

[47] See 5.3.1 in Chapter 5 of this book.

[48] See Hefei IP Lawyer. 2020. Data Analysis of Trade Secret Cases in China (2015–2019). https://hfiplaw.cn/details/20610.html. Accessed 23 March 2025.

The IP Guidelines Should Adopt a Two-Fold Test for the Determination of Bad Faith Litigation of Trade Secrets[49]

This book proposes the following suggestions pursuant to assessments in Chapter 5. Firstly, the IP Guidelines should specify that the bad faith litigation may be determined only if the litigation is objectively baseless. Learning from the EU *ITT Promedia* case, Chinese competition agencies and courts should assess whether the dominant undertaking reasonably believes that the suit is baseless, instead of considering whether there exists a legal right for the dominant firm.[50] Secondly, Chinese competition agencies and courts should consider whether the dominant firm has a subjective intention to restrict competition. For instance, if the dominant firm repetitively files bad faith litigation of trade secrets against competitors, this may indicate the intention of hindering competition.[51]

The IP Guidelines Should Specify Two Particular Circumstances of Bad Faith Litigation of Trade Secrets[52]

One scenario is that of the US *CVD* case analyzed in Chapter 5. If the dominant undertaking does not own a legally-defined trade secret but argues for misappropriation of trade secrets, the litigation is an abuse of dominance.

Another circumstance occurs when the underlying trade secret becomes a de facto standard as shown in the EU *Microsoft* case. *Huawei v InterDigital* reveals that bad faith litigation of SEPs may violate FRAND commitments and constitute the abuse of dominance. Similarly, this situation may happen in trade secrets when the secret information becomes a de facto standard. Chinese competition agencies and courts should determine the bad faith litigation of trade secrets if (1) the dominant firm (e.g. Microsoft) is ordered by the competition authority to disclose secret information to rivals; (2) the antitrust agency imposes FRAND requirement on the dominant company; and (3) the dominant undertaking violates FRAND requirements and sues competitors in bad faith for unreasonable trading conditions.[53]

6.4.3 Non-challenge Clauses in Relation to Trade Secrets

Chapter 5 of this book critically examines non-challenge clauses in relation to trade secrets imposed by a dominant firm as a type of the abuse of market dominance.

---

49 See 5.3.3 in Chapter 5 of this book.

50 Chapter 5 provides an example concerning the characteristic of 'reasonable measures' of a trade secret to explain this requirement. See ibid.

51 Ibid.

52 Ibid.

53 Ibid.

The IP Guidelines provide some provisions on non-challenge clauses. For example, Chapter 3 of the IP Guidelines (Articles 14-19) stipulates relevant practices related to the exploitation of intellectual property that may constitute the abuse of market dominance.

Article 18 of the IP Guidelines prevents unreasonable trading conditions regarding intellectual property imposed by a dominant firm. It says that:

> The imposition of the following transaction conditions by undertakings with dominant market position to transactions involving intellectual property rights without justifiable reasons may lead to effects of eliminating or restricting competition:
>
> ... (2) prohibiting the transaction counterparties from challenging the validity of intellectual property...

The IP Guidelines recognize that the non-challenge clauses for intellectual property may constitute the abuse of dominance under certain circumstances. The book proposes some recommendations for the IP Guidelines in terms of non-challenge clauses of trade secrets.

6.4.3.1 The IP Guidelines Should Explain the Reason Why Non-challenge Clauses of Intellectual Property (Including Trade Secrets) Imposed by a Dominant Company Should Be Prohibited

Chapter 5 critically analyses the NDRC Qualcomm case, which is the only case regarding non-challenge clauses in China. However, as discussed in Chapter 5, the two arguments proposed by the NDRC to explain the anti-competitive effects of non-challenge clauses are not clear.[54]

It is suggested that the IP Guidelines should explain anti-competitive concerns arisen from the non-challenge clause of intellectual property. In accordance with assessments in Chapter 5, the IP Guidelines should specify that intellectual property law does not supply protection to invalid intellectual property, including information that does not constitute a trade secret. The holder of invalid intellectual property (including a trade secret) is not entitled to charge supra-competitive prices to consumers.[55]

The non-challenge clause of intellectual property may result in anti-monopoly concerns because it enables a dominant licensor to charge supra-competitive prices on consumers. As the *Lear* doctrine stated, the licensee is in a good position to challenge the validity of intellectual property, including the existence of a trade

[54] The first argument is that non-challenge clauses of patents may violate Chinese patent law, which is irrelevant to its anti-competitive effects. The second argument is that non-challenge clause may not please actual or potential licensees. However, even a dominant firm does not have an antitrust duty to provide contractual terms that all licensees accept. See 5.4.4 in Chapter 5 of this book.

[55] Ibid.

secret.[56] As the policy of clearing invalid intellectual property prevails, a dominant licensor is prohibited from imposing non-challenge clauses of intellectual property (including trade secrets) on licensees.

6.4.3.2 The IP Guidelines Should Consider the Duration of Non-challenge Clauses of Trade Secrets in Assessing Breach

As examined earlier in Chapter 5, the duration of the non-challenge clause of a trade secret has substantial influences on the anti-competitive effects of the clause.[57] The secrecy is the core element of information constituting a trade secret.[58] The owner of secret information may possess it indefinitely, without the need to disclose it to the public.[59] Even though there is a duration of the license of a trade secret, a dominant licensor may compel the licensee not to challenge the existence of the secret information indefinitely. In this scenario, if the licensed information fails to constitute a trade secret, consumers may suffer from the long-term non-challenge clauses through paying for the invalid secret information. A non-challenge clause of trade secrets with a longer duration may give rise to more anti-monopoly outcomes.

6.4.3.3 The IP Guidelines Should Consider One Exception of the Prohibition of Non-challenge Clauses of Trade Secrets, Which Occurred in the EU *Bayer* Case[60]

If the licensed technology (including trade secrets) is an outdated process that the licensee does not use at all, the license would not have any negative implications on downstream consumers. Under such circumstances, even if there is a non-challenge clause in the license contract, the clause will not have detrimental effects on consumers and competition. China's anti-monopoly rules should not intervene in this situation.

---

[56] In terms of trade secrets, Chapter 5 demonstrates that the licensee is in a good and exclusive position to challenge the existence of a trade secret. See ibid.

[57] Ibid.

[58] Chapter 2 of this book introduces three requirements to constitute a legally-define trade secret. Information that is kept a secret does not necessarily belong to a trade secret. For instance, the information may lack commercial value. In this regard, a licensee can challenge the existence of a trade secret despite the secrecy of the information.

[59] This is different from a patent, which must enter the public domain after the expiration date.

[60] See 5.4.4 in Chapter 5 of this book.

6.4.3.4 The IP Guidelines Should Provide Two Types of Defenses for the Dominant Licensor to Justify the Non-challenge Clauses of Trade Secrets[61]

The anti-competitive effects of a non-challenge clause arise from the potential invalidity of the licensed trade secret. Therefore, the first defence should be that the dominant licensor may prove that there exists a legally-defined trade secret. That is, the dominant licensor may prove that the licensed information has met the three essential requirements of constituting a trade secret (secrecy, commercial values and reasonable precautions taken by secret a holder).

Another defence is related to the characteristic of the secrecy of a trade secret. In comparison to other categories of intellectual property (e.g. a patent), the contents of which are public, a trade secret is maintained in secrecy. A trade secret disappears if its content is disclosed to the public. Consequently, the dominant licensor may justify the non-challenge clause by proving it is an essential method of protecting the secrecy of the licensed information.

6.4.3.5 Chinese Competition Agencies Should Focus on Non-challenge Clauses of Trade Secret Related to Standards

Comparative experience has demonstrated that non-challenge clauses in SEP-related cases may have more severe anti-competitive effects than those in non-SEP cases.[62] This is primarily because consumers have no choice but to use the technology which is incorporated into standards. If the licensed technology consists of invalid intellectual property, consumers are harmed because of paying for needless technology.

Similarly, Chinese competition authorities should investigate non-challenge clauses when a trade secret becomes a de facto standard. For example, supposing Microsoft is ordered by the competition authority to disclose interface information (which is argued by Microsoft constituting a trade secret) to its rivals, Microsoft may compel its licensees not to challenge the existence of the trade secret. This may lead to competition concerns particular if the interface information in essence does not constitute a trade secret.

6.5 Conclusion

After normative analysis about the abuse of market dominance in relation to trade secrets discussed in previous chapters, Chapter 6 details some recommendations for China's anti-monopoly legal practices.

---

[61] Ibid.

[62] See 5.4.2.2 in Chapter 5 of this book.

The AML is the fundamental anti-monopoly rule in China. Provisions of the AML are general provisions and can be applied in all fields. The IP Guidelines are China's anti-monopoly guidelines focusing on competition enforcement in the exercise of intellectual property (including trade secrets) and have close relationship with this book.

Anti-monopoly enforcement in China is divided into public and private enforcement. Chinese anti-monopoly agencies lead the public enforcement by taking investigations against a company. The AML also authorizes individuals who suffer from monopolistic conduct to file civil lawsuits against the monopolist. This is known as the private enforcement of the AML in China.

In order to find an abuse of dominance concerning trade secrets, Chinese competition agencies and courts need to (1) determine whether the company is in a dominant position in the relevant market; and (2) identify whether the dominant undertaking engages in abusive practices that harm competition. To this end, Chapters 4 and 5 critically analyse the market dominance in trade secrets and some abusive practices in relation to trade secrets. This chapter provides specific recommendations according to analysis in Chapters 4 and 5. Among all anti-monopoly rules in China, the IP Guidelines are directly intended to guide anti-monopoly enforcement in the domain of intellectual property, including trade secrets. As a consequence, most suggestions in this chapter are designed to improve the IP Guidelines.

Chapter 6 provides specific suggestions for China's future anti-monopoly legal practices and serves as the last substantive chapter to answer the main research question of this book. The next chapter (Chapter 7) will conclude the whole book.

Chapter 7
Conclusion

7.1 Introduction

As proposed in Chapter 1, the primary research question of this book is: in which circumstances does the use of trade secrets constitute an abuse of market dominance pursuant to China's Anti-monopoly Law and how can the approach analysis be improved? The previous chapters have elucidated the answer to the research question through critical legal analysis.

All chapters in the book are organized so as to better answer the research question. Chapters 2 and 3 provide an overview of the two important subject-matters of the book—namely trade secrets and the abuse of market dominance. Chapter 4 critically analyses the market dominance with regard to trade secrets. After the determination of the dominant position of a firm, Chapter 5 examines three categories of abusive practices in relation to trade secrets: the refusal to disclose trade secrets, bad faith litigation of trade secrets and the non-challenge clauses of trade secrets.

This chapter draws conclusions from the whole book and is divided into four parts. This chapter concludes some key findings relevant to the research questions according to previous chapters. This chapter then proposes some future directions that have not yet been researched in this book.

7.2 Key Findings

Chapters 2 to 6 provide substantive analysis of the abuse of market dominance concerning trade secrets and its proposed regulation in China. Each chapter plays a different but significant role in this book. The following outlines key findings of each chapter of this book.

Chapter 2 defines the landscape of trade secret protection in China. As a type of intellectual property, holders of trade secret information are not required to apply for

P. Wu, *Trade Secrets and Market Dominance*, Contemporary Chinese Civil and Commercial Law, https://doi.org/10.1007/978-981-95-1152-5_7

registration before a national office for the grant of trade secrets. However, there are three requirements essential to the formation of a trade secret from a legal point of view. A trade secret should be unknown to the public (the requirement of secrecy) and with commercial values. Additionally, the secret holder should take reasonable precautions to protect the underlying secret information.

Chapter 2 outlines some characteristics of a trade secret. Firstly, there are different categories of trade secrets—such as technical secrets, business secrets and other new-emerging trade secrets. Secondly, compared with other kinds of intellectual property rights which have expiration dates, the holder of a trade secret may be qualified for the possession of the secret information indefinitely as long as the holder keeps it as a secret. Thirdly, the trade secret, as a type of intellectual property, is an exclusive right. That is, a secret holder is entitled to prohibit other competitors from misappropriation of the secret information. Nevertheless, the exclusivity of the trade secret is limited because it is legal for others to acquire secret information through self-creation and reverse-engineering.

The introductory chapter of the book uses the 'family resemblance' doctrine as one significant theoretical framework. This doctrine helps explain the similarities and differences of the trade secret as opposed to other categories of intellectual property. After analyzing the characteristics of a trade secret, Chapter 2 takes patents (a typical intellectual property) as an example to compare it with the trade secret. In this regard, the following chapters apply existing antitrust experience relevant to other intellectual property to the less discussed trade secret cases due to their similarities. This book also considers the differences between a trade secret and other typical intellectual property in the following antitrust assessments, which makes this book original in the competition law academia.

Chapter 3 provides an overview of another important subject-matter—the abuse of market dominance. The abuse of market dominance, together with monopoly agreements and anti-competitive mergers are three anti-competitive practices prohibited by competition law. Chapter 3 critically examines comparative lessons from the US and the EU on the regulation of the abuse of market dominance. In short, the Chicago School has dominated the US antitrust thinking and led to an effects-based approach. Section 2 of the US Sherman Act is the legal foundation that prohibits both monopolization and attempted monopolization. The ordoliberalism substantially influences the EU competition law, particularly Article 102 TFEU which prevents the abuse of market dominance. The application of Article 102 has transformed from a form-based approach to an effects-based approach, although there are still some disputes on the transformation.

Chapter 3 examines China's AML in which the abuse of market dominance is proscribed. Both the US antitrust law and EU competition law have had effects on the provisions and the application of China's AML. The landmark *Qihoo v Tencent* was a watershed case in China. Prior to *Qihoo v Tencent*, China held a form-based approach without examining the anti-competitive effects of practices in detail. The *Qihoo v Tencent* and its following cases demonstrate that China prefers an effects-based approach when analyzing abusive conduct now. However, Chinese courts and competition agencies may not depend on the effects of consumer welfare only, but will analyse other types of effects on competition.

Chapter 3 sets out a two-step approach to assessing cases of the abuse of dominance, which is commonly used by the US, EU and China. That is, the competition agencies and courts may identify whether the company at issue is in a dominant position in the relevant market. If a dominant undertaking is determined, authorities may assess whether the dominant firm conducts abusive practices that hinder competition. Chapters 4 and 5 are organized according to the two-step approach.

Pursuant to the two-step approach, Chapter 4 examines the market dominance in trade secrets. This book argues the necessity to define the relevant market before assessing market power of a company in the market. The antitrust agency needs to determine the relevant product and geographic market in terms of trade secret products. The trade secret may be licensed in the technology transaction. In cases where the trade secret is licensed as a commodity, it is necessary to define the technology market. The traditional quantitative test (e.g. SSNIP) and the qualitative approach based on characteristics, price and intended use may help define the relevant market. Meanwhile, in circumstances where the consumers are not sensitive to prices or the royalty fees are difficult to determine, the competition agencies or courts may make some adjustment to traditional approaches. To sum up, this book argues that in cases of the abuse of market dominance as to trade secrets, it is necessary to use both quantitative and qualitative methods for market definition on a case-specific basis.

After defining a relevant market, Chapter 4 also outlines market dominance related to trade secrets. This chapter briefly discusses the relationship between trade secrets and market power. It argues that the (limited) exclusivity of the trade secret may result in market dominance of the secret holder when the underlying trade secret becomes essential and a de facto standard. This book proposes two indicators that may reflect the market power of a secret holder: market share and barriers to entry. When it comes to barriers to entry, this book identifies that trade secret protection may act as a type of legal and regulatory barriers. Lack of access to key secret information and advanced technology may also constitute barriers to entry that can influence market power of the secret holder.

Chapter 5 explores three abusive practices relevant to the exploitation of trade secrets. It indicates that the possession of a trade secret by a dominant firm is legal. Only if the dominant company abuses its trade secrets during the exploitation that may constitute the abuse of market dominance.

The refusal to disclose trade secrets, as a sub-set of the refusal to deal, may constitute the abuse of market dominance. This book argues that the EU case-law might be more suitable for Chinese context than the US approach indicated in *Trinko*. That is, a dominant undertaking is in principle entitled to refuse to disclose trade secrets to competitors. Nevertheless, under exceptional circumstances, the refusal to disclose trade secrets conducted by a dominant undertaking might be an abuse, particularly when the secret information has acted as a de facto standard. This book proposes a balance test that was held in the EU *Microsoft* case to determine an illegal refusal to disclose trade secrets. The test takes into account the anti-competitive effects of the refusal to disclose trade secrets, and deals with potential tensions between the antitrust duty to deal and the incentive to innovate.

Chapter 5 identifies bad faith litigation of trade secrets as the second abusive conduct as to trade secrets. The owner of a trade secret is entitled to sue its rivals for misappropriation of his/her trade secret. However, if the dominant secret holder litigates in bad faith in order to enhance competitive advantages, it might constitute the abuse of market dominance (as shown in the US *CVD* case). For the reason of keeping a reasonable balance between the right of access to justice and antitrust intervention, this book proposes a two-prong test which focuses on both objective and subjective aspects to identify bad faith litigation of trade secrets.

The last abusive practice examined in Chapter 5 is non-challenge clauses of trade secrets. The dominant licensor may force the licensee to accept the non-challenge clause of trade secrets. This might constitute the abuse of market dominance under competition law. Comparative lessons demonstrate that the licensor is in a good position to challenge the validity of intellectual property, including the existence of the trade secret. The book argues that consumers should not pay for invalid intellectual property and the public policy of clearing invalid intellectual property should prevail over other considerations. The non-challenge clauses of trade secrets may be proscribed in principle. Nonetheless, the dominant firm may justify the non-challenge clause by proving the existence of the legally-defined trade secret or the fundamental significance of non-challenge clauses in secret protection.

Chapter 6 proposes several suggestions for improvements of anti-monopoly enforcement of the abuse of dominance as to trade secrets in China. This chapter summarizes the existing anti-monopoly rules and enforcement in China. Based on Chinese legal traditions, this chapter provides detailed suggestions on amending Chinese anti-monopoly rules and improving anti-monopoly enforcement in accordance with legal analysis in previous chapters. As the IP Guidelines are the Chinese anti-monopoly rule which mainly concerns the application of the AML in the field of intellectual property, many suggestions in this chapter are proposed for revising the IP Guidelines.

To conclude, this book critically analyses the abuse of market dominance relating to trade secrets in China step by step. Different chapters play a different role in providing key findings as the above. The following section will look at some further research in relation to this book.

7.3 Further Research

This book deals with the legal issue of the abuse of market dominance in relation to trade secrets in China. Arguably, the abuse of dominance in trade secrets is a new-emerging issue not only in China but also in the west. This book is only an inception of the research of this issue from a legal and economic point of view.

In addition to this book, it is projected that there will be further research concerning the antitrust intervention into trade secrets in the future. The following are three aspects that are worth studying in the future.

The first direction is closely related to abusive practices regarding trade secrets. Chapter 5 analyses three categories of abusive practices: the refusal to disclose trade secrets, bad faith litigation of trade secrets and the non-challenge clause trade secrets. This book has analyzed these three abusive practices because there have been some cases and literature in which these practices are identified. Noteworthy is that there might be some new abusive practices concerning trade secrets in the future. This means that it is possible for a dominant firm to abuse its market dominance by conducting abusive practices other than those examined in Chapter 5 of this book. There might be some further research on other possible abusive practices regarding trade secrets in the future.

Secondly, the abuse of trade secrets may exist not only in the form of the abuse of market dominance, but also in the process of anti-competitive mergers and monopoly agreements. As discussed earlier, modern competition law prohibits three types of anti-competitive practices, namely the abuse of market dominance, anti-competitive merges and monopoly agreements. This book concentrates merely on the prevention of the abuse of market dominance. A company might use its trade secrets illegally in the form of other two types of anti-competitive practices. Accordingly, competition lawyers might wish to follow this direction to conduct future research on the abuse of trade secrets in relation to anti-competitive mergers and monopoly agreements.

Last but not least, there are likely to be more case studies of the abuse of market dominance in trade secrets in China. This book primarily relies on doctrinal methodology to study the abuse of dominance in trade secrets, benefiting from comparative lessons from the US and the EU, as well as experience of the abuse of dominance in other intellectual property (e.g. patents). For now, there have been few anti-monopoly cases of the abuse of market dominance relating to trade secrets in China.

If there were more cases of the abuse of market dominance as to trade secrets in China, it might be possible to undertake further case studies and provide additional suggestions on the handling of specific cases for Chinese competition agencies and courts.

Bibliography

Articles/Books/Reports

Adediji, Damola. 2016. United State's law on refusal to deal after the trinko decision of the supreme court. (Seminar Paper, Intellectual Property and Competition Law Seminar under the direction and tutelage of Professor Dr. Josef Drexl, July 2016)

Ahlborn, Christian, David Evans, and A. Jorge Padilla. 2001. Competition policy in the new economy: is European competition law up to the challenge?. *European Competition Law Review* 22(5): 156

Almeling, David. 2012. Seven reasons why trade secrets are increasingly important. *Berkeley Technology Law Journal* 27: 1098–1117

Altman, Louis and Malla Pollack. 2008. *Callmann on unfair competition, trademarks, and monopolies.* Toronto: Thomson Reuters

Ansari, Dina. 2009. The EC essential facilities doctrine, the microsoft case and the treatment of trade secrets. Masters Thesis.

Bai, J. Benjamin, and Da Guoping. 2010. Strategies for trade secrets protection in China. *Northwestern Journal of Technology and Intellectual Property* 9: 351–376

Bain, Joe. 1956. *Barriers to new competition: their character and consequences in manufacturing industries.* Cambridge: Harvard University Press

Bain, Joe. 1968. *Industrial organization 2d ed.* New York: Wiley

Bain, Joe. 1951. Relation of profit rate to industry concentration: American manufacturing, 1936–1940. *The Quarterly Journal of Economics* 65(3): 293–324

Baker, Jonathan. 2007. Beyond schumpeter vs. arrow: How antitrust fosters innovation. *Antitrust Law Journal* 74(3): 575–602

Behrens, Peter. 2018. The ordoliberal concept of 'abuse' of a dominant position and its impact on Article 102 TFEU. In *Abusive practices in competition law,* eds. Fabiana Di Porto and Rupprecht Podszun. 5–25. Cheltenham: Edward Elgar Publishing

Bengtsson, Henrik. 2017. International Report. In *Abuse of dominant position and globalization & protection and disclosure of trade secrets and know-how* eds. Pranvera Këllezi, Bruce Kilpatrick and Pierre Kobel. 291–311. Berlin: Springer

Bergh, Roger van den, Peter D Camesasca, and Andrea Giannaccari. 2017. *Comparative competition law and economics.* Cheltenham: Edward Elgar Publishing

Bone, Robert. 2010. Trade secrecy, innovation, and the requirement of reasonable secrecy precautions. In T*he law and theory of trade secrecy: A handbook of contemporary research,* eds. Rochelle Dreyfuss and Katherine Strandburg. Cheltenham: Edward Elgar Press

Bork, Robert. 1978. *The antitrust paradox: A policy at war with itself*. New York: Basic Books

P. Wu, *Trade Secrets and Market Dominance*, Contemporary Chinese Civil and Commercial Law, https://doi.org/10.1007/978-981-95-1152-5

Brandeis, Louis, Fraenkel, K. Osmond and Clarence M Lewis. 1965. *The curse of bigness*. New York: Kennikat Press

Browne, Michael. 2017. United Kingdom. In *Abuse of dominant position and globalization & protection and disclosure of trade secrets and know-how,* eds. Pranvera Këllezi, Bruce Kilpatrick and Pierre Kobel. 605–620. Berlin: Springer

Burk, Dan and Mark Lemley. 2009. Fence posts or sign posts? Rethinking patent claim construction. *University of Pennsylvania Law Review* 157(6): 1743–1799

Carlton, Dennis W and Jeffrey M Perloff. 2005. *Modern industrial organization. 4th ed*. Boston: Pearson/Addison Wesley

Cheng, Thomas. 2016. Antitrust treatment of the no challenge clause. *Journal of Intellectual Property and Entertainment Law* 5(2): 437–512

Cheng, Thomas. 2012. Convergence and its discontents: A reconsideration of the merits of convergence of global competition law. *Chicago Journal of International Law* 12(2): 433–490

Cheng, Thomas. 2017. The PRC NDRC case against qualcomm: A misguided venture or justified enforcement of competition law. *Journal of Antitrust Enforcement* 5(1): 76–99

Chow, Daniel and Thomas Schoenbaum. 2012. *International trade law: Problems, cases, and materials. 2d ed*. New York: ASPEN Publishing

Clark, JM. 1940. Toward a concept of workable competition. *The American Economic Review* 30(2): 241–256

Cornish, William and Kathleen Liddell. 2016. The origins and structure of the TRIPS agreement. In *TRIPS Plus 20,* eds. Hanns Ullrich, Reto Hilty, Matthias Lamping and Josef Drexl. Berlin: Springer

Crane, Daniel. 2014. Actavis, the reverse payment fallacy, and the continuing need for regulatory solution. *Minnesota Journal of Law, Science & Technology* 15(1): 51–59

Crane, Daniel. 2009. Chicago, post-Chicago, and neo-Chicago. *The University of Chicago Law Review* 76: 1911–1933

Crass, Dirk et al. 2019. Protecting innovation through patents and trade secrets: Evidence for firms with a single innovation. *International Journal of the Economics of Business* 26(1): 117–156

Czapracka, Katarzyna. 2008. Antitrust and trade secrets: The US and the EU approach. *Santa Clara High Technology Law Journal* 24(2): 207–273

Demsetz, Harold. 1973. Industry structure, market rivalry, and public policy. *The Journal of Law and Economics* 16(1):1–9

Dessemontet, Fracois. 1998. Protection of trade secrets and confidential information. In *Intellectual property and international trade. The TRIPS Agreement,* eds. Carlos Correa and A. Yusuf. London-Cambridge: Kluwer Law International

Determann, L., L. Schmaus, and J. Tam. 2017. Trade secret protection measures and new harmonized laws. *Computer and Internet Lawyer* 34(1): 179–189

丁茂中 [Ding Maozhong]. 2020. 我国《反垄断法》的修订路径 [Analysis on revisions of China's anti-monopoly law]. *法学 [Law Science]* 5: 133–150

Drexl, Josef. 2007. Abuse of dominance in licensing and refusal to license-a 'more economic approach' to competition by imitation and to competition by substitution. In *The interaction between competition law and IP law*, eds. Claus Dieter Ehlermann, and Isabela Atansiu, 647–648. Oxford: Hart publishing

Drexl, Josef. 2011. Intellectual property in competition: How to promote dynamic competition as a goal. In *More common ground for international competition law?* eds. Josef Drexl, Warren S. Grimes, Clifford A. Jones, Rudolph J.R. Peritz and Edward T. Swaine, 210. ASCOLA Competition Law series

Drexl, Josef. 2011. *Competition policy and the economic approach: Foundations and limitations.* Cheltenham: Edward Elgar Publishing

Drexl, Josef. 2011. Intellectual property in competition: How to promote dynamic competition as a goal. In *More common ground for international competition law?(ASCOLA competition law series),* eds. Josef Drexl, Warren S. Grimes, Clifford A. Jones, Rudolph J.R. Peritz and Edward T. Swaine, 210. Cheltenham: Edward Elgar Publishing

Drexl, Josef. 2011. Refusal to grant access to trade secrets as an abuse of market dominance. In *Intellectual property and competition law-new frontiers*, 165. Oxford: Oxford University Press

Drexl, Josef. 2008. The Relationship between the legal exclusivity and economic market power. links and limits. In: *Intellectual property, market power and the public interest (College of Europe studies, 8)*, eds. Inge Govaere and Hanns Ullrich. 13–33. New York: Brussels

Dworkin, Ronald. 1980. Is wealth a value? *The Journal of Legal Studies* 9(2): 191–226

Eilam, Eldad. 2011. *Reversing: Secrets of reverse engineering*. Hoboken: John Wiley & Sons

Elhaugec, Einer and Alex Krueger. 2012. Solving the patent settlement puzzle. *Texas Law Review* 91(2): 283–330

Emch, Adrian and Ng, Wendy. 2019. *Wang Xiaoye liber amicorum: The pioneer of competition law in China.* New York: Institute of Competition Law.

Emch, Adrian. 2016. Effects Analysis in abuse of dominance cases in China—Is Qihoo 360 v Tencent a game-changer. *Competition L. Int'l* 12: 11–31

方小敏 [Fang Xiaomin]. 2010. 竞争法视野中的欧洲法律统一 *[Unifications of European laws from the perspective of competition law]*. 北京: 中国大百科全书出版社 [Beijing: Encyclopedia of China Publishing House]

Evans, David and A Jorge Padilla. 2005. Designing antitrust rules for assessing unilateral practices: A Neo-Chicago approach. *The University of Chicago Law Review* 72(1): 73–98

Fialkoff, Michael. 2014. Pay-for-delay settlements in the wake of actavis. *Michigan Telecomm. & Technology Law Review* 20: 523–546

First, Harry. 2019. American express, the rule of reason, and the goals of antitrust. *Nebraska Law Review* 98: 319–343

First, Harry. 2011. Trade secrets and antitrust law. In *The law and theory of trade secrecy: A handbook of contemporary research*, ed. C Dreyfuss Rochelle. Northampton: Edward Elgar

Fox, Eleanor. 2013. Against goals. *Fordham Law Review* 81: 2157–2161

Fox, Eleanor. 2008. An anti-monopoly law for china—scaling the walls of government restraints. *Antitrust Law Journal* 75(1): 173–194

Fox, Eleanor and Daniel Crane. 2017. *Global issues in antitrust and competition law*. Eagan: West Academic Publishing

Fox, Eleanor and Deborah Healey. 2013. When the state harms competition-the role for competition law. *Antitrust Law Journal* 79: 769–820

Fox, Eleanor and Lawrence Sullivan. 1987. Antitrust—retrospective and prospective: Where are we coming from—where are we going. *NYU Law Review* 62: 936–985

Fox, Eleanor. 2017. Competition and democracy (4 April 2018). *OECD Report DAF/COMP/GF* 5

Fox, Eleanor. 2005. Is there life in aspen after trinko? The silent revolution of section 2 of the Sherman Act. *Antitrust Law Journal* 73(1): 153–169

Fox, Eleanor. 2014. Monopolization and abuse of dominance: Why Europe is different. *The Antitrust Bulletin* 59(1): 129–152

Fox, Eleanor. 2005. Monopolization, abuse of dominance, and refusal to license intellectual property to competitors–do antitrust duties help or hurt competition and innovation? How do we know? *European Competition Law Annual*: 633–637

Fox, Eleanor. 2019. Should China's competition model be exported?: A reply to Wendy Ng. *European Journal of International Law* 30(4): 1431–1440

Francioni, Francesco. 2007. *Access to justice as a human right.* Oxford: Oxford University Press

Gallego, Beatriz Conde. 2008. Unilateral refusal to license indispensable intellectual property rights–US and EU approaches. In *Research handbook on intellectual property and competition law.* Cheltenham: Edward Elgar

Gal, Michal and Alan Miller. 2017. Patent challenge clauses: A new antitrust offense? *Iowa Law Review* 102(4): 1477–1532

Gal, Michal. 2015. Licensee patent challenges. *Yale Journal on Regulation* 32(1): 121–160

Gavil, Andrew. 2004. Exclusionary distribution strategies by dominant firms: Striking a better balance. *Antitrust Law Journal* 72: 3–81

Gebicka, A. and A. Heinemann. 2014. Social media and competition law. *World Competition* 37: 149–172
George, Alexandra. 2012. *Constructing intellectual property*. Cambridge: Cambridge University Press
George, Alexandra. 2015. The metaphysics of intellectual property. *The WIPO Journal* 7: 16–28
Geradin, D., A. Layne-Farrar, and N. Petit. 2012. *EU Competition Law and Economics*. Oxford: Oxford University Press
Gerber, David. 2019. Comparative competition law. In *The Oxford handbook of comparative law*, eds. Mathias Reimann and Reinhard Zimmermann, 1184–1185. Oxford: Oxford University Press
Gerber, David. 2014. Searching for a modernized voice: Economics, institutions, and predictability in European competition law. *Fordham International Law Journal* 37(5): 1421–1450
Gestel, Rob van and Hans-W. Micklitz. *Revitalizing doctrinal legal research in Europe: What about methodology*? (Working Paper, European University Institute, May 2011)
Glick, Mark, Lara Reymann and Richard Hoffman. 2002. *Intellectual property damages: Guidelines and analysis*. Hoboken: John Wiley & Sons
Gormsen, Liza Lovdahl. 2010. *A principled approach to abuse of dominance in European competition law*. Cambridge: Cambridge University Press
Graef, Inge. 2015. Market definition and market power in data: The case of online platforms. *World competition* 38(4): 473–506
Gugliuzza, Paul. 2015. Patent Trolls and Preemption. *Virginia Law Review* 6: 1579–1647
郭德忠 [Dezhong Guo]. 2015. 商业秘密滥用的反垄断规制 [The anti-monopoly regulation of the abuse of trade secrets]. 情报理论与实践 *[Information Studies: Theory & Application]*, 38: 36–39
Healey, Deborah. 2008. An anti-monopoly law for China: Weapon or mirage? *Competition & Consumer Law Journal* 16: 220–245
Healey, Deborah. 2020. The ambit of competition law: Comments on its goals. In *Research handbook on models and methods of competition law*, eds. D. Healey, M. Jacobs and R. Smith. Cheltenham: Edward Elgar
Hoeren, Thomas. 2017. Germany. In *Abuse of dominant position and globalization & protection and disclosure of trade secrets and know-how*, eds. Pranvera Këllezi, Bruce Kilpatrick, and Pierre Kobel, 425. Berlin: Springer
Hou Liyang. 2012. The essential facilities doctrine—what was wrong in Microsoft? *IIC International Review of Intellectual Property and Competition Law* 43 (4): 451–471
Hou Liyang. 2015. The influence of EU and US legal theory on competition law in China: divergence and convergence. https://ssrn.com/abstract=2586859. Accessed 26 March 2025
Hovenkamp, Herbert. 2020. *Federal antitrust policy: the law of competition and its practice*. Sixth edition. St. Paul, Minnesota: West Academic Publishing
Hovenkamp, Herbert. 2019. Intellectual property and competition. https://scholarship.law.upenn.edu/faculty_scholarship/1807/. Accessed 26 March 2025
Hovenkamp, Hebert, Janis, Mark, and Mark Lemley. 2003. Anti-competitive settlement of intellectual property disputes. *Minnesota Law Review* 87 (6):1719
Hovenkamp, Herbert, Janis, Mark, et al. 2010. *IP and antitrust: An analysis of antitrust principles applied to intellectual property law*. Austin: Aspen Publishers. § 1.3
Hovenkamp, Herbert. 2001. Post-Chicago antitrust: A review and critique. *Columbia Business Law Review*
Hovenkamp, Herbert. 2008. The Harvard and Chicago schools and the dominant firm. In *How the Chicago school overshot the mark the effect of conservative economic analysis on U.S. antitrust*, ed. Robert Pitofsky, 110. Oxford: Oxford University Press
Hu, Christopher. 2014. Some observations on the patent troll litigation problem. *Intellectual Property & Technology Law Journal* 26 (8):10–19

胡良荣 [Hu Liangrong]. 2016. 利益平衡: 论商业秘密的竞争法保护与规制 [Balance of interests: Research on the protection and regulation of trade secrets from a competition law perspective]. 知识产权 *[Intellectual Property]* 12:52–57

Hutchinson, Terry, and Nigel Duncan. 2012. Defining and describing what we do: Doctrinal legal research. *Deakin Law Review* 17 (1):83–119

Hutchinson, Terry. 2015. The doctrinal method: Incorporating interdisciplinary methods in reforming the law. *Erasmus Law Review* 8:130–138

Jones, Alison, and R. Nazzini. 2019. The effect of competition law on patent remedies. In *patent remedies and complex products: Towards a global consensus, eds.* B. Biddle et al. Cambridge: Cambridge University Press

Jones, Alison, Sufrin, BE, and Niamh Dunne. 2019. *EU competition law: Text, cases, and materials.* 7th ed. Oxford: Oxford University Press

Jones, Alison. 2014. Standard-essential patents: FRAND commitments, injunctions and the smartphone wars. *European Competition Journal* 10 (1):1–33

Jorda, Karl. 2007. Trade secrets and trade-secret licensing. In *Intellectual property management in health and agricultural innovation: A handbook of best practice,* eds. Krattiger A. Mahoney RT and Nelsen L., 1043. Oxford: MIHR

Juckniess, Frederick, and Suzanne Larimore Wahl. 2012. Antitrust and intellectual property rights—the ultimate counter-weapon? *Michigan Bar Journal* 23

Kaczorowska-Ireland, Alina. 2016. *European Union Law.* London: Routledge

Kaplow, Louis. 2012. On the choice of welfare standards in competition law. In *The Goals of Competition Law, ed.* Daniel Zimmer. Cheltenham: Edward Elgar

Kolasa, Magdalena. 2018. *Trade secrets and employee mobility: volume 44: in search of an equilibrium. vol. 44.* Cambridge: Cambridge University Press

Korah, Valentine. 2000. *An introductory guide to EC competition law and practice.* Oxford: Hart Publishing

Kovacic, William. 2008. Competition policy in the European Union and the United States: Convergence or divergence in the future treatment of dominant firms. *Competition Law International* 4:8

Lang, Temple. 2003. Anti-competitive non-pricing abuses under European and national antitrust law. *Fordham Corporate Law Institute* 235

Lawrance, Sophie. 2014. The competition law treatment of no-challenge clauses in licence agreements: An unfortunate revolution? *Journal of Intellectual Property Law & Practice* 9 (10):802–811

Lemley, Mark A., and Mark P. McKenna. 2012. Is Pepsi really a substitute for coke? market definition in antitrust and IP. *Georgetown Law Journal* 100 (6):2055–2118

Lemley, Mark. 1994. Antitrust counterclaims in patent and copyright infringement cases. *Texas Intellectual Property Law Journal* 3 (1):1–8

Lemley, Mark. 2008. The surprising virtues of treating trade secrets as IP rights. *Stanford Law Review* 62:311–353

Lerner, AP. 1934. The concept of monopoly and the measurement of monopoly power. *The Review of Economic Studies* 1 (3):157–175

Lianos, Ioannis, and Pierre Regibeau. 2017. "Sham" litigation: When can it arise and how can it be reduced? *Antitrust Bulletin* 62 (4):643–689

刘贵祥 [Liu Guixiang]. 2016. 滥用市场支配地位的司法考量 [How can courts handle cases of the abuse of market dominance]. 中国法学 *[China Legal Science]* 5:260–280

李剑 [Li Jian]. 2014. 中国反垄断法实施中的体系冲突和化解 [System conflict and resolution in the implementation of China's anti-monopoly law]. 中国法学 *[China Legal Science]* 6:138–153

林平 [Lin Ping]. 2019. 假冒/盗版情况下的市场界定 [Market definition in passing off/ piracy]. In 反垄断法的相关市场界定及其技术方法 *[Market definition in the anti-monopoly law and its technical methods],* ed. 王晓晔 [Wang Xiaoye]. 北京: 法律出版社 [Beijing: Law Press China], 268

刘磊 [Liu Lei]. 2009. 浅析滥用商业秘密权的反垄断法规制 [Research on the anti-monopoly regulation of trade secrets]. 科学之友 *[Friend of Science Amateurs]* 145–146

龙柯宇 [Long Keyu]. 2016. 滥用知识产权市场支配地位的反垄断规制研究 *[The anti-monopoly regulation on the abuse of the dominant market position of intellectual property rights]*. 武汉: 华中科技大学出版社 [Wuhan: HUST Press]

Maggiolino, Mariateresa. 2012. *Intellectual property and antitrust—a comparative economic analysis of US and EU law.* Cheltenham: Edward Elgar

Mahnke, Robert. 2015. Big data as a barrier to entry. *Antitrust Chronicle* 5

Ma Jingyuan. 2020. *Competition law in China: A law and economics perspective.* Berlin: Springer

Marshall, Alfred. 2009. *Principles of economics.* Eighth edition. Cosimo, Inc.

Mason, Edward. 1964. *Economic concentration and the monopoly problem.* New York: Atheneum

McGinn, Colin. 2011. Definition and family resemblance. In *Truth by Analysis: Games, Names and Philosophy,* ed. Colin McGinn, 15. Oxford: Oxford University Press

Menell, Peter, Lemley, Mark, and Robert Merges. 2018. *Intellectual property in the new technological age 2018: Volume i: perspectives, trade secrets and patents.* Clause 8 Publishing

Mestmacker, Ernst-Joachim. 1972. Concentration and competition in the EEC. *Journal of World Trade Law* 6:615–647

Mezzanotte, Félix, and Hou Liyang. 2015. The role of presumptions of market dominance in civil litigation in China. *Journal of Antitrust Enforcement* 3 (1):i108-i131

Morton, Fiona M. Scott, and Carl Shapiro. 2014. Strategic patent acquisitions. *Antitrust Law Journal* 79 (2):463–499

Muller, Ulf, and Anselm Rodenhausen. 2008. The rise and fall of the essential facility doctrine. *European Competition Law Review* 29 (5):310

Niebel, Rembert, Lorenzo de Martinis and Birgit Clark. 2018. The EU trade secrets directive: All change for trade secret protection in Europe? *Journal of Intellectual Property Law & Practice* 13 (6):445–457

Niels, G. 2004. The SSNIP test: some common misconceptions. *Competition Law Journal* 3 (4):267

Office of the United States Trade Representative Executive Office of the President. 2018. findings of the investigation into china's acts, policies, and practices related to technology transfer, intellectual property, and innovation under section 301 of the trade act of 1974. https://ustr.gov/about-us/policy-offices/press-office/press-releases/2018/march/section-301-report-chinas-acts. Accessed 25 March 2025

Oke, Emmanuel Kolawole. 2018. Territoriality in intellectual property law: Examining the tension between securing societal goals and treating intellectual property as an investment asset. *SCRIPTed* 15 (2):313–348

Oliverira, Gesner, and Thomas Fujiwara. 2007. Intellectual property and competition as complementary policies. https://www.wipoforcreators.org/export/sites/www/competition-policy/en/docs/study_ip_competition_oliveira.pdf. Accessed 25 March 2025

Oliver, Michael. 1989. Comments: Antitrust liability for bad faith assertion of trade secrets. *University of Baltimore Law Review* 3:544–569

Ong, Ryan. 2013. Trade secret enforcement in China: Options and obstacles. *China Business Review* 40 (1):49

Ørstavik, Inger Berg. 2005. Technology transfer agreements: Grant-backs and no-challenge clauses in the new EC technology transfer regulation. *IIC: International Review of Intellectual Property and Competition Law* 36 (1):83

Patterson, Mark. 2007. The peculiar "new product" requirement in European refusal to license cases: A US perspective. *European Competition Law Annual* 707

Pejovic, Caslav. 2001. Civil law and common law: Two different paths leading to the same goal. *VUWLR* 32:819

Pooley, J. 1997. The top ten issues in trade secret law. *Temple Law Review* 70:1181–1189

Report by the Max Planck Institute for Intellectual Property and Competition Law. Drexl, Josef. Copyright, competition and development. 2013. https://www.accessiblebook.org/export/sites/www/competition-policy/en/docs/copyright_competition_development.pdf. Accessed 25 March 2025

Report of the Working Group on the Interaction between Trade and Competition Policy to the General Council. 1998. WT/WGTCP/2

Rose, V., and D. Bailey. 2013. *European union law of competition.* 7th edn. Oxford: Oxford University Press

Samuelson, Pamela, and Suzanne Scotchmer. 2001. The law and economics of reverse engineering. *Yale Law Journal* 111:1575–1663

Sandeen, Sharon, and Christopher Seaman. 2017. Toward a federal jurisprudence of trade secret law. *Berkeley Tech. Law Journal* 32: 829–914

Schmidt, Hedvig, and Steven Anderman. 2011. *EU competition law and intellectual property rights, the regulation of innovation.* Oxford: Oxford University Press

Schumpeter, Joseph. 1976. *Capitalism, socialism and democracy.* New York: Harper Perennial

Shelanski, Howard A. 2013. Information, innovation and competition policy for the internet. *University of Pennsylvania Law Review* 161 (6): 1663–1705

Silva, Nuno Sousa e. 2014. What exactly is a trade secret under the proposed directive? *Journal of Intellectual Property Law & Practice* 9 (11): 923–932

Sokol, Daniel. 2017. Introduction. In *Patent assertion entities and competition policy,* 1. Cambridge: Cambridge University Press

Su Pan. 2021. The court as a market regulator: Proactive rule-making of the Supreme People's Court of China on economic regulation. *China Information* 35 (2): 219–238

Surblyte, Gintare. 2011. *The refusal to disclose trade secrets as an abuse of market dominance-microsoft and beyond*. Bern: Stämpfli

Taylor, Christian Chadd. 1993. No-challenge termination clauses: Incorporating innovation policy and risk allocation into patent licensing law. *Indiana Law Journal* 69 (1):215–254

Trenor, John A. 2018. *Guide to damages in international arbitration.* London: Law Business Research Ltd.

Unctad-Ictsd, et al. 2005. *Resource book on TRIPS and development.* Cambridge: Cambridge University Press

Varanini, Emilio. 2017. United States of America. In *Abuse of dominant position and globalization & protection and disclosure of trade secrets and know-how.* eds. Pranvera Këllezi, Bruce Kilpatrick and Pierre Kobel, 622. Berlin: Springer

Vezzoso, Simonetta. 2012. Towards an EU doctrine of anti-competitive IP-related litigation. *Journal of European Competition Law & Practice* 3 (6):521–535

Vickers, John. 2006. Market power in competition cases. *European Competition Journal* 2 ((1) Supp (Special issue)):3–14

王博闻 [Wang Bowen]. 2016. 德国反不正竞争法私法属性的历史和理论建构 [The historical and theoretical constructions of the private law nature of German anti-unfair competition law]. 竞争政策研究 *[Competition Policy Research]* 4:19–30

王先林，吴佩乘 [Wang Xianlin, and Wu Peicheng]. 滥用市场支配地位案例评析 [Assessment of cases of the abuse of market dominance in China]. In 中国竞争法律与政策研究报告*2018–2019*年 *[Report on Competition Law and Policy of China 2018–2019]*

王先林 [Wang Xianlin]. 2018. 竞争法学 *[Chinese competition law].* 北京: 中国人民大学出版社 [Beijing: Press of Renmin University of China]

王先林 [Wang Xianlin]. 2016. 知识产权领域反垄断中相关市场界定的特殊问题 [The special problem of anti-monopoly market definition in the field of intellectual property]. 价格理论与实践 *[Price Theory and Practice]* 2:49–53

王先林 [Wang Xianlin]. 2020.知识产权与反垄断法 *[Intellectual property and anti-monopoly law].* 北京: 法律出版社 [Beijing: Law Press China]

王先林 [Wang Xianlin]. 2014. 3Q垄断纠纷案终审判决的行业意义与法律影响 [Meanings and legal effects of *Qihoo v Tencent*]. 中国审判 *[China Trial]* 11:78–80

Wang Xianlin. 2017. Recent developments in China's anti-monopoly regulations on abuse of intellectual property rights. *Antitrust Bulletin* 62 (4): 806–814

王先林 [Wang Xianlin]. 2015. 关于制定我国滥用知识产权反垄断指南的若干思考 [Relevant thoughts on the enactment of the anti-monopoly guidelines of the abuse of IPRs in China]. 价格理论与实践 *[Price Theory & Practice]*10: 25–29

Wang, Xianlin. 2017. Some key issues concerning further development of China's anti-monopoly law. In *Competition policy for the new era: Insights from the BRICS countries,* eds. Tembinkosi Bonakele, Eleanor Fox and Liberty Mncube, 224. Oxford: Oxford University Press

王晓晔, 张素伦 [Wang Xiaoye, and Zhang Sulun]. 2013. SSNIP测试法运用于互联网行业的思考 [Thoughts of how SSNIP test can be applied in Internet-based Sector]. 法制日报 *[Legal Daily]*, September 18

王晓晔 [Wang Xiaoye]. 2011. 反垄断法 *[Chinese anti-monopoly law]*. 北京: 法律出版社 [Beijing: Law Press China]

王晓晔 [Wang Xiaoye]. 2018. 论相关市场界定在滥用行为案件中的地位和作用 [Functions of market definition in cases of the abuse of market dominance]. 现代法学 *[Modern Law Science]* 3: 57–69

王晓晔 [Wang Xiaoye]. 滥用知识产权限制竞争的法律问题 [Legal issues surrounding the misuse of intellectual property rights to restrict competition]. 中国社会科学 *[Social Sciences in China]* 4: 130–144

王晓晔 [Wang Xiaoye]. 2019. 反垄断法的相关市场界定及其技术方法 *[Market definition in the anti-monopoly law and its technical methods]*. 北京: 法律出版社 [Beijing: Law Press China]

王晓晔 [Wang Xiaoye]. 2018. 市场界定在反垄断并购审查中的地位和作用 [The function and status of market definition in merger control cases]. 中外法学 *[Peking University Law Journal]* 5: 1324–1338

Wang Xiaoye. 2008. Highlights of China's new anti-monopoly law. *Antitrust Law Journal* 75 (1): 133–150

Wang Yong. 2019. Interpreting US–China trade war background, negotiations and consequences. *China International Strategy Review* 1 (1): 111–125

Wang, Yuting. 2020. The anti-monopoly regulation of reverse payment patent settlement agreements in the pharmaceutical industry in China. *Asia Pacific Law Review* 28 (1): 202–224

WIPO. 2011. Study on the anti-competitive enforcement of intellectual property rights. CDIP/9/INF/6.https://www.wipo.int/export/sites/www/meetings/en/2011/wipo_ip_ge_11/docs/study.pdf. Accessed 23 March 2025

WIPO. 2015. Successful technology licensing. *IP Assets Management Series*. https://www.wipo.int/edocs/pubdocs/en/licensing/903/wipo_pub_903.pdf. Accessed 23 March 2025

Witt, Anne. 2010. The commission's guidance paper on abusive exclusionary conduct-more radical than it appears? *European Law Review* 35: 214–235

Wittgenstein, Ludwig. 2003. *Philosophical investigations*, trans. G.E.M. Anscombe. Oxford: Blackwell

World Intellectual Property Organization (WIPO) and SPC (2019) *WIPO Collection of leading judgment on intellectual property rights: People's Republic of China (2011–2018)*. https://www.wipo.int/publications/en/details.jsp?id=4477. Accessed 23 March 2025

Wu Peicheng and Charlie Xiao-chuan Weng. 2020. Implications of the China-US trade agreement on the civil protection of trade secrets in China: Is it a game changer? *Asia Pacific Law Review* 28(2): 316–336

吴佩乘 [Wu Peicheng]. 2018. 反垄断法中纵向垄断协议的解释学澄清 [Clarifications of RPM in China's anti-monopoly law]. 知识产权 *[Intellectual Property]* 11: 44–51

Wu Peicheng. 2021. How does China prohibit the abuse of market dominance? A comparative analysis with the US and EU approaches. *Journal of Law and Economy of China* 1: 4–16

吴佩乘 [Wu Peicheng]. 2019. 欧盟与德国商业秘密立法及对中国的借鉴 [Legislation on trade secrets in the EU and Germany and its implications on China]. 中德法学论坛 *[China-Germany Law Review]* 2:23–35

吴佩乘 [Wu Peicheng]. 2020. 论作为私人实施方式的反垄断民事纠纷仲裁 [On the civil anti-monopoly dispute arbitration as the private enforcement]. 北京仲裁 *[Beijing Arbitration Quarterly]* 4: 27–46

Wu Changqi, and Liu Zhicheng. 2012. A tiger without teeth? Regulation of administrative monopoly under China's anti-monopoly law. *Review of Industrial Organization* 41: 133–155

Xiong Ping and Philip Griffith. 2014. Protecting trade secrets in China: history and context. *Queen Mary Journal of Intellectual Property* 4 (1): 30-56
Yoerg, Norman Jr. 1977. Should a trade secret misappropriation claim lie in the procrustean antitrust bed. *Antitrust Bull* 22 (1): 1
曾雄 [Zeng Xiong]. 2018.商业秘密滥用行为的反垄断适用规则之完善研究 [Research on improvements on the application of anti-monopoly law in the abuse of trade secrets]. 研究生法学 *[Graduate Law Review] 5:* 77–85
张鸽，黄琳琳 [Zhang Ge, and Huang Linlin]. 2018. 以知识产权管理体系保护企业商业秘密 [Protecting trade secrets of enterprises through intellectual property management sytem]. 上海商学院学报 *[Journal of Shanghai Business School]* 19: 49–59
张卫平 [Zhang Weiping]. 2016. 民事诉讼法 *[Civil procedure law].* 北京: 法律出版社 [Beijing: Law Press]
郑鹏程，刘长云 [Zheng Pengcheng, and Liu Changyun]. 2016. 我国反垄断相关市场执法实践检讨与反思 [Rethinking on the practice of relevant market definition in Chinese anti-monopoly]. 中南大学学报*(社会科学版) [Journal of Central South University (Social Science)] 22:* 46–51
朱理 [Zhu Li]. 2015. 互联网领域竞争行为的法律边界: 挑战与司法回应. [Legal boundaries of competition in Internet area: challenges and responses]. 竞争政策研究 *[Competition Policy Research]* 7: 11–19
Zhu, Li. 2017. Punitive damages under patent law: where should we go after Halo? *China Patents & Trademarks* 1: 25–35

Legislative Instruments & Regulations

Anti-monopoly Law (PRC) (2008)
Anti-monopoly Guidelines in the Field of Intellectual Property Rights (PRC) (2019)
Agreement on Trade-Related Aspects of Intellectual Property Rights (WTO) (1995)
Antitrust Guidelines for the Licensing of Intellectual Property (US) (2017)
Anti-unfair Competition Law (PRC) (2019)
Civil Code (PRC) (2021)
DG Competition Discussion Paper on the Application of Article 82 of the Treaty to Exclusionary Abuses (EU) (2005)
Guidelines for the Definition of Relevant Markets (PRC) (2009)
Guidelines on the Application of Article 81 of the EC Treaty to Technology Transfer Agreements (EU) (2004)
Guidance on the Commission's Enforcement Priorities in Applying Article 82 of the EC Treaty to Abusive Exclusionary Conduct by Dominant Undertakings (EU) (2009)
Interim Provisions on Prohibition of the Abuse of Market Dominance (PRC) (2019)
Provisions on Several Issues concerning the Application of Law in the Trial of Civil Cases involving Trade Secret Infringement (PRC) (2020)
Regulation on the application of Article 101(3) of the Treaty on the Functioning of the European Union to Categories of Technology Transfer Agreements (EU) (2014)
Regulation on the Application of Article 81 (3) of the Treaty to Categories of Technology Transfer Agreements (EU) (2004)
Rules of the Supreme People's Court on Guidance Cases (PRC) (2010)
Sherman Antitrust Act (US) (1890)
Treaty on the Functioning of the European Union (EU) (2009)

Cases

阿里巴巴滥用市场支配地位案 [Alibaba—The Abuse of Market Dominance Case], 国家市场监管总局 [SAMR], 国市监处 [2021]28号 [Administrative Decision of the SAMR No 28], 10 April 2008
Aspen Skiing Co. v Aspen Highlands Skiing Corp., 472 U.S. 585 (1985)
Bayer AG and Maschinenfabrik Hennecke GmbH v Heinz Süllhöfer, Case 65/86, EU:C:1988:448
北京奇虎科技有限公司诉腾讯科技(深圳)有限公司、深圳市腾讯计算机系统有限公司滥用市场支配地位纠纷案 [Beijing Qihoo Technology v Shenzhen Tencent Technology—Abuse of Market Dominance Case], 最高人民法院 [Supreme People's Court], 2013民三终字第4号 [Economic Judgement No 3], 8 October 2014
Bendix Corporation v Balax, Inc., 471 F.2d 809 (7th Cir. 1970)
Broadcom Corp. v Qualcomm, 543 F.3d 683
Case AT. 3974, Google Search (Shopping) Decision of 27 June 2017
Case AT. 40099, Google Android Decision of 18 July 2018
Case C-170/13, Huawei Technologies Co. Ltd v ZTE Corp. and ZTE Deutschland GmbH., EU:C:2015:477
Case C-418/01, IMS Health GmbH & Co. OHG v NDC Health GmbH & Co. KG EU:C:2004:257
Case C-457/10 P, AstraZeneca EU:C:2012:770
Case C-7/97, Oscar Bronner GmbH & Co. KG v Mediaprint EU:C:1998:569
Case 27/76 United Brands v Commission [1978] ECR 207
Case 311/84, Télémarketing EU:C:1985:394
Case 66/86, Ahmed Saeed Flugreisen and Silver Line Reisebüro GmbH v Zentrale zur Bekämpfung unlauteren Wettbewerbs e.V., EU:C:1989:140
Case 85/76 Hoffmann-La Roche & Co. AG v Commission [1979] ECR 461
Case T-111/96, ITT Promedia NV v Commission of the European Communities EU:T:1998:183
Case T-219/99, British Airways EU:T:2003
Centrafarm BV et Adriaan de Peijper v Sterling Drug Inc (Case 15–74.)
City of Columbia v Omni Outdoor Advertising, 499 U.S. 365 (1991)
CVD, Inc. v Raytheon. Co., 769 F.2d 842, 850 (1st Cir. 1985)
Deutsche Telekom AG v European Commission (C-280/08) [2010] ECR 09555
D.I. du Pont deNemours & Co. v Christopher, 431 F.2d 1012, 1970 U.S
Eastern R. Conference v Noerr Motors, 365 U.S. 127 (1961)
Établissements Consten S.à.R.L. and Grundig-Verkaufs-GmbH v Commission of the European Economic Community (Joined cases 56 and 58–64) [1966]
FTC v. Actavis, Inc., 570 U.S. 136 (2013)
FTC v Watson Pharmaceuticals, Inc., et al., No. 10–12729 (11th Cir. 2012)
Globetrotter Software v Elan Computer Group, 63 F. Supp. 2d 1127 (N.D. Cal. 1999)
HiQ Labs, Inc. v LinkedIn Corp., 273 F. Supp. 3d 1099 (N.D. Cal. 2017)
华为公司与交互数字公司滥用市场支配地位案 [Huawei v InterDigital—Abuse of Market Dominance case], 广东省高级人民法院 [Guangdong High People's Court], (2013)粤高法民三终字第306号 [Economic Appeal No 306], 21 October 2013
汇力公司诉壳牌公司横向垄断协议纠纷案 [Huili v Shell—Horizonal Monopoly Agreement Case],最高人民法院 [Supreme People's Court] (2019)最高法知民辖终47号 [Economic No 47], 21 August 2019
海能达与摩托罗拉滥用市场支配地位纠纷案 [Hytera v Motorola—Disputes of the Abuse of Market Dominance], 北京知识产权法院 [Beijing Intellectual Property Court, People's Republic of China], 北京知识产权法院(2017)京73民初1671号 [Economic Appeal No 1671], 31 December 2019
Joined Cases 6 and 7–73, Istituto Chemioterapico Italiano S.p.A. and Commercial Solvents Corporation v Commission EU:C:1974:18
Joined Cases C-241/91 P and C-242/91 P, Radio Telefis Eireann (RTE) and Independent Television Publications Ltd (ITP) v Commission EU:C:1995:98

Kewanee Oil Co. v Bicron Corp., 416 U.S. 470 (1974)
Kinsman v Parkhurst, 59 U.S. 289 (1855)
Intel Corporation Inc v. European Commission [2017] (Case-C-413/14 P)
Lear, Inc. v Adkins, 395 U.S. 653 (1969)
MCI Communications Corp. v AT&T Co., 708 F.2d 1081 (7th Cir. 1983)
Microsoft v European Commission (T-201/04) [2007] ECR II-3601
高通公司滥用市场支配地位案 [NDRC v Qualcomm—Abuse of Market Dominance case].国家发展和改革委员会 [National Development and Reform Commission of the PRC], (2015)发改办价监处罚 [2015]1号 [Decision of the NDRC [2015] No. 1], 9 February 2015
Novell v. Microsoft, 731 F. 3d 1064 (10th Cir. 2013)
NV Nederlandsche Banden-Industrie Michelin v Commission (Case 322/81) [1983] ECR 3461
Octane Fitness, LLC v ICON Health & Fitness, Inc., 572 U.S. 545 (2014)
Professional Real Estate Investors, Inc. v Columbia Pictures Industries, Inc., 508 U.S. 49 (1993)
Queen City Pizza, Inc. v Domino's Pizza, Inc, 124 F.3d 430, 436 (3 Cir., rd 1997)
State Oil Co. v Khan, 522 U.S. 3 (1997)
Swift & Co. v United States, 196 U.S. 375 (1905)
Times-Picayune v United States, 345 U.S. 594 (1953)
United Mine Workers v Pennington, 381 U.S. 657 (1965)
United States v Arnold, Schwinn & Co., 388 U.S. 365 (1967)
United States v Colgate & Co., 250 U.S. 300 (1919)
United States v Paramount Pictures, Inc., 334 U.S. 131, 68 S. Ct. 915 (1948)
United States Steel Corp. v Fortner Enterprises, Inc., 429 U.S. 610 (1977)
United States v Grinnell Corp., 384 U.S. 563 (1966)
Verizon v. Trinko, 540 U.S. 398 (2004)
Walker Process Eqpt., Inc. v Food Machinery Corp., 382 U.S. 172 (1965)
Windsurfing International Inc. v Commission of the European Communities, Case 193/83, EU:C:1986:75
徐书青诉深圳市腾讯计算机系统有限公司滥用市场支配地位纠纷案 [Xushuqing v Shenzhen Tencent Technology—Abuse of Market Dominance Case], 最高人民法院 [Supreme People's Court], (2017)最高法民申4955号 [SPC Economic Judgement No 4955], 14 September 2018
云南盈鼎生物能源股份有限公司、中国石化销售有限公司云南石油分公司拒绝交易纠纷 [Yunnan Ying Ding v Sinopec Group—Refusal to Deal Dispute Case], 最高人民法院 [Supreme People's Court], (2017)最高法民申5063号 [Economic No 5063], 11 November 2019
裕泰公司与海南省物价局垄断纠纷案 [Yutai v Hainan Price Administration—Monopoly Dispute Case], 最高人民法院 [Supreme People's Court], (2018)最高法行申4675号 [Administrative No 4675], 18 December 2018

Online Resources

Access to justice. *United Nations.* https://www.un.org/ruleoflaw/thematic-areas/access-to-justice-and-rule-of-law-institutions/access-to-justice. Accessed 25 Mar 2025
A forum was held in memory of the enforcement of the anti-monopoly law for 10 years by the supreme people's court. *Supreme people's court.* https://www.court.gov.cn/fabu-xiangqing-130481.html. Accessed 25 Mar 2025
Antitrust: commission finds that motorola mobility infringed EU competition rules by misusing standard essential patents. *European commission.* https://ec.europa.eu/commission/presscorner/detail/en/IP_14_489 Accessed 25 Mar 2025
Antitrust: commission opens proceedings against samsung. *European commission.* https://ec.europa.eu/commission/presscorner/detail/en/IP_12_89. Accessed 25 Mar 2025

Barbe, Andre and Linton, Katherine. Trade secrets: international trade policy and empirical research. *OECD*. https://www.oecd.org/sti/144%20-%20OECD%20Trade%20Secrets%202016-8-5.pdf. Accessed 25 Mar 2025

Barnett, Thomas (assistant attorney general of the US department of justice). Interoperability between antitrust and intellectual property. *US department of justice*. https://www.justice.gov/atr/speech/interoperability-between-antitrust-and-intellectual-property#N_3_. Accessed 25 Mar 2025

Bona, Jarod. What is noerr-pennington immunity and is this doctrine a defense to an antitrust case. *Bona law PC*. https://www.theantitrustattorney.com/what-is-noerr-pennington-immunity-and-is-this-doctrine-a-defense-to-an-antitrust-case/. Accessed 25 Mar 2025

Brant, Jennifer and Lohse, Sebastian. Trade secrets: tools for innovation and collaboration. *ICC*. https://iccwbo.org/publication/trade-secrets-innovation-process.
Accessed 25 Mar 2025

Clover, Juli.95% of Chinese users surveyed would rather give up their iPhones than lose WeChat. *MacRumors*. https://www.macrumors.com/2020/08/13/china-iphone-users-prefer-wechat. Accessed 25 Mar 2025

Comments of the American bar association sections of antitrust law, intellectual property law, and international law on the draft anti-monopoly guidelines on abuse of IP rights. *ABA* https://www.americanbar.org/news/abanews/aba-news-archives/2017/04/aba_sections_comment/. Accessed 25 Mar 2025

Competition and monopoly: single-firm conduct under section 2 of the sherman act. *The US department of justice*. https://www.justice.gov/atr/competition-and-monopoly-single-firm-conduct-under-section-2-sherman-act-chapter-1. Accessed 25 Mar 2025. Competition policy and Intellectual property rights. *OECD* https://www.oecd.org/regreform/sectors/2376247.pdf. Accessed 25 Mar 2025

Court of justice of the European Union. *European Union*. https://europa.eu/european-union/about-eu/institutions-bodies/court-justice_en.
Accessed 25 Mar 2025

Data analysis of trade Secret cases in China (2015–2019). *Hefei IP lawyer*. https://hfiplaw.cn/details/20610.html. Accessed 25 Mar 2025

Does China have common law. *China justice observer*. https://www.chinajusticeobserver.com/a/does-china-have-common-law. Accessed 25 Mar 2025

Executive Order on Promoting Competition in the American Economy', *The White House*. https://www.whitehouse.gov/briefing-room/presidential-actions/2021/07/09/executive-order-on-promoting-competition-in-the-american-economy/>Accessed 25 Mar 2025

Feng, Zhaoyin and Joshua Cheetham, 'Trump WeChat ban "an unwelcome signal" for Chinese community', *BBC* (Web Page) <https://www.bbc.com/news/world-asia-china-53686507>Accessed 25 Mar 2025

French autorité de la concurrence and the German bundeskartellamt. Competition law and data. *Bundeskartellamt*. https://www.bundeskartellamt.de/SharedDocs/Publikation/DE/Berichte/Big%20Data%20Papier.html. Accessed 25 Mar 2025

Frequently asked questions: patents. *WIPO*. https://www.wipo.int/patents/en/faq_patents.html. Accessed 25 Mar 2025

Gugliuzza, Paul. patent trolls and patent litigation reform. *Oxford handbooks online*.https://www.oxfordhandbooks.com/view/https://doi.org/10.1093/oxfordhb/9780199935352.001.0001/oxfordhb-9780199935352-e-15. Accessed 25 Mar 2025

Hines, Doris Johnson and Yang, Ming-Tao. Worldwide activities on licensing issues relating to standard essential patents. *WIPO*. https://www.wipo.int/wipo_magazine/en/2019/01/article_0003.html. Accessed 25 Mar 2025

Intellectual property owners association. Survey on strategic management of intellectual property. *MITSloan*. https://sloanreview.mit.edu/article/strategic-management-of-intellectual-property. Accessed 25 Mar 2025

Intellectual property: protection and enforcement. *WTO.* https://www.wto.org/english/thewto_e/whatis_e/tif_e/agrm7_e.htm. Accessed 25 Mar 2025

IP and competition policy. *WIPO.* https://www.wipo.int/ip-competition/en/. Accessed 25 Mar 2025

Kharel, Amrit. Doctrinal legal research. *SSRN.* https://papers.ssrn.com/sol3/papers.cfm?abstract_id=3130525. Accessed 25 Mar 2025

Leonte, Andreea and Crivat, Valentina. 2017. A civil code for China: a great leap forward for the rule of law. *The diplomat.* https://thediplomat.com/2017/03/a-civil-code-for-china-a-great-leap-forward-for-the-rule-of-law. Accessed 25 Mar 2025

Mansell, Robin and Steinmueller, Edward. Intellectual property rights: the development of information infrastructures for the information society. *LSE research online.* http://eprints.lse.ac.uk/24969/1/Intellectual_property_rights_report_%28LSERO%29.pdf. Accessed 25 Mar 2025

Competition policy and intellectual property rights. 1989. Licensing of IP rights and competition law. Research Paper. *OECD* https://www.oecd.org/daf/competition/licensing-of-ip-rights-and-competition-law.htm.

Accessed 25 Mar 2025

Office of the United States trade representative. Update concerning China's acts, policies and practices related to technology transfer, intellectual property, and innovation. https://ustr.gov/sites/default/files/enforcement/301Investigations/301%20Report%20Update.pdf. Accessed 25 Mar 2025

Oliveira, Gesner and Thomas Fujiwara. Intellectual property and competition as complementary policies: a test using an ordered probit Model(WIPO) https://www.wipo.int/export/sites/www/ip-competition/en/studies/study_ip_competition_oliveira.pdf. Accessed 25 Mar 2025

Outline of the 14th Five-Year Plan (2021–2025) for national economic and social development and long-range objectives for 2035. *State council of China* http://www.gov.cn/xinwen/2021-03/13/content_5592681.htm. Accessed 25 Mar 2025

Overview: The TRIPS agreement. *WTO* https://www.wto.org/english/tratop_e/TRIPS_e/intel2_e.htm#tradesecrets. Accessed 25 Mar 2025

Paragraph IV challenges: exploring 2017 trends, developments and updates. *MINTZ* https://www.mintz.com/insights-center/events/2017/paragraph-iv-challenges-exploring-2017-trends-developments-and-updates. Accessed 25 Mar 2025

Principles of the Trading System. *WTO.* https://www.wto.org/english/thewto_e/whatis_e/tif_e/fact2_e.htm. Accessed 25 Mar 2025

'Resume of Judge Li Zhu. *Supreme People's Court.* http://ipc.court.gov.cn/zh-cn/news/view-126.html. Accessed 25 Mar 2025

Special 301 Report.2021. *Office of the US trade representative* https://ustr.gov/sites/default/files/files/reports/2021/2021%20Special%20301%20Report%20(final).pdf. Accessed 25 Mar 2025

Standard Setting Organizations and Processes: Challenges and Opportunities for Competition and Innovation. *Concurrences.* https://www.concurrences.com/en/review/issues/no-3-2015/conferences/standard-setting-organizations-and-processes-challenges-and-opportunities-for. Accessed 25 Mar 2025

Statement by Vice President Joaquín Almunia following General Court Judgement in Case T-167/08 Microsoft vs Commission', *European commission.* https://ec.europa.eu/commission/presscorner/detail/en/MEMO_12_498. Accessed 25 Mar 2025

Study on trade secrets and confidential business information in the internal market.

European commission. https://ec.europa.eu/growth/publications/study-trade-secrets-and-confidential-business-information-internal-market_en. Accessed 25 Mar 2025

Thayer, Ken. How does reverse engineering work. *Engineering360.* https://insights.globalspec.com/article/7367/how-does-reverse-engineering-work. Accessed 25 Mar 2025

The essential facilities concept. *OECD.* https://www.oecd.org/competition/abuse/1920021.pdf. Accessed 25 Mar 2025

The future of ISI for PMR TETRA network is now. *LTE technology.* https://www.criticalcommunicationsreview.com/lte/news/33962/the-future-of-isi-for-pmr-tetra-networks-is-now. Accessed 25 Mar 2025

工商总局对微软的反垄断调查正深入进行 [The SAIC is investigating further into Microsoft's monopolistic behaviour]. *State council of PRC*. http://www.gov.cn/xinwen/2014-08/26/content_2739925.htm. Accessed 25 Mar 2025

The Socialist System of Laws with Chinese Characteristics. *Supreme people's court of China*. http://english.court.gov.cn/2015-07/17/content_21312781_2.htm. Accessed 25 Mar 2025

US Imposes Technology Transfer and Export Restrictions on Dozens of Chinese Companies, including Top Chipmaker and Drone Manufacture. *Mondaq*. https://www.mondaq.com/unitedstates/export-controls-trade-investment-sanctions/1019498/us-imposes-technology-transfer-and-export-restrictions-on-dozens-of-chinese-companies-including-top-chipmaker-and-drone-manufacturer. Accessed 25 Mar 2025

What are intellectual property rights. *WTO*. https://www.wto.org/english/tratop_e/TRIPS_e/intel1_e.htm. Accessed 25 Mar 2025

MIX
Papier aus verantwortungsvollen Quellen
Paper from responsible sources
FSC® C105338

If you have any concerns about our products,
you can contact us on
ProductSafety@springernature.com

In case Publisher is established outside the EU,
the EU authorized representative is:
Springer Nature Customer Service Center GmbH
Europaplatz 3, 69115 Heidelberg, Germany

Printed by Libri Plureos GmbH
in Hamburg, Germany